America, Amerikkka

Religion and Violence

Series Editors
Lisa Isherwood, University of Winchester, and
Rosemary Radford Ruether, Graduate Theological
Union, Berkeley, California

This interdisciplinary and multicultural series brings to light the ever increasing problem of religion and violence. The series highlights how religions have a significant part to play in the creation of cultures that allow and even encourage the creation of violent conflict, domestic abuse and policies and state control that perpetuate violence to citizens.

The series highlights the problems that are experienced by women during violent conflict and under restrictive civil policies. But not wishing to simply dwell on the problems the authors in this series also re-examine the traditions and look for alternative and more empowering readings of doctrine and tradition. One aim of the series is to be a powerful voice against creeping fundamentalisms and their corrosive influence on the lives of women and children.

Published:

Reweaving the Relational Mat
A Christian Response to Violence against Women from Oceania
Joan Alleluia Filemoni-Tofaeono and Lydia Johnson

Forthcoming in the series:

Weep Not for Your Children
Essays on Religion and Violence
Lisa Isherwood and Rosemary Radford Ruether (eds.)

In Search of Solutions
The Problem of Religion and Conflict
Clinton Bennett

Meditations on Religion and Violence in the United States
T. Walter Herbert

America, Amerikkka
Elect Nation and Imperial Violence

Rosemary Radford Ruether

LONDON   OAKVILLE

Published by
Equinox Publishing Ltd., Unit 6, The Village, 101 Amies St., London SW11 2JW, UK
DBBC, 28 Main Street, Oakville, CT 06779, USA

www.equinoxpub.com

First published 2007

© Rosemary Radford Ruether 2007

British Library Cataloguing-in-Publication Data
A catalogue record for this book is available from the British Library.

ISBN-10   1 84553 157 4   (hardback)
             1 84553 158 2   (paperback)

ISBN-13   978 184553 157 7   (hardback)
             978 184553 158 4   (paperback)

Library of Congress Cataloging-in-Publication Data

Ruether, Rosemary Radford.
America, Amerikkka : elect nation and imperial violence / Rosemary
Radford Ruether.
       p. cm. — (Religion and violence)
Includes bibliographical references and index.
ISBN-13: 978-1-84553-157-7 (hbk.)
ISBN-10: 1-84553-157-4 (hbk.)
ISBN-13: 978-1-84553-158-4 (pbk.)
ISBN-10: 1-84553-158-2 (pbk.)
1. United States — Foreign relations. 2. United States — Territorial
expansion. 3. Imperialism — History. 4. Messianism, Political — United
States — History. 5. Religion and politics — United States — History. 6.
United States — Politics and government. 7. National characteristics,
American. 8. Racism — Political aspects — United States — History. 9.
United States — Race relations — Political aspects. 10. Protest
movements — United States — History. I. Title. E183.7.R895 2007
973 — dc22
                        2006019370

Typeset by S.J.I. Services, New Delhi
Printed and bound by Antony Rowe, Chippenham, Wiltshire

*This book is dedicated to Maryknoll Sisters,
Joan Uhlen, Rita Owczarek and Elizabeth Solmon,
faithful witnesses to justice and solidarity
with the Nicaraguan people*

CONTENTS

INTRODUCTION

THE TWO FACES OF AMERICA: THE IDEAL AMERICA AS
DECEPTION AND AS PROTEST

In his major book, *Killing Hope: U.S. Military and CIA Interventions since World War II*, William Blum explains why so many Americans are so ignorant of the history of their nation and have a hard time believing that it has continually intervened in the lives of other nations in destructive ways. '...It is because the American people see and hear their leaders expressing the right concern at the right time, with just the right catch in their throat to convey, "I care!" they see them laughing and telling jokes, see them with their families, hear them speak of God and love, of peace and law, of democracy and freedom — it is because of such things that the idea that our government has done to the world's huddled masses what it did to the Seminoles has such a difficult time penetrating the American consciousness. It's like America has an evil twin.'

This book, with its double name, *America, Amerikkka*, is about that double identity of America. It is about the ideology of God and love, peace and law, democracy and freedom, and the evil twin that is concealed behind this rhetoric of positive national values and beliefs. This concealment could not happen if it were not that Americans genuinely believe in these national values, and they believe that American actions in the world are motivated by and express these values. Moreover, American leaders know that they touch a deep root of national faith when they use these words. But often they are doing something very different when they intervene in Guatemala, Chile and Nicaragua, Korea and Vietnam, Iraq and Iran. They are pursuing what they regard as policies of national self-interest that many Americans would regard as unacceptable. Thus, these unacceptable realities must be cloaked in the language of national values rooted in a belief that America is uniquely innocent and good, chosen by God to defend freedom and democracy around the world.

Mark Twain, American author read by most Americans for his boy stories, was himself a sharp critic of American imperialism in the era of the Spanish American wars. In his satiric essay, 'To the person sitting in darkness,' where he assumes the voice of the colonized Filipino of that period, he had this person 'sitting in darkness' say: 'There is something curious about this—curious and unaccountable. There must be two Americas; one that sets the captive free and one that takes the once-captive's new freedom away from him and picks a quarrel with him with nothing to found it on, then kills him to get his land.'[1]

This study of the two Americas is not only about the evil twin and its concealment behind justifying ideologies of American goodness and righteousness. If it were only this, then it would be only about American hypocrisy. It is also about America's deep faith in these positive national values. This means that national leaders are often believers in their own ideological rhetoric. They *both* pursue murderous policies motivated by what they see as American self-interest and *also* manage to sincerely believe that they are serving the best interests of these colonized and exploited people as well. Few American politicians are pure hypocrites who know that what they say to justify their policies has little to do with what they are doing. Most politicians are deeply self-deluded by their own rhetoric. Indeed, to combine being both practitioners of *real politik* and also self-deluded believers in the rhetoric of America's messianic role is the basic requirement of an effective American politician.

Yet, when some Americans see through this ideological smokescreen and discover the very different realities that are happening to these other people who we are 'liberating' by killing and taking their land, they often are outraged. Precisely because they believe in these national values of 'liberty and justice for all,' they both have difficulty believing that something else is happening, but also, when it becomes evident to them that the reality is very different from the ideology, they can become mobilized as critics and reformers.

1. 'To the Person Sitting in Darkness,' in Walter Blair (ed.), *Selected Shorter Writing of Mark Twain* (Boston: Houghton Mifflin Company, 1962), p. 299.

Thus the contrast between American ideals and reality has sparked continual movements for change in the United States. Such movements have engaged in trenchant criticism of American racism and injustice to minority peoples, to workers and to women within this society, as well as movements to withdraw from unjust policies toward other peoples; to get out of Vietnam, to stop the contra war against Nicaragua, to engage in genuine nuclear disarmament, to withdraw from the occupation in Iraq, among other issues in different periods of national history.

This book traces the 350-year history of this double American identity and its consequences, both for unjust policies within and without this society and also the continual uprising of movements of protest and reform.

In Chapter One, 'Elect Nations of Europe and the Making of the American Myth of Chosenness,' I trace the roots of the ideology that America is a uniquely chosen people with a mission from God to redeem the world. The Spanish, the French and the British all shared aspects of this ideology about themselves as rival defenders of different versions of the 'true church,' and as rival colonizers who claimed to be bringing that true church to benighted indigenous people 'sitting in darkness.' It is the British version of the myth of chosenness that is the immediate background for the American myth. The American myth was acquired both as an extension of, and in opposition to, the seventeenth century British version of this myth.

In Chapter Two, 'The Rights of Man and the Excluded Others,' I trace the new stage of the founding myth of American identity as the redeeming people of 'liberty and justice for all,' in the period of the American revolution, Declaration of Independence and writing of the Constitution. These events and documents are the founding 'scriptures' of American political identity by which the 'constitutionality' of every law is judged. At the same time the decisions of this period and its founding documents laid the basis of those exclusions of major sectors of American people from equal citizenship, women, American Indians and African slaves. The founding evil of American history is rooted in the long historical process of near genocide of American Indians and the confiscation of their land. Both African slaves and women would struggle for inclusion in equal citizenship from the 1830s, winning some approximation of equality before the law only in the 1960s–70s.

The third chapter, 'Manifest Destiny and Anglo-Saxon Racism' traces the process of expansion of white settlers across the continent to California. In the American revolutionary period the idea of the rights of man was seen as both universal and at the same time uniquely the rights of Englishmen. But as white settlers embarked on eliminating American Indians, and shoving aside the claims of Mexicans to much of the Southwest from Texas to California, the rights to the land come to be framed as explicitly that of 'Anglo-Saxons,' of white Protestant English-speaking males and their families. This process can be viewed clearly in the white settlement of California after 1848 as the California Indians were exterminated, the Mexicans turned into landless aliens and the immigration of free African-Americans and of Chinese blocked, thus claiming California for the white man.

The fourth chapter, 'Manifest Destiny and American Empire,' charts the next stage of this expansion of American claims to land, power and wealth. Having expanded across the continent, America begins to set its eyes on the rest of the world. The immediate target of this imperial expansion was the remnants of the Spanish Empire in the Caribbean and the Pacific Islands, but the U.S. also saw itself as competing for global spoils with the European empires in China. In that era the ideology of Anglo-Saxon racism purports to scientific status in Social Darwinism. At the same time the implicit masculinist ideology of Americanism becomes explicit as imperialists, such as Theodore Roosevelt, respond to the growing demands of women for citizenship, perceived as a threat to American male war-making virility.

The fifth chapter, 'America's Global Mission: The Cold War Years,' traces the shaping of the American national security state and its global military and economic hegemony under the aegis of the anti-communist crusade. Anti-communism as the war of the American 'way of life' against 'totalitarian' communism becomes the American civil religion, justifying endless interventions in national revolutionary struggles around the world, most notably in Vietnam, but also throughout Latin America.

The sixth chapter, 'American Empire and its Denouement' brings the story of the claims of American global hegemony to the contemporary period, from 1990 to 2006. Refusing to accept the scaling down of the American military after the end of the Cold War, American military and political leaders search for new 'enemies' against whom to justify their expansion of global control to every part of the earth. The war against terrorism after the 9/11 attacks on the World Trade buildings and the Pentagon provide the justification for this new stage of the war of America the Good against the evil forces of the world.

The seventh chapter, 'Alternative Visions of America: The Protest Tradition,' turns to that other side of American identity, to those who in every era of U.S. history have recognized the contradictions between ideals and reality, and have voiced their protests and mobilized movements for social and political change. This chapter parallels the first five chapters of this book from the perspective of key figures of prophetic critique of the failures of America to live up to its 'calling.' One could have written several chapters to chart this protest tradition, but in the interests of space I have chosen a male and a female paradigmatic figure and/or movement from five periods of American history: the colonial era, the revolutionary war period, the abolitionist and civil war era, the progressive era and the civil rights period. I do not have paradigmatic representatives for the current era discussed in Chapter Six. While protest figures abound today, just who might be seen as representative is unclear. The many American critics of American history cited in this book are perhaps the best representatives of this ongoing protest tradition that I know.

The concluding chapter, 'Toward an American Theology of Liberation/Letting Go,' seeks to summarize the purposes of this book in two ways. First, I attempt a theological critique of the religious themes that underlie the American claim to be God's elect nation. This critique includes four key themes: the idea of a chosen nation, what idea of God underlies the notion of an elect nation, the concept of good and evil in play in such a claim, and finally what is useful and what is destructive for a just society in the tradition of messianic hope.

This critique is enunciated not simply as personal opinion, but also what I believe the Christian church should be saying about these themes. The claims to be God's elect nation, the view of God, of good and evil and of messianic hope behind such claims are, in strict theological terms, idolatrous. Christians, far from collaborating with such claims, should be making clear criticism of them, much as the Confessing Church in Germany at the time of the rise of Hitler repudiated the false messianic claims made by German Christianity.

Christian churches should be issuing new Barmen Declarations,[2] defining what is unacceptable in such idolatrous religious claims and calling their members to repudiate them.

At the same time, the churches should be enunciating authentic visions of a society that would truly represent the hopes of the earth for justice, peace and sustainable living. Thus, the second half of the concluding chapter attempts a resume of how we should re-imagine America's place in the world community, in terms of curbing militarism, overcoming poverty and curing environmental devastation. How do we get there from here? This book hardly attempts or even knows any very full answer to this question. But it is the question of the hour, the question of our generation, with which we must all grapple in our time.

2. The Barmen Declaration was issued by protesting mostly German theologians in 1934 to define what was unacceptable in the German Christianity that emerged to justify the messianic claims of the Hitler regime. The Confessing Church was those churches that endorsed this criticism of the Barmen Declaration and thus set themselves as opponents of the Hitler regime.

Chapter One

ELECT NATIONS OF EUROPE AND THE MAKING OF THE AMERICAN MYTH OF CHOSENNESS

The Christian Bible combines the literatures of two religious communities, the Hebrew Bible and the New Testament. The second claims to inherit, perfect and supersede the first, yet the relation between the two remains in constant tension and reinterpretation within Christianity. One of these themes of reinterpretation is the idea of an elect nation, God's chosen people. For the ancient Hebrews, as well as the Jewish people through the ages, the chosen people are Israel, a particular people created by a religiously defined ethnicity. Israel is those who covenant with the God of Israel to be his people, yet Jewishness is also an inherited ethnicity. This national God gave his people the law as a way of life through whose observance obedience to God is fulfilled.

This God also promised his people a land and a flourishing future in relation to all the other nations in the Middle East. But these promises remained continually postponed. The people of Israel were a small nation or federation of tribes, who only in brief periods were politically independent and ruled over a few neighboring tribes. For most of their history to the first century BCE they were ruled by other empires. After the Jewish Wars of 66–73 CE and 132–36 CE, the Jews were scattered in or migrated to other areas within and beyond the borders of the Roman Empire. The vision of being a great nation ruling from their own land (Palestine) was transferred to a future horizon of messianic hope. In this vision, when Israel learns to obey the law fully, it will be restored to its land, rebuild its ancient temple and peace and justice will reign throughout the earth under the true God of Zion whose law goes forth from Jerusalem (Isa. 2:2–4).[1]

1. See Rosemary Ruether and Herman Ruether, *The Wrath of Jonah: The Crisis of Religious Nationalism in the Israeli-Palestinian Conflict* (Minneapolis, MN: Fortress Press, 2002), pp. 6–20.

Early Christianity denationalized, universalized, spiritualized and eschatologized these ideas of an elect nation and its future hopes. God's chosen people were no longer the Jews but the Church, a people drawn from all nations through the redemption won for humanity in Christ. In Christ there is no more Jew or Greek (Gal. 3:28); that is, division between nations is overcome. A new universal community is gathered together in Christ. The Promised Land is no longer one particular land of a particular people, but the heavenly kingdom to come where all people redeemed in Christ will be gathered together after death. The whole earth will be renovated and become immortal, freed from sin and death. The New Jerusalem is the redeemed city that comes out of heaven as the manifestation of God's dwelling with humanity on a renovated earth. (Rev. 21:2-4).

The Christian people have been given the mandate to make disciples of all nations (Mt. 28:19). When the 'full number' of the gentiles has been gathered into the Christian church, then the Jews too will be converted. This will be followed by the unfolding of the final messianic events: Christ will return as conquering Lord, there will be a resurrection of all humans from the dead, the evil doers will be judged and thrown into Hell, and the elect from all nations translated into a redeemed New Heaven and Earth.

This vision, with its expectation of an imminent coming of Christ and defeat of the Roman Empire as the Kingdom of Satan, was revised in the fourth century with the conversion of the Roman Emperor Constantine. Through Constantine, Christianity was transformed into the religion of a Christianized Roman State that ruled over many nations, but hardly the whole world. The pretensions of the Roman Empire to universal rule were married to Christian universalism. Imperial Christians, such as Bishop Eusebius of Caesarea, the eulogist of Constantine, interpreted the *Pax Romana* as the universal Kingdom of God on earth and Constantine as the godly king who represented Christ's reign on earth.[2]

This vision of Christian empire as the manifestation of Christ's reign on earth through a godly emperor was transferred to the two heirs of that empire, the Byzantine Empire centered in Constantinople in the East and the empire founded by Charlemagne in the West in the eighth century. Crowned Western Roman

---

2. Eusebius, *Oration on Constantine* 10.7.

Emperor by Pope Leo III in Rome in 800 CE, Charlemagne's empire united the German and Frankish heartland of Europe, and included Lombard North Italy. The heritage of this empire was continued by the Saxon king, Otto I, in 936 who established the Holy Roman Empire, again with the blessings of the Pope. Thereby Western Europeans sought to maintain the idea of a universal Christian empire that united many nations. Reverberations of this idea continued into Western Europe until Napoleon, who in 1804 crowned himself Holy Roman Emperor as an expression of his ambition to unite Europe in an empire ruled from Paris.[3]

With the fall of the Western Roman Empire in the fifth century, Western Europe disintegrated into local kingdoms. A process of reintegrating regions began in the thirteenth to fifteenth centuries. Several large nation states emerged, France, England and Spain. In the Reformation/Counter-Reformation in the sixteenth century these nations struggled against each other in the wars of religion in Europe, each claiming to represent the 'true' Church. France, England and Spain (also Portugal) set themselves, not only in rivalry with each other as representatives of true Christianity, but also competed for world trade, seeking monopolies on the luxury trade with India and China. When the American continent was inadvertently 'discovered' in this process, they sought to establish overseas empires in this region. Each claimed to be God's chosen people commissioned to convert the newly discovered 'pagans' of the Americas to true Christianity. Thereby they believed that they were fulfilling the New Testament mandate to 'convert all nations,' bringing about the final redemption of the earth.[4]

The rest of this chapter will briefly summarize these rival claims to national election and divine mandate to imperial expansion and conversion of the 'natives' held by the Spanish, French and English in the sixteenth and seventeenth centuries. The chapter will then focus on how Anglo-America, most specifically the Puritans of New

3.   Napoleon summoned the Pope to his crowning, but at the last minute seized the crown from the Pope's hands and crowned himself.

4.   See Edmundo O'Gorman, *The Invention of America: An Inquiry into the Historical Nature of New World and the Meaning of its History* (Westport, CT: Greenwood Press, 1961). O'Gorman argues that America is an historical construct of the ideologies of Europe. He also sees a sharp contrast between the ideologies of America created by the Spanish and by the English, resulting in different historical developments of these areas of America.

England, reshaped this claim to be an elect people commissioned by God to renew their God's true church and holy people in the 'wilderness' of North America. It is the Puritan version of this claim to be God's elect people, translated to a new 'Promised Land' in America, that is the root of the concept of the United States as an elect nation, a claim that continues to be central to U.S. American identity long after the European nations that once held such views have left them behind. This chapter thus seeks to set the historical foundations for this U.S. American claim to be God's elect nation in comparative perspective.

Spain: Elect Nation and Messianic World Ruler

The date 1492 represents a fateful conjunction of events in the history of Spain. On that date the long struggle of the Spanish to expel the Muslims from Spain was completed with the fall of the Kingdom of Granada. At the same time, those Jews who had failed to convert to Catholicism were expelled from Spain. Spain had been united in 1469 with the marriage of Ferdinand II and Isabella who brought together the kingdoms of Aragon and Castile. In 1492, Columbus set out with the endorsement of these joint monarchs of Spain to find a Western route to the Indies. Instead, he stumbled upon an unknown continent, thus initiating Spain's colonial empire in the Americas.

With the outbreak of the Protestant Reformation in Germany a quarter century later, Spain became the center of the Counter-Reformation that sought to re-conquer Europe for Catholicism. In this same period Spain was expanding and consolidating a vast empire from Mexico to Peru. The sixteenth century also was the golden age of Spain's intellectual vitality. When Charles V united the crowns of Spain with the Holy Roman Empire in 1520, Spain could also claim this heritage of universal Christian empire. In the mid-sixteenth century Spain saw itself as shouldering multiple world historic tasks: the repression of Protestantism and the reuniting of Catholic Europe under Spanish hegemony, the defeat of the Turks whose rapid expansion brought about the Fall of Constantinople in 1453 and who continued to be seen as a threat to Western Europe; and the conquest of the Americas, converting the Indians to Catholic Christianity, while blocking the rival expansion of Protestant powers in the Americas (Holland and England).

The multiple aspects of this vast mission led to intense philosophical and theological reflection among Spanish intellectuals on the meaning of Spain's role in world history at this time. It was not enough to wield the sword in these struggles. For Spaniards these roles must be interpreted and justified as part of a redemptive mission bestowed on Spain by God. Philosophers, jurists, canon lawyers, historians, missionaries and theologians were all engaged in this work of defining Spain's divinely chosen role in what was understood as the final era of world history.

The Franciscan, Gerónimo de Mendieta's *Historia eclesiástica Indiana*,[5] on which he labored in Mexico in the second half of the sixteenth century, brings together a synthesis of many of these ideas of Spain's unique election. For Mendieta the Spanish are God's chosen people, the heirs of the election of Israel. They have been uniquely chosen, under their 'blessed kings,' Ferdinand and Isabella and Charles V, to undertake the final conversion of the world. Having dealt with the Jews and Muslims, who either converted or left Spain, they are commissioned by God to defeat the 'heretics,' (Protestants) and convert the last remaining 'gentiles' or pagans to whom the Gospel has not yet been offered; namely, the American Indians. When these tasks are completed, history will be completed and the redemptive Kingdom of God will dawn.

For Mendieta, Spain not only inherited the election of Israel, but its kings fulfill the promise of a Messianic world ruler of the end of days who will defeat the minions of Satan and complete the conversion of the world on the eve of the Last Judgment, thereby bringing about the millennial kingdom of redemption.

> ...as Ferdinand and Isabella cleansed Spain of these wicked sects (Jews and Muslims) in like manner their royal descendants will accomplish the universal destruction of these sects throughout the whole world and the final conversion of all the peoples of the earth to the bosom of the church...[6]

Mendieta's efforts to interpret the theological meaning of Spain's world historic role was one of many similar efforts of his time.

---

5.   O.F.M. Gerónimo de Mendieta, *Historia eclesiástica indiana*, 4 vols. (Mexico: Editorial Salvador Chávez Haydoe) 1945.

6.   Gerónimo de Mendieta, *Historia eclesiástica indiana*, p. 17, quoted in John Leddy Phelan, *The Millennial Kingdom of the Franciscans in the New World* (Berkeley, CA: University of California Press, 1970), p. 13.

Columbus himself shared apocalyptic and messianic speculations about his own 'discoveries.' He came to believe that the lands he had come upon (which he imagined to be the Eastern side of the Island of the World where lay Asia and India) were the sites of the original Garden of Eden.[7] Some saw the Indians as the lost tribes of Israel, and so in converting them Spain was completing the mandate to convert those Jews who had not yet been offered the gospel of Christ.[8]

Views of the nature of the Indians varied and were the source of deep conflicts over the means of conversion. For some, Indians were childlike and naturally virtuous, retaining the innocent nature of the original Adam in the Garden of Paradise.[9] They should be protected by the friars and converted in a gentle and persuasive manner, without force. The Dominican, Bartolomé de las Casas,[10] especially took the lead in insisting on this naturally virtuous nature of the Indians. For Las Casas coercive methods of conversion contradict the mandate of the Gospel, which can only be authentically accepted as an act of free will. Conversion can never justify taking Indian land and subjugating them to forced labor.

Others saw the Indians as vicious idolaters, worshippers of demons, as evidenced by practices of human sacrifice. Violent conquest and subjugation to forced labor is due punishment for their sins and the means of bringing them to a better level of civilization. Some Spaniards even saw the epidemics that began to wipe out the Indian population in the sixteenth century as divine punishment for their previous sins.[11] Mendieta allows for moderate coercion, as against Las Casas. He idealized Hernan Cortés, the conqueror of Mexico, as a new Moses who liberated the Indians from bondage to demonic powers.[12] Conversion of the Indians was also seen as compensating the (true) church for its losses to 'heresy'

7. The geographical assumptions of Columbus' time posited one great continent or island of the world surrounded by water in which Europe, Africa and Asia were all connected. See O'Gorman, *Invention of America*, pp. 58–61.

8. See Phelan, *Millennial Kingdom*, pp. 24–25.

9. Phelan, *Millennial Kingdom*, p. 59.

10. Bartolomé de las Casas, *Del único modo de atraer a todos pueblos a la verdadera fe* (Mexico: Fondo de cultura económica, 1942), cited in Phelan, *Millennial Kingdom*, p. 9.

11. Phelan, *Millennial Kingdom*, p. 93. On the diverse European views of the Indian, see Olive Patricia Dickason, *The Myth of the Savage and the Beginning of French Colonialism in the Americas* (Edmonton, Canada: University of Alberta Press, 1984), pp. 61–84.

12. Phelan, *Millennial Kingdom*, pp. 29–38.

in the Reformation. The places of those lost to heresy have been taken by the new converts in the Indies. Through the conversion of the Indians the purity of the apostolic church is being restored.[13]

To those who saw the Indians as naturally virtuous, their conversion might be seen as perfecting natural goodness with supernatural grace. Views of the Indian as naturally disposed to Christianity thus built on Thomistic and Renaissance views of natural reason and natural religion.[14] The Friars saw themselves as both restoring an unfallen church of apostolic times and inaugurating the millennial kingdom of the end of history. For both Jesuits and Franciscans, protecting the Indians and segregating them from the vices of the Spaniards is necessary to preserve their natural innocence and to bring them into a Christianity renewed in its original apostolic purity. But, by the later decades of the sixteenth century, these hopeful visions of a restored apostolic Christianity and the beginnings of the millennial Kingdom of Christ began to give way to discouragement. Mendieta saw the golden age of the Franciscan missions having already given way to a new Babylonian captivity under Charles V's son, Philip II.[15]

France: Holy Land, Chosen People and Most Christian King: French Canada

Although the Saxon kings had claimed the title of emperors of the Holy Roman Empire in the tenth century, France also traced the lineage of its kings to Charlemagne and to earlier Merovingian kings, such as Clovis and Pepin. Some French ideologues of the late Middle Ages looked back even earlier and traced their roots to the Trojans who were said to have taken refuge in France, thus rivaling the claims of the Romans to be descendents of the Trojans.[16] France was one of the earliest areas in Western Europe to consolidate a state under a national monarch in what became its defined territory.

13. Phelan, *Millennial Kingdom*, pp. 44–58.
14. See the chapter on 'Natural Reason and Natural Religion,' in J.H. Kennedy, *Jesuit and Savage in New France* (New Haven, CT: Yale University Press, 1950), pp. 133–52.
15. Phelan, *Millennial Kingdom*, pp. 41, 81–85.
16. See Colette Beaume, *The Birth of an Ideology: Myths and Symbols of Nation in Late–Medieval France* (trans. Susan Ross Huston; Berkeley, CA: University of California Press, 1991), pp. 226–44.

A unified French Kingdom emerged by the end of the thirteenth century, providing the basis for religious claims to its identity.

Alternatively to Trojan ancestry, French nationalists claimed that the French were God's chosen people superseding and replacing the people of Israel. Robert the Monk at the end of the twelfth century could speak of 'the holy race of the Franks who God has chosen as his people and his heritage.'[17] The French people were seen as uniquely pious, its King a paradigm of saintliness and its land uniquely favored by God. Saintly kings, such as the crusader Louis IX, canonized as Saint Louis, and his grandson Philip the Fair, were said to be sons of David and even types of Christ.[18] As 'eldest daughter of the Church' French Catholicism of the late Middle Ages saw itself as the defender of the faith. This view of itself was renewed in the sixteenth century as France vied with Spain as the defender of the true Catholic Christianity against Protestant 'heretics.'

However, unlike Spain, France faltered in establishing a sizable empire in America where it could act out its claims to expand its 'civilizing mission' on the world stage, defeat the Protestants, convert the Indians to the true faith, thereby replacing those lost to heresy, and bring about the completion of history, although all these claims would be made by the French missionaries to North America in the seventeenth century. In the sixteenth century, while Spain was consolidating a huge empire in Central and South America, French seamen, explorers and merchants roamed the coasts of both North and South America. French fishermen long plied the rich fishing areas off the North Atlantic coast, bringing back huge hauls of fish needed for the 153 fast days a year in Catholic France.[19]

But France was hampered in claiming an empire by the papal bull of Pope Alexander VI (1493) and subsequent Treaty of Tordesillas (1494), which divided the American lands between Spain and Portugal. By 1533, France succeeded in persuading Pope Clement VII that this division only applied to lands already explored. Lands not yet explored were open to trade and land claims by other

17. Beaume, *The Birth of an Ideology*, p. 19.

18. Joseph R. Strayer, 'France: the Holy Land, the Chosen People and the Most Christian King,' in *Action and Conviction in Early Modern Europe*, Theodore K. Rabb and Jerrold E. Seigel (eds.), Essays in Memory of E.H. Harbison (Princeton, NJ: Princeton University Press, 1969), pp. 6–10; also Beaume, *The Birth of an Ideology*, pp. 96–125.

19. W.J. Eccles, *France in America* (East Lansing, MI: Michigan State University Press, 1990), pp. 1–2.

Catholic nations.[20] These efforts to open American lands to French trade and settlement were, of course, intended to exclude 'heretics'; namely, the Dutch and English who were already laying down substantial claims along the Atlantic coast of North America. These efforts to exclude Protestants who would spread heresy, not the true faith, were embarrassed by the fact that some of the most adventurous French explorers of the sixteenth century, such as Admiral Gaspard de Coligny, were Huguenots (French Protestants).[21] However, the St. Bartholomew slaughter of Huguenots in 1572, and the conversion of Henry IV to Catholicism, ended the wars of religion in France.

Blocked from land claims by both Spain and Portugal in Latin America and the Dutch and English in North America, the French began to focus their efforts to create a New France in the Eastern half of North America north of New England, an area which none of the other European powers seemed to want (due in part to its long cold winter). In 1625, Cardinal Richelieu, King Louis XIV's first minister, formed a new trading company to exploit the resources of New France, to establish agricultural settlements and promote missionary activity. Huguenots were excluded.[22] Eight Jesuits were sent to New France in 1625–26 to begin the conversion of the Indians to the (French) Catholic faith.

The religious interpretation of New France in the seventeenth century bears similarities to that of New Spain, but more modestly, perhaps reflecting the poverty and weakness of the French efforts, compared to the huge empire being founded by the Spanish, as well as the much greater numbers of settlers flooding from England to the Anglo-American settlements to the south. In 1689, the English settlers numbered 200,000 compared to only 10,000 French, and by 1756 when New France fell to England, there were 1,500,000 English settlers and only 70,000 French.[23] Moreover, France itself was sporadic in its financial support for New France, ignoring it for long periods. The French nobility and merchant classes also had minimal interest. Voltaire dismissed New France as 'a few acres of

20. Eccles, *France in America*, pp. 1, 3.

21. Eccles, *France in America*, pp. 8–10, 12.

22. Eccles, *France in America*, p. 28; also Mason Wade, *The French Canadians, 1760–1945* (London: Macmillan and Co., 1955), p. 14.

23. Eccles, *France in America*, p. 28; Wade, *The French Canadians*, p. 20.

snow.'[24] The missionary orders of the Catholic Church were its more faithful supporters. It would be they who would primarily shape its culture.

Like Spain in the sixteenth century, seventeenth century France was experiencing a renaissance of Catholic humanistic scholarship. The Jesuits who arrived in New France as missionaries were well educated in languages, the classics and history. They quickly decided that there could be no authentic conversion of the Indians except through learning their languages and worldview and translating the doctrines of the faith into terms that the Indians could understand.[25] They devoted themselves to years of learning the indigenous languages, often at great peril to their own lives, as the basis for winning real converts. They also developed schools from the primary level to universities for Indian girls and boys, as well as the French settlers.

Conversion to Christianity and the French civilizing mission were seen as going hand in hand. While beginning in the Indian's own language, the French missionaries also assumed that making the Indians Christians meant making them French. This meant not only learning to speak French, but also abandoning their nomadic way of life for agricultural settlement and absorbing a French Catholic culture. So closely were conversion and becoming French identified, that Christian Indians were even offered the option of living in France as French subjects, although few Indians seemed to be interested in this.[26]

As the missionaries deepened their understanding of the Indian peoples, their view of them as savage barbarians was often tempered by an admiration of them as eloquent and possessed of a deep sense of morality and community ethic. Indians were seen by some Jesuits as possessing a simple morality superior to the corrupted French.[27] This stirred hopes that the conversion of the Indians, protected in their own enclaves from French vices, might be the basis of a renewal of apostolic Christianity. Thus, the Jesuit, Paul le Jeune, reflects in his report of missionary activity in 1637: 'The more this infant church has in common with the primitive one, the greater the hope it gives

24. Voltaire, *Candide*, p. 23, cited in Wade, *The French Canadians*, p. 3.
25. Kennedy, *Jesuit and Savage*, pp. 61–62.
26. Eccles, *France in America*, pp. 40–41.
27. Kennedy, *Jesuit and Savage* , pp. 109–24.

us of seeing it produce flowers and fruits worthy of Paradise.'[28] The Jesuit missionaries supported policies of screening the settlers from France, excluding the vicious, so Indian innocence might mingle with the best of a morally renewed French Christianity, and New France become a paradigm of the New Jerusalem to come. As Le Jeune puts it, 'There will arise here a Jerusalem blessed of God composed of citizens destined for heaven.'[29]

By the mid-eighteenth century these tentative hopes for a New Jerusalem in Quebec crashed against the harsh realities of New France's poverty, lack of numbers of settlers or adequate military and financial support from France. In 1759, after a devastating destruction of Quebec, the English General, James Wolfe, defeated the Comte de Montcalm on the Plains of Abraham. New France was incorporated under English rule of North America. The Jesuits, already being suppressed in Europe, were left to die out in New France. The descendants of the French settlers turned from hopeful visions of a French Catholic redemption of the world to a determination to 'survive,' to preserve their Catholic faith and French language and culture in a world ruled by English Protestants. This struggle would shape what it would mean to be French Canadian.

England: God's True Church and Chosen People

England's sense of itself as the people chosen by God to preserve the true faith was forged in the context of the sixteenth century English Reformation. Legends of God's special favor on England had existed before, such as the belief that after the resurrection of Christ, the Apostle, Philip, had sent Joseph of Arimathea to England, bearing the chalice of the last supper, to establish the first church there, a claim found already in William of Malmesbury in the twelfth century and central to the medieval English Holy Grail legends. The British also had their Trojan legend. The Trojan Brutus was said to have been the founder of Britain. The emperor Constantine was also seen as British through his English mother Helena and was crowned on British soil. These legends had been gathered together in the *Anglica Historia* of the Italian humanist, Polydore

28. *Jesuit Relations and Allied Documents: Travels and Explorations of the Jesuit Missionaries of New France, 1636–37*, XI, p. 43.

29. *Jesuit Relations, 1634–35*, X, pp. 217, 273.

Vergil, resident in Britain as the deputy collector of Peter's Pence in the reign of Henry VII.[30] Such ideas took on a new meaning in the context of sixteenth century English Protestant apologetic historiography.

English reformers felt stung to answer the Catholic claim that their church was schismatic, a breakaway sect from the one true church founded by Christ. They forged an alternative interpretation of church history to defend the Church of England as the successor of the true church of apostolic times, while the 'Romish' church was the corrupt 'synagogue of Satan' that had fallen away from the true faith of Christ. This perspective was hammered out in various tracts in the 1530s–60s during the tumultuous reigns of Henry VIII and his break with the Roman church, the brief reign of his son, Edward VII (1547–53), then his daughter Mary's efforts to restore Roman Catholicism (1553–58). This was followed by the forty-four year reign of Henry's second daughter Elizabeth I, in which the Church of England was consolidated as the 'middle way' between Catholics and Puritans.

One of the most influential works to argue for English Protestantism as the true church of Christ is Bishop John Bale's commentary on the book of Revelation, *Image of Both Churches* (1550). Here is laid out the unending war between the true church of Christ and the false church of the anti-Christ. For Bale this war is not only the guiding theme for understanding this New Testament book, but undergirds Christian history from its beginnings to the triumph of God's true people in the English Reformation.

> Herein is the true Christian church, which is the meek spouse of the Lamb without spot, in her right-fashioned colors described. So is the proud church of the hypocrites, the rose-colored whore, the paramour of antichrist and the sinful synagogue of Satan, in her just proportion depainted, to the merciful forewarning of the Lord's elect.[31]

Bale traces this conflict between the true and false church in vivid detail through the pages of the book of Revelation. The dragon from which the woman clothed with the sun flees (Rev. 12), the beasts that rise from the sea and from the earth (Rev. 13) and the harlot seated on the scarlet beast (Rev. 17) are identified as the

30. William Haller, *The Elect Nation: The Meaning and Relevance of Foxe's Book of Martyrs* (New York: Harper and Row, 1963), p. 143.

31. 'Image of both Churches,' in *Select Works of John Bale* (Cambridge: Cambridge University Press, 1849), p. 251.

church of Rome, source of all abominations, while the reformed church of England is that people of the lamb called to come out of Babylon, who are being vindicated in the Reformation and who will inherit the new heaven and earth when Satan and his minions are thrown into the lake of fire to be tormented day and night forever (Rev. 20:10). Commenting on the description of the Whore of Babylon in Revelations 17, Bale says:

> This beast is the great antichrist that was spoken of afore, or the beastly body of the devil, comprehending in him popes, patriarchs, cardinals, legates, bishops, doctors, abbots, priors, priests and pardoners, monks, canons, friars, nuns and so forth; temporal governors also, as emperors, kings, princes, dukes, earls, lords, justices, deputies, judges, lawyers, mayors, bailiffs, constables and so forth, learning their own duty-offices as to minister rightly, to serve their abominations.
>
> Full of blasphemous names is this beast also, as your holiness, your grace, your lordship, your fatherhood, your mastership, your reverence...Upon this beast sitteth a woman. For what else advanceth or bareth out this malignant muster in their copes, crosses, oils, mitres, robes, relics, ceremonies, vigils, holy days, blessings, censings and fooling, but a wanton, foolish and fantastical religion, a vain-glorious pomp, and a shining pretence of holiness in superstition, calling it their holy church?
>
> Moreover in her hand, which is her exterior ministration, she hath a golden cup full of abominations and filthiness of her execrable whoredom. This cup is the false religion that she daily ministereth, besides the chalice whom her merchants most damnably abuse and it containeth all the doctrine of devils, all beastly errors and lies, all deceitful power, all glittering works of hypocrites, all crafty wisdom of the flesh and subtle practices of man's wit, besides philosophy, logic, rhetoric and sophistry; yea, all prodigious kinds of idolatry, fornication, sodomitry and wickedness... Full of abominations is the drink of the execrable faith of the Romish religion...[32]

In this polemic Bale goes considerably beyond identifying the Pope with the Anti-Christ and Whore of Babylon, a view which had become standard among Protestants. He not only condemned the entire Catholic Church in all its ministries and ceremonies as evil, but also attacked the nobility and merchant classes as part of the same system of abomination. Such a sweeping condemnation of the leadership classes of church, state and society would lead to new civil war in the seventeenth century, as radical Protestants called for deeper reforms and began to apply the rhetoric of

---

32. 'Image of both Churches,' in *Select Works of John Bale*, pp. 496, 497.

demonization to the Church of England and English social hierarchies.[33]

The saga of this struggle between the English true church of Christ and the false Church of Rome was laid out in every expanding detail in Foxe's book of martyrs. This work began in 1559 with the assembly of the testimonies of the martyrs of the reign of 'bloody Mary,' but soon gathered many more stories of English martyrs back to the time of Wycliffe and the Lollards of the fourteenth century. An expanded version appeared in 1563, a few years after the accession of Elizabeth I, in a folio of 20 pages of introduction, followed by 1800 pages of text, entitled: *Actes and Monuments of these latter and perillous days, touching matters of the Church, wherein are comprehended and described the great persecutions & horrible troubles, that have been wrought and practiced by the Romish Prelates, speciallye in this Realme of England and Scotlande, from the yeare of our Lord a thousande, unto the tyme nowe present. Gathered and collected according to the true copies & wrytings certificatorie as wel of the parties them selves that suffered, as also out of the Bishops Registers which wer the doers thereof, by John Foxe.*

This title was enclosed in an engraved border showing the last judgment on the two churches according to the view found in Bale's *Image of the Two Churches*. At the top, the Lord is enthroned surrounded by trumpeting angels. On his right are the risen saints with trumpets and palms. Below them the martyrs blowing trumpets while burning at the stake and below them the people listening to the Word with the (English) Bibles in their laps. On the left are the priests of the false church of Rome being thrown out of heaven by demons, while below them people kneel at the elevation of the host, march toward a crucifix and tell their beads while listening to a vested priest. Fifty-six woodcut illustrations are scattered through the volume showing the martyrs, often at the moment of being burned at the stake.[34]

Further expanded editions appeared through the sixteenth century adding more martyrs' stories, giving more detail on the times of Henry and Mary and tracing the history of the Church of England back to apostolic times. In recounting earlier church history from its beginnings, Foxe followed the patterns found in Eusebius'

33. See Christopher Hill, *Antichrist in the Seventeenth Century* (London: Oxford University Press, 1971).

34. Haller, *Elect Nation*, pp. 118, 119.

Ecclesiastical History (340 CE) as a struggle between orthodoxy and heresy, as well as Augustine's *City of God*, as a conflict between the two cities, the city of God and the city of Satan. But he adapted these earlier understandings to the English Protestant view of church history.

Church history was divided into five periods. The first era, which ran from the Apostles to Constantine, was a struggle of the true church to keep the faith against heresy and persecution, an account largely drawn from Eusebius, but with the claims to apostolic foundations of the Church of England through the apostle Philip and Joseph of Arimathea. The second era, from the Constantinian foundation to 600, was seen as one of flourishing of the church. Constantine was seen as British and a defender of the true faith to whom Elizabeth is compared. The third era from 600–1,000 is one of decline in which the church of the anti-Christ begins to make inroads. From 1,000 to the time of Wycliffe, Satan is unloosed and the church of the anti-Christ predominates.

With Wycliffe come the beginnings of the struggle against the false church and the new time of the martyrs. Thus, Foxe makes Wycliffe the primary source of the Reformation, subordinating Luther and Calvin to an English foundation of the reform of the church. This era continues through the conflicts of the first half of the sixteenth century to the martyrs of Mary's time and is concluded with Elizabeth I in whom the true Church of Christ is reestablished. It is suggested that her reign is the time of the last struggle for redemption on earth leading to the millennial kingdom. The English church, founded in apostolic times, has always sought to defend the true faith, and its true kings and prelates have fought off continual efforts from Rome to take it over and submerge it. Augustine of Canterbury, sent by Pope Gregory the Great in 597 CE, far from being the true founder of the English church, is interpreted as one of the efforts of the false Church of Rome to subordinate the apostolic church preserved in Britain.

The greatest detail is reserved for the story of the martyrs and the struggle for reform from Wycliffe through the Marian martyrs, leading to the triumphant reign of Elizabeth. The story of Wycliffe opens with the words:

> We will begin our history with the story of John Wickliffe our countryman and the other men of his time and country, whom the Lord (with the like zeal and power of the spirit) raised up here in

England, to detect more fully the poison of the Pope's doctrine and false religion set up by the friars.[35]

Wycliffe's story continues through his posthumous condemnation at the Council of Constance and the decree to burn his bones. The burning of Wycliffe's bones and the pouring of his ashes into the river is illustrated with a woodcut. Comparing Wycliffe with Christ whom the Pharisees killed in order to silence him forever, but who defeated their intentions by rising again, Foxe comments:

> ...so there is no keeping down verity, but it will spring and come out of dust and ashes, as appeared right well with this man. For though they digged up his body, burnt his bones and drowned his ashes, yet the word of God and the truth of his doctrine, with the fruit and success thereof, they could not burn.

The story of the struggle for the reformation and restoration of the true church is continued from Wycliffe's time to that of Elizabeth. Hundreds of martyrs for the faith, both from the highest station to the lowliest village woman are recounted, with many an illustrating woodcut, typically featuring the final burning at the stake. The pictures of the martyrs falls into a recurring type, despite great variety of detail. The martyrs are depicted as devoted to the true Christianity of faith alone, without ceremonies, and expressed in the Word of God in English, both the English Bible and prayers in English. Although totally inoffensive except for their unwavering perseverance in the true faith, they are seized by malicious clerics and authorities. They are tormented but refuse to yield. Finally, they are sent to the stake, dying in total tranquility and surrendering their soul to God in a manner edifying to those neighbors disposed to the truth. So the martyrdom of the unlettered but steadfast Kerby Clarke of Mendlesham in 1546 is told thus:

> The next day about 10 o'clock Kerby was brought to the marketplace, where a stake was ready, wood, broom, and straw, and did off his clothes unto his shirt, having a nightcap on his head, and so was fastened to the stake with irons, there being in the gallery Lord Wentworth with most of the justices of those quarters, where they might see the execution and hear what Kerby did say; and a great number of people, about two thousand, by estimation. Then said the under-sheriff to Kerby, "Hast thou anything to say?" "Yea, sir," said he, "if you will give me leave." "Say on," said the sheriff. Then Kerby taking his

35. G.A. Williamson (ed.), *Foxe's Book of Martyrs*, (Boston: Little, Brown and Company, 1965), p. 1.

nightcap from his head was putting it under his arm, as though it should have done him service again; but remembering himself he cast it from him, and lifting up his hands he said the *Te Deum* and the Belief with other prayers, in English. Lord Wentworth, whilst Kerby was thus doing, did shroud himself behind one of the posts of the gallery and wept, and so did many others. Then said Kerby, "I have done: execute your office, good Mr Sheriff." Then the fire was set to the wood, and with a loud voice he called unto God, knocking on his breast, and holding up his hands, as long as remembrance would serve, and so ended his life; the people giving shouts and praising God, with great admiration for his constancy, being so simple and unlettered.[36]

The greatest detail is reserved for the Marian martyrs, particularly leading figures such as Thomas Cranmer, Nicholas Ridley and Hugh Latimer, all of whom had written and published their own testimonies while in the Tower before their executions.[37] The story of the martyrs culminated with the sufferings of the Princess Elizabeth under her hostile sister Mary. Although not actually executed, her constant imprisonments, harassment and threats of being put to death, even while maintaining her steadfast faith, counts for Foxe as a kind of martyrdom, as well as a testimony to the providential work of God who thus 'miraculously' preserved her.

Elizabeth's pivotal role in Foxe's book of the election of the English Church and nation is summed up thus:

...never was there any example wherein the Lord's mighty power hath more admirably and blessedly showed itself, to the glory of his holy name, the comfort of all good hearts, and the felicity of this whole realm, than in the miraculous custody and outscape of this own sovereign Lady, now Queen, then Lady Elizabeth, in the strait time of Queen Mary her sister. We have first to consider in what extreme misery, sickness, fear and peril her Highness was; into what care, what trouble of mind, and what danger of death she was brought, first with great routs and bands of armed men being fetched up as the greatest traitor in the world, clapped in the Tower, and again tossed from thence, and from house to house, from prison to prison, then post to pillar, guarded with a sort of cut-throats which ever gaped for the spoil. Secondly, to consider we have how strangely, or rather miraculously, from danger she was delivered, what favor she found with the Almighty; who, when with all help of man and hope of delivery was past, stretched out his mighty protection and preserved

36. Williamson (ed.), *Foxe's Book of Martyrs*, p. 161.
37. Haller, *Elect Nation*, pp. 25–47.

her Highness, and placed her in this princely seat wherein now she sittith; and long may she sit, the Lord of his glorious mercy grant, we beseech him.[38]

Although Foxe might hymn Elizabeth I as a godly prince and a second Constantine, the Puritan wing of the Church of England was quickly made aware that her ideas of religion were far from their hopes for a reformed English Christendom. Elizabeth wanted a church firmly under her own control, but otherwise retaining many traditional elements. The reformers hoped to gradually effect those changes necessary for what they saw as a truly 'purified' church. They would struggle against a wily but intransigent queen for the forty-four years of her reign. Their hopes for further reform would also be disappointed under her successor James I, while his son, Charles I, moved back toward an even more Catholic church under his archbishop Laud. The struggle was political and international, as much as religious and national. Elizabeth and the Stuarts wanted to position England in a positive relation to the Catholic powers of France and Spain, including marriage alliances, not ally England with a rigid Protestantism that would make these powers their enemy.

The desired reforms included a long list of demands. First, there were a number of changes in rites that might today appear petty, but for the reformers separated a truly reformed church from 'papist idolatry.' This meant eliminating vestments and surplice, distinctive outdoor dress for the clergy, signing the cross, addressing questions to the infant in baptism, baptism by midwives, the rite of confirmation, kneeling at communion and the use of wafers, giving the ring in marriage, purification of women after childbirth, use of terms such as 'priest' and 'absolution,' observance of saints' days, bowing at the name of Jesus, organs and singing in parts.[39]

But the list went on to a number of other matters. The Puritans wanted a more strictly Calvinist theology in the Prayer Book, one that clearly taught predestination and limited election. An educated and better-paid clergy was needed that would instruct the people through regular sermons. The scandal of bishops living in princely luxury, while local clergy could barely feed their families, must

38. Williamson (ed.), *Foxe's Book of Martyrs*, p. 429.
39. See Patrick Collinson, *The Elizabethan Puritan Movement* (London: Jonathan Cape, 1967), p. 36.

change; also the practice of plurality of livings, so that local churches were left with untrained delegates of the priest. While abolishing Saints Days (which allowed medieval society over a hundred holidays), Puritans wanted a strict observance of the Sabbath. They would go toe to toe with James I on banning sports on Sunday.[40] Relief was sought from the system of church courts that prosecuted humble people for minor offenses while serious problems were ignored. The Court of the High Commission was a tool of the royal bureaucracy. Excommunication was used for political as much as religious purposes. Books were banned. Preachers were hauled before the court for minor infractions of ritual. The Puritans sought a far-reaching reform of the whole system of church and state relations.[41]

One of the early conflicts between the Puritan clergy and Elizabeth was over vestments. Reformers want to eliminate vestments as setting the clergyman apart from the people. Some bishops were allowing their clergy freedom of choice in the matter. But Elizabeth insisted on the surplice. In 1565, she instructed Matthew Parker, her Archbishop of Canterbury, to enforce uniformity in clerical dress. Many clergy were deprived of their positions for refusing to conform.[42] In this struggle Elizabeth and the Puritan reformers shared a common presupposition; namely, the unity of church and nation. There should be one national church, and all parts of that national church should follow the same regulations. Only with difficulty over the ensuing three centuries would this presupposition be given up, allowing both a diversity of separate churches to exist without civil discrimination, as well as some diversity of practices within the Church of England.

The intransigence of Elizabeth toward these demands for reform led many Puritans to sponsor their own lectureships. Reform-minded laymen and women from the nobility and wealthy merchant classes, as well as bands of more humble workers, might fund a Puritan-style preacher who would lecture on Sunday afternoon or during the week. Circles gathered within parishes for study and conversation. All this was seen as subversive and incipiently sectarian. There were waves of repression of such lecturers. Groups

40. Christopher Hill, *A Century of Revolution, 1603–1714* (Edinburgh: Thomas Nelson and Sons, 1961), pp. 84–86.
41. Hill, *A Century of Revolution*, pp. 79–80.
42. Collinson, *The Elizabethan Puritan Movement*, pp. 67–83.

gathering in their own halls were arrested.[43] Churches within the church sprang up all over England, yet most of these engaged in such practices had no desire to be 'separatists.' They saw themselves as reformers within the Church of England.

New England: God's New Elect Nation and Promised Land

Some reformers became discouraged and decided that the Church of England was not reformable. In their mind it had become simply another branch of the 'papistical anti-Christ' little different from the Church of Rome. True Christians are called to separate from this great Whore of Babylon, to 'come out of her, my people, lest you take part in her sins, lest you share in her plagues' (Rev. 18:4). They should form truly purified church congregations, escaping to some safe place where they might await the outpouring of divine wrath that was soon to come. Henry Barrow and John Greenwood were leaders of such separatists in the 1580s. They were arrested in 1587 and executed in 1593. To escape persecution some separatists moved to Holland. But they quarreled among themselves and found some aspects of Dutch society uncongenial.

In 1620, an English separatist group in Leiden began to negotiate with a group of English investors to form a joint stock company to finance immigration to America. There the separatists hoped to form a Christian community according to their fullest ideals. After several false starts, the *Mayflower* left on September 6, 1620, overcrowded with 102 passengers. Not all of these belonged to the Leiden separatist group. Some, like Captain Miles Standish and the cooper John Alden, were engaged by the London investors to provide the colony with needed skills. Although the Mayflower's destination was the northern part of the Virginia territory, the boat went astray and landed on Cape Cod. After various explorations of the coast, they chose Plymouth harbor as the place to stay.

Because they had no legal right to settle in New England, they drew up a covenant signed by 41 men, later called the 'Mayflower Compact,' on November 11, 1620, agreeing to 'covenant and combine ourselves together into a Civil Body Politic, for our better ordering and preservation...and frame such just and equal Laws, Ordinances, Acts and Constitutions and Offices, from time to time, as shall be

---

43. *The Elizabethan Puritan Movement*, pp. 88–91.

thought most meet and convenient for the general good of the Colony, unto which we promise all due submission and obedience.'[44]

Although half of the group died over the long winter, in spring the colonists were able to begin to build and plant crops. William Bradford was elected governor, a post he held to his death in 1657. The colony grew slowly, was able to stabilize itself and buy out the investors so that they could own their own land. Although the original Mayflower Compact had not been explicitly religious, the separatist core of the immigrants soon formed a church, reinforced by the arrival of more members of the Leiden congregation. This small beginning of colonization of New England would soon be greatly expanded by the arrival of non-separatist Puritans in the 1630s.

In 1625, James I was replaced by his son Charles I who was even less disposed to church reform. His French Catholic queen, Henrietta Maria, was the center of a pro-Catholic party at court. Charles' Archbishop of Canterbury, William Laud, championed an anti-Calvinist movement, forbidding predestinarian theology and emphasizing liturgical devotion, thus deepening the polarization between the preferred church of the court and the Puritan reformers. Independent corporations to finance Puritan preachers were suppressed by the government. Charles also pressured Dutch authorities to crack down on English dissidents resident there. It was in this context that Puritan groups turned to migration in New England. In 1628, the New England Company was formed with rights to settle from three miles north of the Merrimac River to three miles south of the Charles River. Its first ship, the *Abigail*, departed with forty colonists, including Charles Endecott, a leader of the company, later named governor of the colony.

The next year, the charter for the Massachusetts Bay Company was issued by the king. That year Charles I also dissolved Parliament, eliminating Puritan hopes for parliamentary redress of their grievances. A group of Puritan leaders from East Anglia, including John Winthrop, formed the Cambridge Agreement in August 1629, pledging to emigrate if the company's government and charter were transferred to the colony. This was completed in October, and seven vessels, led by the flagship *Arbella*, departed Southampton

44. Francis J. Bremer, *The Puritan Experiment: New England Society from Bradford to Edwards* (Hanover: University Press of New England, 1995), p. 33.

on 29 March 1630, after the Puritan preacher, John Cotton, preached the departure sermon to the voyagers. Thousands more would follow in the next few years, reaching some 21,000 colonists in New England by the end of the decade.

Cotton's sermon, 'God's Promise to his Plantations,' struck major themes of a theological justification for the migration. Cotton took as his text 2 Sam. 7:10, 'Moreover I will appoint a place for my people Israel, and I will plant them, that they may dwell in a place of their owne and move no more.' Thus the Puritan colonists were identified with God's chosen people Israel, and the land to which they were going was one given to them by God as their land of promise. For Cotton, this land was itself being created as a land of promise by the very process of planting the purified ordinance of God in this land: 'When God wrappes us in his Ordinances and warms us with the life and power of them as with wings, there is a land of promise.'[45]

John Winthrop, first governor of the Massachusetts Bay colony, struck the major themes of his understanding of the godly commonwealth that they hoped to plant in New England in his 'A Modell of Christian Charity,' written on board the Arbella during the journey. This was not to be an egalitarian society. God had ordained society to consist of rich and poor, rulers and ruled:

> God Almightie in his most holy and wise providence hath soe disposed of the Condicion of mankinde, as in all times some must be rich, some poore, some highe and eminent in power and dignitie; others mean and in subjeccion.

However, such distinctions between persons do not allow for some to be unjust to others. For Winthrop, the godly society must be a covenant of mutual help ruled by the two principles of justice and mercy. Winthrop declared that the colonists have entered into a covenant with God to create such a just and merciful society. They have drawn up the terms of this agreement with God, and God will 'expect a strickt performance of the Articles contained in it.' Such a covenant with God carries with it the threat of dire punishment if it is not faithfully observed:

45. John Cotton, *God's Promise to his Plantation* (1634), pp. 6–7: see Avihu Zakai, *Exile and Kingdom: History and Apocalypse in the Puritan Migration to America* (Cambridge: Cambridge University Press, 1992), p. 168.

...but if wee shall neglect the observation of these Articles which are the ends we have propounded, and dissembling with our God, shall fall to embrace this present world and prosecute our carnall intentions seekeing great things for ourselves and our posterity, the Lord will surely breake out in wrathe against us, be revenged of such a perjured people and make us knowe the price of the breache of such a Covenant.

The onlely way to avoyde this shipwracke and to provide for our posterity is to followe the counsell of Micah, to doe justly, to love mercy, to walke humbly with our God.

Such faithfulness to their covenant will demand that the colony be 'knitt together in this worke as one man.' This means a community of 'brotherly affection' where some 'abridge' their 'superfluities for the supply of others' necessities.' Through this bond of mutual help they might create a truly godly society, ruled by justice and mercy, Winthrop warns that the eyes of the whole world will be upon them as a model for subsequent plantations:

...the Lord make it like that of New England: for wee must Consider that wee shall be as a Citty on a Hill, the eies of all people are uppon us, soe that if we shall deale falsely with our God in this worke wee have undertaken and soe cause him to withdrawe his present help from us, wee shall shame the faces of many of gods worthy servants, and cause their prayers to be turned into Cursses upon us till wee be consumed out of the good land whither wee are goeing. And so to shutt up his discourse with that exhortacion of Moses, that faithful servant of the Lord in his last farewell to Israell, Deut. 30. Beloved there is now sett before us life and good, deathe and evil in that wee are Commaunded this day to love the Lord our God and to love one another, to walke in his wayes and keepe his Commaundements and his Ordinance, and his lawes and the Articles of our Covenant with him that wee may live and be multiplied, and that the Lord our God may blesse us in the land whither we goe to possesse it. But if our heartes shall turne away soe that wee will not obey, but shall be seduced and worship ...other Gods, our pleasures and proffitts and serve them, it is propounded unto us this day, wee shall surely perishe out of this good Land whither wee passe over this vast Sea to possesse it: Therefore lett us choose life, that wee and our Seede may live, by obeyeing his voyce and cleaveing to him for he is our life and our prosperity.[46]

46. From the *Winthrop Papers*, II (The Massachusetts Historical Society, 1931), pp. 282, 292–95: taken from Conrad Cherry (ed.), *God's New Israel; Religious Interpretations of American Destiny* (Chapel Hill, NC: The University of North Carolina Press, 1998), pp. 37–41.

Modern interpreters have developed several ways of looking at the religious self-understanding of this first generation of Puritan colonists. For Perry Miller, the Puritans defined their migration as an 'errand into the wilderness,' modeled after Rev. 12.6, by which the true church flees from the Dragon of worldly evil and takes refuge in the wilderness until God has poured out his wrath against the Kingdoms of Satan and delivered God's people into millennial blessing.[47] Others have seen the Puritans as continuing their hope of reform of the English nation and church long distance. They hoped that by developing a model of the true godly commonwealth, others in England might be inspired to follow. In some more propitious time the model could be brought back for the reform of the English church and society.

Winthrop's reflections, however, contain neither an immediate apocalyptic expectation of a divine advent nor hopes for reform back in England. Rather his attention is riveted on the colony he and his group propose to found in Massachusetts Bay. He does speak of it as a 'citty on a Hill' in the sense of being an experiment under scrutiny by others seeking to found other 'plantations' in the New World. Winthrop claims the identity of this people as God's Israel in a way that is compounded of equal measures of promise and warning. If they are faithful to their covenant with God, they will be a model of God's true people for others to follow. But if they 'deale falsely with our god,' divine wrath will be poured out on them, they will become cursed and a source of calumny for others. Self-understanding as God's elect people carries no assurance of divine blessing for Winthrop . Only if they are truly just and faithful will they fulfill the covenant as God's people. But if they fail and descend into the opposite of all these hopes, they will become, like ancient Israel, a people upon whom God will pour out punishment and even expel from the land.

The notion claimed by Spain, France and England in the sixteenth and seventeenth centuries of being God's New Israel, an elect nation chosen to bring redemption to the world, could thus lend itself to a variety of interpretations. For the most part this claim carried the assumption of entitlement. Because God had elected them, this nation both monopolizes a knowledge of true Christianity and has

47. Perry Miller, *Errand into the Wilderness* (Cambridge, MA: Harvard University Press, 1956).

a right to expand, to colonize the land of the Americans and to bring true Christianity to its indigenous people, while defeating and driving away competitors, understood as God's enemies. Colonization and conversion of the Indians are expansions of the privileged status of this people. This expansion includes spreading their national language, culture and other institutions, as well as their church.

Such views are also found among other English colonists. Alexander Whitaker, a clergyman of the Church of England who arrived in the colony of Jamestown, Virginia in 1611, recommends investment in the colony to Sir Thomas Smith, treasurer of the colony in England, through a combination of the promise of conversion of the benighted Indians to the true faith and the expectation of great prosperity to be found in cultivating this new land. Like the promise of the land of Canaan to Abraham, so the promise of the land of Virginia to Englishmen will reap the fruits of economic as well as spiritual benefits.[48]

Avihu Zakai has argued that two radically distinct models of being the elect nation: the Genesis model and the Exodus model were operative in this period. The Genesis model was based on Abraham's migration to the Promised Land of Canaan. It was a model of expansion from a base of divine election to a larger empire. This model governed French and Spanish colonization, as well as that of the English of Virginia. The Puritans, however, worked with an Exodus model, in which England had sinned and lost its election. It had fallen to become an anti-Christ, like the Church of Rome. Thus, the true people of God are called to exodus from the land of slavery, Egypt, to flee from the city of evil, Babylon, to prepare them for a future redemption to be brought about by God, one that they would anticipate by their godly plantings in America.

While this distinction is insightful, I find it too simple. A Spanish Franciscan like Mendieta could speak sorrowfully of the high hopes of his order to plant the millennial kingdom as having fallen into a new 'Babylonian captivity.' Bartolomé de las Casas could pour out impassioned judgment against his fellow Spaniards for their oppression of the Indian in tones that far surpassed the Jeremiads of any Puritan preacher on his fellow colonists. On the other hand, Puritan settlers in Massachusetts Bay never doubted that their elect

48. See Cherry, *God's New Israel*, pp. 30–36.

status as God's New Israel entitled them to colonize the land of New England. When Roger Williams in 1633 asserted that the King of England had no right to grant land to the Puritans because the land belonged to the Indians, his opinion was treated as simply outrageous. He was censured by the General Court and eventually expelled from the colony.

The Puritans' view of those things, which should be judged as failures in their covenant with God, did not include taking the land from the Indians. Nevertheless, they did entertain a keen sense of their own fallibility and the possibility that they could fail in their venture of building a godly commonwealth, instead becoming a model of sinful apostasy meriting divine wrath. American civil religion, as we will trace in subsequent chapters of this book, will find both of these aspects of the ideology of divine election operative. There will be much in this claim that is primarily an assumption of entitlement, an assumption of a superiority that merits wealth and power over other peoples and nations of the world. But, again and again, there will break out in the language of American reformers the tones of the Puritan Jeremiad, rooted in a horrified conviction that America has failed in her claims to godliness, even turned them to their opposite and become a scandal to the world, an epitome of oppressive violence, not unlike the other evil kingdoms of the world that have set themselves against authentic goodness, truth and justice. Such reformers will issue a call to repent and to return to America's true vocation. In both these stances, of adulation and of judgment and call to repentance, America remains, to the American puritan mind, a 'city set on a hill' for the instruction of other nations.

Chapter Two

THE RIGHTS OF MAN AND THE EXCLUDED OTHERS — THE REVOLUTIONARY ERA AND BEYOND

The founders of the godly commonwealths came to North America to pursue their vision of the true church and society, but they had no more intention of including Christians of other views in their communities than the English establishment was willing to include them. Both shared an exclusive view of the true church coterminous with the nation, or, in the case of the Puritan settlers, coterminous with their own covenanted community. From the beginning of the foundation of the Massachusetts Bay colony, there were clashes with Christians of other persuasions.

Catholics were, of course, totally excluded as the demonic alien of the Puritan worldview, and the French Catholic settlement to the North was regarded as its sworn enemy. Anglicans were looked on with suspicion and classified as dissenters in New England. When the Church of England developed the Society for the Propagation of the Gospel in Foreign Parts in 1701 to evangelize the colonies, and especially when there was talk of founding an American episcopacy, this was seen as part of an English conspiracy to subject the Puritans of Massachusetts to the joint power of bishops and crown.[1] There were also constant efforts by the Puritan divines to exclude any tendency toward Presbyterianism in their midst.[2]

Separatists and more radical dissenters were rigorously excluded. The Separatists of Plymouth colony were regarded with suspicion, but since they were a self-governing colony, the Massachusetts ministry and magistracy had no direct jurisdiction over them. Punitive measures were taken against 'heretics' who either arose within the Puritan community or attempted to settle in it. In 1635,

1. Francis J. Bremer, *The Puritan Experiment: New England Society from Bradford to Edwards* (Hanover, NH: University Press of New England, 1995), pp. 225–27.

2. Bremer, *The Puritan Experiment*, pp. 133–34.

separatist dissenter, Roger Williams, was banished for a variety of heresies, including his view that the English crown had no right to allot Indian lands to Englishmen. Anne Hutchinson and her supporters were put on trial for preaching a doctrine of grace separated from good works and claiming direct revelations from God. She and her supporters were banished in 1637.[3] Baptist views were not allowed, and in 1651 three Baptists found in the colony were fined and banished.[4]

The Massachusetts Bay colony would be further challenged by the arrival of Quakers in 1656. These were fined and banished. But when the Quakers insisted on continuing to show up and witnessing to their views despite these measures, the Massachusetts court decreed the death penalty against them. In 1659, the Quakers William Robinson and Marmaduke Stevenson were hung in Boston under this law, as was Mary Dyer in 1660. In 1661, Charles II ruled against the execution of Quakers, although Puritan law continued to punish Quakers by strapping them to a cart and whipping them all the way out of town.[5]

In May of 1692, a witch hysteria arose in Salem, Massachusetts. Before it was over at the end of that year one hundred and fifty-six people had been imprisoned, nineteen were hung and four died in prison. Another fifty confessed to witchcraft and so were saved from execution. This was not directly a question of religious dissent, since all agreed that witches who made pacts with the devil existed and could cause 'maleficia' (evil), and they were to be executed if they failed to repent. There was dispute over whether particular persons actually were witches and the evidence for such convictions. The incident stands rather as a testimony to the extent to which a society bent on banishing demonic enemies outside, is itself prone to discover devils within.[6]

3. Bremer, *The Puritan Experiment*, pp. 62–70. See also Edmund Morgan, *Roger Williams: Church and State* (New York: Harcourt, Brace and World, 1967). For Anne Hutchinson and the Antinomian Controversy, see Emery Battis, *Saints and Sectaries: Anne Hutchinson and the Antinomian Controversy in the Massachusetts Bay Colony* (Chapel Hill, NC: University of North Carolina Press 1962).

4. Bremer, *The Puritan Experiment*, pp. 135, 137.

5. Bremer, *The Puritan Experiment*, pp. 154–56. See also Carla Pestana, *Quakers and Baptists in Colonial Massachusetts* (New York: Cambridge University Press, 1991).

6. Bremer, *The Puritan Experiment*, pp. 181–64: See also Marion Starkey, *The Devil in Massachusetts* (New York: A.A. Knopf, 1949). On the gendered aspects of the conflict, see Carol Karlsen, *The Devil in the Shape of a Woman: Witchcraft in Colonial New England* (New York: Norton, 1987).

Perhaps contributing to the hysteria was the growing reality of the inability of the Puritan colonies to control dissent in their own midst. Moreover, across the English colonies the full spectrum of English Christianity was becoming represented. English Catholics settled Maryland, declaring a policy of religious liberty to all, although they themselves became classified as dissenters when the Church of England became the established church there. Quakers settled Pennsylvania and their policy of religious tolerance would continue through the colonial period. The Church of England was the established church in Virginia, also in North and South Carolina, Georgia and New York, but laws against dissenters were lightly enforced, or not at all. The Great Awakening and the advent of Methodist preachers in the 1730–40s added to the religious diversity. By 1710, Massachusetts extended tolerance to what they regarded as more acceptable dissenting groups within the Puritan family of theology; i.e., Presbyterians, although groups like Separatist Baptists still had to pay church taxes for an established church to which they did not belong.

This reality of Christian diversity in the English colonies would eventually lead to the disestablishment clause of the 1791 Bill of Rights of the new Revolutionary government: 'Congress shall make no law respecting an establishment of religion or prohibiting the free exercise thereof'. Complete religious tolerance and separation of church and state were not elements of the agenda of most of the American revolutionaries in the 1770's. James Madison was an exception in his construction of the 1776 Virginia Declaration of Rights, which decreed that religion 'can be directed only by reason and conviction' and 'all men are equally entitled to the free exercise of religion according to the dictates of conscience.' But the reality of pluralism clearly was leading in this direction for the colonies as a whole.[7]

Both the protests of Quakers and Separatist Baptists against the remnants of a Puritan established church in Massachusetts, as well as the Puritans' own fears of an established Church of England, finally left no option but to negate any established church and to allow freedom of conscience for all. Yet, although no longer legally established, a general Protestant Christianity would continue to be

7. See particularly the section of the development of religious tolerance in American revolutionary thought in Bernard Bailyn, *The Ideological Origins of the American Revolution* (Cambridge: Harvard University Press, 1967), pp. 246–72.

seen as culturally established in the United States into the twentieth century, creating patterns of discrimination against Catholics and Jews. In the twenty-first century the suspicion that their religion was incompatible with 'Americanism' would plague the growing community of American Muslims. As we shall see later in this chapter, American Indians would struggle well into the twentieth century for freedom of religion (which, for Indians, is an integral part of their culture).

The gap between the Puritan covenant theology of the seventeenth century and the ideology of the American Revolution in the late eighteenth century might seem considerable. The language of the Declaration of Independence and Constitution is resolutely secular, except for a passing reference to 'the laws of Nature and Nature's God' and 'the protection of Divine Providence' in the Declaration of Independence, both statements are more compatible with Enlightenment natural religion than with revealed biblical faith. The signers of the Declaration of Independence were mostly lawyers, farmers and merchants. Only one, John Witherspoon of New Jersey, was a clergyman. This question of the Christian faith of the founding fathers would become a new subject of controversy in the twenty-first century, as a newly politicized Protestant right argues for the Christian foundations of the United States.[8]

Religion, the American Revolution and the Rights of Man

Protestant clergymen were major supporters of the American Revolution. The sermons of clergymen that identified the American Revolution as a new stage of the election and destiny of God's elect people of Israel were an integral part of the public discourse of American society in the revolutionary era. Nicolas Street, pastor of East Haven Congregational Church, raised money for the continental army and preached sermons advocating its support. His sermon, 'The American States Acting over the Part of the Children of Israel in the Wilderness and Thereby Impeding their Entrance into Canaan's Rest,' preached in April 1777, followed the lines of the traditional jeremiad, but applied it to the revolutionary situation.

8. For an example of the claim that the Founding Fathers were Christians and intended the United States to be a Christian nation, see David Barton, *Original Intent: The Courts, the Constitution and Religion* (Aledo, TX: Wallbuilders Press, 1996).

In this sermon, Street argued that the sufferings of the colonists at the hands of the English crown should be seen as divine punishment for their sins. Only if they repent and return to humble obedience to God can they hope for God to 'Restore to us our liberties as at the first and our privileges as at the beginning.'[9]

The sermon preached by Ezra Stiles, president of Yale University, before the General Assembly of Connecticut, 8 May 1783 directly identified the United States with the elect people of Israel and the millennial church. George Washington is the new Joshua and the Lord's anointed. America has been raised high above all other nations and is called upon to lead all humanity to God's millennial reign on earth. America's flight into the wilderness has prepared her for this millennial role. Stiles even suggested that the twelve stars in the woman's crown (Rev. 12:1) have been expanded to thirteen; i.e., the thirteen colonies. Now this purified church and people is advancing to an ultimate conquest of the whole world for Christ 'with the ultimate subserviency to the glory of God, in converting the world.'[10]

Samuel Langdon's sermon, 'The Republic of the Israelites an Example to the American States,' preached at Concord, New Hampshire, before the General Court at the Annual Election, 5 June 1788, advocating the ratification of the American Constitution, identified this law with Israel's law given by God. Israel, however, disobeyed this law and was punished by God. God's new Israel, America, now expanded from twelve tribes to thirteen colonies, must be faithful to its laws. Only if it does so will God give it prosperity and lead it to exalted power over all other nations. 'May the general government of these United States, when established, appear to be the beset (*sic*) which the nations have yet known and be exalted by uncorrupted religion and morals! And may the everlasting gospel diffuse its Heavenly light and spread Righteousness, Liberty and Peace throu' the whole world.'[11]

The contemporary American debate over whether the Founding Fathers were orthodox Christians or secular naturalists misses the diversity of traditions of thought in late eighteenth century United States. As Bernard Bailyn has shown in his magisterial *The Ideological*

9. Printed in Conrad Cherry, *God's New Israel: Religious Interpretations of American Destiny* (Chapel Hill, NC: University of North Carolina Press, 1998), pp. 67–81.

10. Cherry, *God's New Israel*, pp. 82–92.

11. Cherry, *God's New Israel*, pp. 93–105.

Origins of the American Revolution, the language of the American revolutionary war era drew on an eclectic mix of traditions, with different thinkers utilizing different combinations of these traditions. The sources for these ideas included classical antiquity, especially the history of Rome (seen as a cautionary tale against the corruption of empire), writers of the European Enlightenment, especially Locke and Montesquieu, English legal thought, Puritan covenantal theology and English radical critics of King and Parliament from the Civil War into the eighteenth century.[12]

This mixture of ideas carried within it some basic contradictions, largely overlooked at the time, but which would come back to haunt later American historical development. One of these contradictions was the simultaneous appropriation of universalist and English particularist claims of American identity. On the one hand, the American Revolution based its revolutionary separation from England, and its establishment of an independent government and laws, on the claims of universal natural rights. This is stated in the second paragraph of the Declaration of Independence: 'We hold these truths to be self-evident that all Men are created equal, that they are endowed by their Creator with certain inalienable Rights, that among these are Life, Liberty and the Pursuit of Happiness' (this last 'right' itself being a revision of the standard Enlightenment claim that the inalienable rights of man are life, liberty and property).[13]

The Declaration goes on to argue that the English crown has violated these natural rights, setting up laws that deny them and subjecting the colonists to 'absolute despotism' and 'absolute tyranny.' Such despotism and tyranny thus justifies the colonists throwing off such government and setting up their own independent government whose laws will be modeled after the universal 'rights of man' that are the inalienable possession of all human beings, derived, not from the sovereignty of any crown or parliament, but from the 'Laws of Nature and Nature's God'. The legitimacy of any legal code, whether that imposed by the British crown, or the one, which the Americans were about to construct, therefore is to be judged by its compatibility with these natural rights possessed

12. Bailyn, *Ideological Origins*, op. cit., pp. 22–54.

13. The French Declaration of the Rights of Man and the Citizen (1789) makes property one of the three Rights of Man. Jefferson was responsible for the term 'pursuit of happiness' in the American Declaration.

by all humans without exception. When the laws violate these rights, the people have the right to rebel and to set up new laws compatible with their natural rights.

But threaded through these universalist claims in American revolutionary thought is a very different discourse that is historically particularist and nationalist. Although not explicitly present in the Declaration of Independence, it was prominent in the thought of many of the advocates of the revolution and was rooted in English radical political thought of the seventeenth and eighteenth centuries. It was destined to have a long life in the ideology of American manifest destiny into the twentieth century. In this discourse America claimed that their revolution was distinctively English, or 'Saxon.'

Englishmen were believed to have a unique heritage of liberty that is the underlying basis of English common law. This liberty was said to have been the legacy of the Saxon people who are the authentic root of English identity and character. The Saxon people were a uniquely free and virile society thanks to its distinct laws and customs. These liberties were submerged by the conquest of England by the Normans who brought with them corrupt royal despotism that reached its apogee in the reign of the Stuart kings in the seventeenth century.[14] The Glorious Revolution of 1688 overthrew Stuart despotism and partly restored the liberties of free Englishmen, but this revolution is incomplete and threatened by a corrupt king and Parliament.

In promoting further reforms English radicals claimed to be restoring the full liberties of Englishmen rooted in their Saxon heritage. U.S. Americans adopted a version of this same myth of the rights of Englishmen (or Saxons), claiming that the parliament and king had become so corrupt as to be irredeemable. Therefore in the name of the true rights of Englishmen, they could depart from this despotic system, restoring in their own revolutionary society those true Saxon-English liberties, which are destined both to reform England itself and also transform all nations under the guidance of the superior English people.[15] Seen as uniquely English,

14. See Christopher Hill, 'The Norman Yoke,' in *Puritanism and Revolution: Studies in Interpretation of the English Revolution of the Seventeenth Century* (London: Seeker and Wartburg, 1958), pp. 50–122.

15. For the English or Saxon roots of American liberty see particularly Bailyn, *Ideological Origins*, pp. 80–82.

the American liberties could be regarded as an endowment to be extended primarily to people of English heritage and perhaps to other Northern European Protestants of similar background, but not to people of entirely different ethnic heritages; i.e., Indians or Africans.

Such a Saxon-English myth of original liberties was itself a political expression of an earlier myth of origins found in Puritan covenantal theology. According to this theology, the true apostolic church was taken to England in the first century and preserved there against Roman despotism. The reformed church that threw off its allegiance to Rome in the sixteenth century, therefore, is a restoration of that original apostolic Christianity preserved among the English. This combined religious-political myth of church and nation reflected the basic Christian pattern of an original Eden, a long historical fall and a dawning redemption destined to extend itself throughout the earth to a millennial Reign of Christ over all nations in the last age of world history.

This original Eden, fall and redemption myth found ready expression in American revolutionary thought, either in its more political form or its more religious form or some syncretism of the two, as is evident in the three sermons of Street, Stiles and Langdon mentioned earlier. The original Eden can be understood either as the original liberties of the Saxon English, or they can be traced to Nature's God as the heritage of all humanity from its original creation. In religious terms this original Eden is the apostolic church founded by Christ.

These liberties have been corrupted by a long despotism: of Rome, in the case of the church; by royal tyrants and a corrupt Parliament, in the case of the English liberties; and by tyrannical governments throughout the world, in the case of the rights of man. Americans, in throwing off the despotism of a corrupted England and world, are restoring the original 'rights of man,' Saxon liberties and, for some, the apostolic church. They are destined to spread this heritage of liberty and the true faith to all humanity, bringing about a millennial reign of justice and peace.

This enthusiastic language of America's future destiny to bring liberty to the whole world did not eschew the language of empire, even in the eighteenth century. Quoting American revolutionary literature, Barnard Bailyn continually alludes to this millennialist discourse, as in the following: 'For while the greatest part of the nations of the earth are held together under the yoke of universal slavery, the North American provinces yet remain the *country of free men: the asylum,* and the last, to which such may flee the common deluge… "Our native country…bids fairest of any to promote the *perfection and happiness of mankind."* … "the foundation of a great and mighty empire, the largest the world ever saw to be founded on such principles of liberty and freedom, both civil and religious…which shall be the principal seat of that glorious kingdom which Christ shall erect on earth in the latter days."'[16]

The United States was thus founded on a basic contradiction. Although claiming to be based on a universal 'rights of man,' the founders held an implicit and often explicit assumption that these rights were the peculiar legacy of Anglo-Saxon Protestant (males). Despite separation of church and state, Catholics and Jews would fight a long fight to be regarded as fully 'American,' and Muslims are not fully accepted today. Women were originally excluded from the public exercise of civil rights as well. But the most central contradiction in this legacy was the implicit racism of the view that the rights of man are peculiarly the rights of Englishmen.

There were two major populations of North America, which the Founding Fathers had no intention of including in the rights of man; Africans brought to North America as slaves and Native Americans, the original peoples of the land. The United States would be fundamentally shaped from its inception by this continuing effort to exclude these two groups of 'others' from American citizenship and even from equal humanness. In the following sections of this chapter I will briefly detail something of the history of these two excluded others in the shaping of the United States.

The ill treatment of these two major populations of 'excluded others' goes back to the very founding of the English colonies in the early sixteenth century. The revolutionary generation inherited a two century legacy of slavery and racism toward Africans and racist, genocidal treatment of the Native Americans. It was not willing to challenge this legacy, but essentially confirmed it, making it an integral part of the ongoing history of the nation.

16. Bailyn, *Ideological Origins,* pp. 139, 141.

The Excluded Other of North America: the American Indians

In the first years of the settlement of the English colonists in New England and Virginia, relations with the Indians were fairly amicable. The colonists at this time were few and endangered by the rigors of the land to which they had immigrated. Help from Indians for both food and skills in managing the new world were vital to their survival. The areas which the colonists settled were already well inhabited by Indians, who were agriculturalists, not simply hunters, a point typically ignored in later white stereotypes of the Indians as 'primitives' who merely used the land for hunting and must be either removed, so whites could use it for farming, or turned into farmers.

However, Indians were not farmers in the manner recognized by the English colonists. Most important, they understood land as communal rather than private property.[17] Reconstructing the understanding of land as private property was what was central to the colonists dealing with the Indians as they sought to either buy or expropriate Indian land. This took the form of a variety of strategies which soon chilled relations with Indians, such as allowing cattle to trample the Indians' corn fields and then declaring it uncultivated land, getting an Indian drunk and forcing him to sign a deed in English he could not read, or levying fines based on various purported crimes and offering to pay the fine in exchange for land.[18]

Before colonial settlement the native population of what was to become Southern New England: Massachusetts, Connecticut and Rhode Island, is estimated to have been 70,000–90,000.[19] However, devastating epidemics of small pox, contracted from Europeans and to which Indians had no immunity, killed tens of thousands of natives in 1616–17 and 1633–34. Although there is no evidence that the colonists intentionally spread these diseases to Indians,[20] (as did

17. See Francis Jennings, *The Invasion of America: Indians, Colonialism and the Cant of Conquest* (Chapel Hill, NC: North Carolina University Press, 1975), chapter 8.

18. See Charles M. Segal and David C. Stineback, *Puritans, Indians and Manifest Destiny* (New York: G.P. Putnam's Sons, 1977), p. 43.

19. See Francis Jennings, *The Invasion of America*, pp. 28–29. Jennings' figures differ markedly from those of Frances Bremer who puts the number of indians in Southern New England at 25,000 in 1615, *The Puritan Experiment*, p. 201.

20. Ward Churchill raises the question of whether this was the case: see his *A Little Matter of Genocide* (San Francisco, CA: City Lights Books, 1997), pp. 169–70.

happen later when disease-infected blankets were deliberately given to Indians[21]), Puritan divines were quick to regard this dying off of the Indians as providential, turning vast tracks of formerly inhabited Indian land into what the English defined as *vacuum domicilium* available for confiscation. As the Puritan divine John Cotton argued: 'Where there is a vacant place, there is liberty for the sons of Adam or Noah to come and inhabit, though they neither buy it nor ask their leaves…In a vacant soil, he that taketh possess of it and bestoweth culture and husbandry upon it, his right it is. And the ground for this is from the Grand Charter given to Adam and his posterity in Paradise, Genesis 1:28, Multiply and replenish the earth and subdue it.'[22]

From the beginning the Puritans viewed the Indians through a theological lens that divided reality between God and the Devil. In Puritan theology all humanity has fallen and is totally depraved. The wilderness itself was seen as the Devil's domain to which the Indian belongs. God has predestined to election a limited number of humans and redeemed them through divine grace made available through Jesus Christ, but God does not intend universal redemption. The Puritans saw themselves as the exemplification of this elect few, although they did not deny that they themselves had been rescued from the Devil's clutches by divine grace through no merits of their own, and some in their own midst might not truly belong to the elect.

Although this was a topic of sharp debate, generally the Puritans assumed that the elect could be recognized by their converted, rigorously disciplined lifestyle, based on their acceptance of this Calvinist theology. Initially, they sought to restrict church membership and, with it, voting in the godly commonwealth to those who had experienced conversion in a manner that was validated by a church council, although later (by the 1650s) they had to relax these restrictions when the children of the original settlers failed to experience this conversion. [23]

21. The first clear case of this is in 1763 when the English commander Lord Jeffrey Amherst directed his subordinate Colonel Henry Bouquet to send infected blankets to the indians. Over 100,000 died in the outbreak of disease: Churchill, *Genocide*, pp. 152–51.

22. John Cotton, 'God's Promise to his Plantations' (1630) from Segal and Stineback, *Puritans, Indians and Manifest Destiny*, pp. 31–32.

23. This was the famous 'Half-way' covenant: See Bremer, *Puritan Experiment*, pp. 161–65.

The Puritans also did not rule out the possibility that Indians might be converted and thus prove themselves to be members of the elect, although they had little interest in actual mission work to the Indians, unlike the Spanish and French. Generally, they assumed that their own godly lifestyle should convey to the Indians their self-evident superiority. Those whom God had elected should be attracted to the Puritan way and come for conversion. If they did not, and even showed aversion to conversion (which for the Puritan meant a total assimilation into the English culture and way of life), this simply proved that they were the Devil's spawn.

However, some English clergymen had a keener interest in the conversion of the Indians, especially as this was seen as a way of rivaling the French who were active in both conversion of, and alliance with, Indian tribes. Like the Spanish and French, some Puritans believed that the conversion of the Indians, as the last outpost of gentiles to whom the Gospel had not yet been preached, was a prerequisite for the dawning of the millennium. Some of these clergy shared the idea that the Indians were the lost tribes of Israel, and so converting them fulfilled the mandate to convert the Jews, necessary for the return of Christ. For others, conversion of these last gentiles was the necessary preamble to converting the Jews (of Europe).[24]

Several Puritan divines dedicated themselves to the conversion of the Indians. John Eliot of Roxbury was one such missionary who began his work in 1646; although only in 1663 did Eliot produce a Bible in the Algonquian language. Until then it was assumed that the Indian could only be converted by learning English. John Mayhew of Martha's Vineyard also began such work even before Eliot and was more successful than he. Roger Williams of Rhode Island was the first minister to become fluent in the local Indian language, but he rejected proselytism of the Indians.

By contrast, the Massachusetts General Court passed laws that attempted to force Indians to convert, making it illegal for them to work on Sunday or to practice their own religion. Towns of 'praying Indians' were set up, although when war broke out between Indians and Puritans, the Indians in these towns were not given special protection, but were slaughtered along with the others.[25]

24. See Segal and Stineback, *Puritans, Indians and Manifest Destiny*, pp. 141–42.
25. Segal and Stineback, *Puritans, Indians and Manifest Destiny*, pp. 143–48.

Puritan policy was expansionist from the first, seeking to acquire more and more land and to remove the Indian presence from these lands. This led to the first major war with the Pequots in 1636–37. The Pequots themselves sought peace with the Massachusetts Bay Colony. In November of 1634, a delegation of Pequot chiefs tried to negotiate a trade treaty with the colony, but the magistrates demanded a huge tribute of wampum (bead work used as money), beaver and otter skins as the price of this treaty.

The Pequot tribal council refused these demands. Relations worsened as Puritans began to settle more areas of Connecticut and the Pequots refused various demands for complete subservience to Massachusetts. By 1636, total war had broken out, with John Endecott sent to destroy Indian villages on Block Island. This was followed by a total massacre of Pequots at Mystic Fort and then at Sadqua Swamp near New Haven, slaughtering men, women and children and burning villages and crops. The Pequots, already decimated by the plague of 1633–4, were all but wiped out by the war.[26]

These experiences stiffened Indian resistance to Puritan expansion. Several major groups, led by the Wampanoag chief Metacom (King Philip), sought to ally against these encroachments. The first strike in the war, that came to be known as King Philip's War, took place when the Commissioners of the New England colonies, meeting in Boston in December, 1675, authorized an attack against the Narragansetts of Rhode Island who were not at that time at war with the colonies. The Puritan army surprised a Narragansetts gathering, burning the village to the ground and killing 100 men and more than 300 women and children.

In the ensuing warfare with the Indian tribes, the Puritan settlements themselves would suffer great losses, with some 52 English villages attacked and 12 destroyed. Countless Indians villages were leveled. About three thousand English settlers, and 6,000 Indians died. Many captured Indians were sold into slavery to the West Indies. The Indian presence was all but destroyed in New England.[27]

In the colony of Virginia relations between the settlers and Indians were at first amicable, when the settlers' numbers were small and

---

26. Segal and Stineback, *Puritans, Indians and Manifest Destiny*, pp. 105–40.

27. On King Philip's war, see Segal and Stineback, *Puritans, Indians and Manifest Destiny*, pp. 181–214. Also Russell Bourne, *The Red King's Rebellion: Racial Politics in New England, 1675–1678* (New York: Atheneum, 1990).

dependent on the Indians for survival. The famous marriage of John Rolfe to Pocahontas, daughter of Powhatan, who headed the Indian Confederation in eastern Virginia, reflected this early alliance. But as colonists grew in numbers and began to encroach on more and more Indian land, war broke out. The Virginia colonists' policy then became one of extermination or expulsion of the Indians from the region. By 1700, fewer than 3,000 indigenous people remained in the area between the Chesapeake Bay and the Appalachian Mountains, an area once densely populated by Native Americans.[28]

Between 1641–44 a war of extermination or removal was waged against the local Indians by the Dutch based at New Amsterdam, killing thousands outright, burning villages and shipping off captives to slavery in the West Indies. War between the Dutch and Swedes from 1655–63 eliminated further groups of tribes, although in the process both the Swedes and the Dutch were knocked out of North American colonization by the English who took over New Netherlands in 1644.[29]

The late seventeenth and first three-quarters of the eighteenth century saw further wars of competition for hegemonic dominance of North America between European powers, particularly between France, England and sometimes Spain: the King William's War (1689–97), Queen Anne's War (1702–13), King George's War (1744–48) and the Seven Years' War (1749–63), the so-called 'French and Indian Wars.' The upshot of these wars was the elimination of the French colonial empire in North America. With the treaty of Paris of 1763, France ceded its vast Louisiana territory to Spain and its other North American territories to England. In these wars the Indian tribes generally allied with the French, seen as less aggressively expansionist than the English, although some Indians at times allied with the English or tried to remain neutral.

In the context of these wars Indian groups were continually destroyed or expelled. For example, the Cherokees, although they had been English allies and had well settled agricultural towns, were virtually eliminated from the Carolinas. The English sought to deprive the Cherokees of their economic basis of life by burning

28. Churchill, *Genocide*, p. 168. See also Henry E. Dobyns, *Their Number Became Thinned: Native American Population Dynamics in Eastern North America* (Knoxville: University of Tennessee Press, 1983), p. 44.

29. Churchill, *Genocide*, pp. 196–99. See also Allen W. Trelease, *Indian Affairs in Colonial New York: The Seventeenth Century* (Ithaca, NY: Cornell University Press, 1960).

their towns, crops and orchards. By 1761 the Cherokees were forced to cede a huge area of land on the Western frontiers of the Carolinas. An alliance of Indian tribes that sought to resist further encroachments was largely eliminated by bacteriological war by the English commander, Lord Jeffery Amherst in the Ohio River area by spreading infected blankets that set off a plague among the Ottowas, Potawatomies, Wyandots and Lenni Lenâpés.[30]

William T. Hagan summarizes the pattern of relation to the Native Americans established by the British Empire from 1610–1770. First, the tribes were used to gather furs for the fur trade, receiving in turn metal tools, firearms, and also alcohol, which both corrupted traditional Indian life and exacerbated warfare between Indians and with the settlers. As settlers expanded their claims and game diminished, wars of extermination or removal broke out against the Indians. These wars soon crushed Indian resistance, forcing them to sign treaties to cede more land and to move further west, often with promises that Indian rights to these areas would be respected. But this meant decimated tribes were pushed into territories of other tribes, or located in a reservation, often carrying diseases, which caused them to die off rapidly.[31]

The new American nation, founded in the American Revolution, would continue and build on this pattern as white settlers expanded from the Eastern seaboard to California in the next seventy-five years. From the American Revolutionary war through the War of 1812, the British posed as protectors of the Indians against the expansionist rapacity of the colonists. The result was that many tribes allied with the English, seeing them as the lesser of evils. This alliance justified renewed hostility toward the Indians as savage enemies of the new nation to be eliminated, a view that found its way into the Declaration of Independence, where, among the grievances against the King of England, it is said that: 'He has…endeavored to bring on the Inhabitants of our Frontiers, the merciless Indian savages, whose known Rule of Warfare is undistinguished Destruction, of all Ages, Sexes and Conditions.'

30. Churchill, *Genocide*, p. 206; also Russell Thornston, *American Indian Holocaust and Survival: A Population History since 1492* (Norman, OK: University of Oklahoma Press, 1987).

31. William T. Hagan, *American Indians* (3rd edn; Chicago: University of Chicago Press, 1993), p. 36.

We see here what will become a typical pattern of 'white' rhetoric against indigenous peoples. By blaming Indians as those who wage savage warfare against whole populations, the United States justifies their right to wage such wars of extermination against them.[32] Indians are also defined as those 'Inhabitants of our frontiers,' not as people to be included in the nation as citizens deserving of the 'rights of man.'

This definition of the Indians as enemies on the side of the British justified George Washington and General John Sullivan's campaigns during the Revolutionary War to demolish Iroquois towns, crops and orchards in Pennsylvania and New York. Two of the Indians killed in these attacks were flayed to provide boot tops for the troops. In a toast drunk by Sullivan's officers during this campaign, they pledged, 'Civilization or death to all American savages.'[33] In the peace treaty that concluded the war, the Indian allies of the British were totally abandoned. The entire Northwest Territories were ceded by the British to the United States who claimed that the Indians had forfeited any rights to the land by aiding the British. Some of the same pattern was found in the War of 1812 in which the British first promised protection of the Indians and then abandoned them in final negotiations with the U.S.

During this whole period from 1776–1812, Indians east of the Mississippi were continually harried and pressed to sign treaties ceding more land. Much of the Indian land in Indiana, Illinois, Ohio, Michigan and Wisconsin was taken over in this period. Here one finds two conflicting rhetorics at work. The Federal Government, particularly spokesmen such as Thomas Jefferson, continually appealed to the Indians to assimilate into white ways, settling down as farmers, taking on private property and dissolving their identity as nations, becoming educated (in Anglo-American culture). Once thus assimilated Jefferson suggested that Indians could become fully 'Americans:' 'You will become one people with us; your blood will mix with ours and will spread with ours over this great island.'[34]

32. For the development of this rhetoric of justification of 'savage war' against the indians, see particularly Richard Slotkin, *Regeneration through Violence: Mythology of the American Frontier, 1600–1860* (NY: Harpers, 1996).

33. Hagan, *American Indians*, p. 46.

34. See Reginald Horsman, citing statements from Jefferson's state papers: *Race and Manifest Destiny: The Origins of American Racial Anglo-Saxonism* (Cambridge, MA: Harvard University Press, 1981), pp. 108–109.

A very different rhetoric predominated among the frontiersmen who overwhelmingly expressed the assumption of their right to confiscate Indian land and either remove or exterminate Indian people. Major John Hamtramck's represented the views of white Kentuckians in his comment in 1790 that 'even if treaties were signed with the Indians, the people of our frontier will certainly be the first to break it. The people of Kentucky will carry on private expeditions against the Indians and kill them whenever they meet them, and I do not believe there is a jury in all Kentucky who would punish a man for it.'[35] Although echoing Enlightenment views of universal humanity in his official statements, Jefferson in practice supported the frontiersmen's policies of Indian removal.[36]

The period from 1816–1850 saw the implementation of the policy of Indian removal, not only by private campaigns of frontiersmen, but by states and the federal government. The leaders of Georgia were particularly adamant that all Indians should be removed West of the Mississippi River. This policy gained Federal approval under the presidency of 'Indian fighter' Andrew Jackson, who believed that the Indians were in no way independent nations with whom the American government need negotiate treaties, nor did they have any rights to land. His support persuaded Congress to pass the Indian Removal Bill of 1830. Many Indian groups were already so defeated that they acceded to this demand without resistance.

The Cherokees, however, were among those who resisted the removal order. They had, in fact, accepted Jefferson's plea to become settled farmers. Well-cultivated fields, brick and stone houses, schools and gristmills abounded in their areas. The Cherokees appealed to the federal courts and retained former Attorney General William Wirt to represent them. The case was brought to the Supreme Court, where Chief Justice John Marshall at first ruled that the Cherokees could not sue states, but in 1832 reversed himself and declared that the Indian nations were self-governing political communities. But his decision could not halt the drive to remove the Cherokees. President Andrew Jackson is said to have remarked, 'John Marshall has made his decision; now let him enforce it.'[37]

35. Horsman, *Race and Manifest Destiny*, p. 111.
36. Hagan, *American Indians*, pp. 61–66. See also Reginald Horsman, *Expansion and American Indian Policy, 1783–1812* (Lansing, MI: Michigan State University Press, 1967).
37. Hagan, *American Indians*, pp. 84–85.

Although Cherokees clung to their lands, General Winfield Scott was given the task of forcibly removing them. Squads of soldiers surrounded Indian farms and herded the Indians at bayonet point into fortified concentration camps. They were then marched west under armed guard. Sickness, inclement weather and poor rations soon took their toll and thousands died in the process. Not only did whites quickly move in to take over the Indian developed properties, but also some whites even harried the Indians as they were marched west, taking their horses and other possessions they sought to take with them. Some Indians fled south and joined the Seminoles in the swamps of Florida, but most of the land east of the Mississippi was cleared of Indians by 1850.[38]

Even as the United States promised the Indians a permanent Indian country in which to live west of the Mississippi, its own expansionist policies were belying these promises. In 1835, the Texans rebelled against Mexican rule under President Santa Anna, and declared their independence in 1836, becoming a state of the Union in 1845. War with Mexico broke out in 1846, provoking a debate among (white) U.S. leaders about whether the United States should conquer all of Mexico (to be discussed in chapter 3). The prevailing view was that the U.S., as a white Anglo-Saxon Protestant country, could and should not assimilate so many racially mixed and religiously suspect Mexicans. In the treaty of Guadalupe-Hildalgo in 1848, Mexico ceded to the U.S. Texas, New Mexico, California and Arizona (expanded in 1853 with the Gladsen purchase).

White settlers poured across the continent, particularly with the discovery of gold in California in 1848. The inviolability of lands granted to Indians who had been pushed west, as well as the territories of Indians long resident west of the Mississippi, were disregarded by these colonists. Waves of disease further debilitated Indian tribes. Indian tribes were under continual pressure to cede new lands to settlers. The Indians of California were particularly devastated. Uprooted by the California missions founded by the Franciscans in the late eighteenth century, the Indians who had been made dependent on these missions, were abandoned when the missions were secularized at the Mexico revolution of 1820. Californios (Spanish Californians) quickly bought up the mission lands for large ranches and employed some Indians as workers,

38. Hagan, *American Indians*, pp. 87–94.

but the aggressive Anglos who entered the area between 1848–50, soon extracted this land from the Californios.

The Indians were abandoned a second time and treated as useless nuisances to be destroyed. Of former mission Indians, ninety per cent had died by 1860. The 'wild' Indians (those who had not been converted and subjugated by the Spanish) were savagely hunted down. In the 1850's small reservations were allotted to the remaining Indians, with the expectation that they would soon die out. In the words of the California Governor, Peter H. Burnett, 'that a war of extermination will continue to be waged between the two races until the Indian race becomes extinct, must be expected; while we cannot anticipate this result with but painful regret, the inevitable destiny of the race is beyond the power and wisdom of man to avert.'[39] Treating Indian extermination as an unavoidable 'law of nature' and therefore not really to be blamed on their exterminators, was typical of white American rhetoric of the 1850s–1900.

During the American Civil War (1861–5) some Indian tribes allied with the South, again seeking protection from those seen as the lesser of evils. This allowed the Federal Government to regard treaties with Indians as abrogated, allowing removals of Indians from Kansas and much of Oklahoma. The 1860s to 1880s saw a continual series of Indian uprisings and resistance to efforts to remove them from their land and confine them to unproductive reservations. The Sioux uprising in 1862 resulted in their removal from most of Minnesota.[40] Kit Carson led expeditions against the Apaches and Navajos in 1863–4.[41] In November of 1864 a company of Colorado militia happened upon about 500 Indians wintering in Sand Creek, killing a third of them, mostly the aged, women and children, with particular brutality. Colonel Chivington, a former Methodist minister who led the attack, later exhibited a collection of a hundred scalps between acts at a theatre in Denver.[42]

These Indian wars of the Great Plains lasted into the 1880s, led by some of the best- known names among Indian chiefs, such as

39. Robert F. Heizer and Alan F. Almquist, *The Other Californians: Prejudice and Discrimination Under Spain, Mexico and the United States* (Berkeley, CA: University of California Press, 1977), p. 26.

40. See Dee Brown, *Bury my Heart at Wounded Knee: An Indian History of the West* (NY: Holt, Rinehart and Winston, 1970), pp. 37–66.

41. Brown, *Bury my Heart*, pp. 13–36.

42. See Hagan, *American Indians*, p. 119. Also Brown, *Bury my Heart*, pp. 83–94.

Red Cloud of the Oglala Dakotas, Apache chiefs Cochise and
Geronimo (who allied himself with Cochise) and Sioux leaders Little
Crow, Crazy Horse and Sitting Bull. There were moments of glory
for the Indian warriors, such as the defeat of General George Custer
who rode into an ambush and died with all his men at Little Big
Horn on June 26, 1876, a defeat all the more enraging to white
Americans since it occurred shortly before the celebration of the
first centennial of the United Nations. The mythologizing of Custer
and his 'last stand' would live long in white American folklore.[43]

But despite some victories the defeat of remaining independent
Indian tribes and their herding into dwindling reservations was
largely accomplished by 1885. The coming of the railroad facilitated
the movement of white settlers across the Plains and to the Pacific
coast. The dwindling buffalo were all but annihilated by sports
hunters firing from railroad cars, eliminating a main source of Indian
food and hides. The pathetic denouement of Indian independence
is symbolized by the December 1890 massacre at Wounded Knee of
300 of the small band of 350 Sioux led by Chief Big Foot, after
having peacefully surrendered to the army in an effort to get to
safety at the Pine Ridge Reservation.[44]

Having crushed Indian militant resistance, American policy from
1880–1934 was to assimilate the remaining Indians, extinguishing
them as a people with a separate culture and communal existence.
Indigenous ceremonies and spiritual practices were outlawed in
1894. At the same time Christian missionaries, mostly Protestants,
were assigned to the reservations. Despite separation of church
and state, the Federal Government continued to assume that
Christianization was an integral part of the assimilation of the Indian
into white culture.[45] Indian children were removed at a young age
to boarding schools, often run by church agencies, and kept there
through their teens, forbidden to speak their own languages or
follow Indian customs. Training was primarily for domestic service
for girls and rote labor for boys. Discipline was harsh at such schools,

43. See Richard Slotkin, *The Fatal Environment: The Myth of the Frontier in an Age of
Industrialization, 1800–1890* (Norman OK: Oklahoma University Press,1998) on the
Custer Myth.

44. See Brown, *Bury my Heart*, pp. 439–45.

45. For a highly critical view of the role of Christian missionaries among Indians, see
George E. Tinker, *Missionary Conquest: The Gospel and Native American Cultural Genocide*
(Minneapolis, MN: Fortress Press, 1993).

and the death rates of the children were high. Those who managed to survive and return to their families were often deeply disturbed, unable to adjust to either Indian or white society.[46]

In 1887, the Dawes Severality Act sought to break up communal land holding in reservations. Each head of family would be allotted title to 160 acres, and the rest sold on the market. High taxes and fraud often deprived Indians even of these allotments.[47] Indians were declared US citizens in 1924. By the 1940s the Indian population, according to the US Census, had dwindled to a third of a million, and it seemed that soon they would disappear altogether. However, the New Deal and particularly the 1960s brought modest revivals in Indian life. Efforts to break up communal property under the Severality Act were rescinded. Day schools began to replace boarding schools, and Indians were granted some amount of self-government. Native ceremonies and crafts were revived, although full religious freedom would await the Religious Freedom Act of 1978.[48]

Inspired by the Civil Rights Movements, Indians organized the American Indian Movement in 1968.[49] Some tribes, such as the Piquots of Massachusetts, and the Passamaquodies of Maine, defeated in the seventeenth century, were able to reconstitute themselves as tribes and buy land for their communities. The legality of the many treaties (and the breaking of treaties) by which land was taken from Indians in the past began to be challenged in the courts.[50] By 1990, the American census recorded an Indian population

46. See, for example, David Wallace Adam, *Education for Extinction* (Topeka, KS: University of Kansas, 1995).

47. The tragic effects of the Dawes Severality Act are recounted in Janet A. McDonnell, *The Dispossession of the American Indian, 1883–1934* (Bloomington, IN: Indiana University Press, 1991). Also Frederick Hoxie, *A Final Promise: The Campaign to Assimilate the Indians, 1880–1920* (Lincoln: University of Nebraska Press, 1985).

48. See Katherine Pettipas, *Severing the Ties that Bind: Government Repression of Indigenous Religious Ceremonies on the Prairies* (Winnipeg: University of Manitoba Press, 1994) for the Canadian version of this story.

49. For a biography of one of the founders of AIM, see Kim Cheatham, *Dennis Banks: Native American Activist* (Springfield, NJ: Enslow Press, 1997). For the conflict of AIM with the Federal Government, see Kenneth Stern, *Loud Hawk: The United States versus the American Indian Movement* (Norman, OK: Oklahoma University Press, 2002).

50. On these legal struggles see Russel Lawrence Barsh and James Youngblood Henderson, *The Road: Indian Tribes and Political Liberty* (Berkeley, CA: University of California Press, 1980) and Vine Deloria and Clifford M. Lytle, *American Indians, American Justice* (Austin, TX: University of Texas Press, 1983).

of 2 million, a six-fold increase. This increase perhaps reflects a previous undercount of Indian people, as well as some people of mixed Indian and white ancestry choosing to identify themselves as Indians after the 1960s, a change that is expressive of renewed pride in Indian identity.[51]

But Indian problems with the American government and society are hardly over. The government and transnational corporations sought to create puppet chiefs in place of real self-government on reservations and to use tribal land for weapons testing and dumping of toxic waste.[52] When valuable minerals, such as uranium, are discovered on Indian land, corporations make haste to deprive Indians of the profits, while employing them to bear the brunt of the toxic conditions of mining.[53] Although some Indians profit from new opportunities, such as casinos, the Indian population as a whole remains deeply demoralized, culturally conflicted, and educationally deprived. They rank among those with the highest poverty level in the U.S. population.[54]

The African Excluded Other: Slavery and Segregation

The slave trade that would bring Africans to North America as slaves began in the fifteenth century. At first monopolized by the Portuguese, other Europeans quickly got into this lucrative trade, with the British dominating it by the late sixteenth century. It is estimated that about 15 million Africans arrived in the Americas between the 1450s and 1850s, with at least an equal number dying in the process of capture and transportation on ships where the enslaved were tightly packed without room to stand. Thus Africa

51. See Nancy Shoemaker, *American Indian Population Recovery in the Twentieth Century* (Albuquerque, NM: New Mexico University Press, 1999).

52. Indians are active in the environmental racism network. See Robert D. Bullard, *Confronting Environmental Racism: Voices from the Grassroots* (Boston: South End Press, 1993).

53. These contemporary issues of the exploitation of Native American lands are well covered in Churchill's chapter 'Cold War Impacts on Native North America: The Political Economy of Radioactive Colonization,' in *Genocide*, pp. 289–362.

54. In the 2000 census Native Americans and Native Alaskans, which includes those who name these identities along with another race, had a medium income slightly higher than the medium for American blacks: $31,799 compared with $28,679. But Native Americans and Native Alaskans had the highest level of lack of medical insurance of any U.S. population: See American Indian Census Facts from the American Indian Graduate Center: www.aigc.com/articles/ai-census-facts.html.

was emptied of some thirty or more million people. The English colonies of North America would receive about 1 million Africans. This number had grown to 4.5 million by 1860 at the time of the outbreak of the Civil War, more than 14 per cent of the total U.S. population, most of them concentrated in the southern states.

The first slaves to come to an English colony in North America, twenty men and women, arrived in Jamestown in 1619 in a ship flying a Dutch flag. Africans were at first treated as occupying the same legal status as European indentured servants who served a term of labor and then were free to marry, buy land and otherwise function as free colonists. But this status as temporary servants quickly deteriorated. By the 1660s African slaves were defined throughout the colonies as slaves for life, their status inherited by their children. Since interracial sex and reproduction happened from the first contact with whites, this was defined as following the status of the mother; i.e., the child of a white father and an African slave mother inherited the mother's slave status, despite being 'half white.'

As Jordan Winthrop makes clear in his magisterial study, *White over Black*,[55] Englishmen, from their first contact with Africa, developed an exaggerated reaction to the physical differences between themselves and Africans, particularly the difference in skin color. By adopting the color metaphor of 'white' and 'black,' the difference in skin color was assimilated into other dualisms which were a part of English culture, such as beautiful/ugly, good/evil, rational/irrational, being/non-being; ultimately God and his angels versus the Devil and his demons as light versus dark. White/black as a metaphor obviously exaggerates actual skin-color difference, which more accurately might be described as dark to middle-brown and a pinkish/tan.

The adoption of the white/black metaphor for skin color difference (the light-dark dualism probably arose originally from the alternation of day and night[56]) imposed a cultural construction on the English perception of English-African difference as a dualism of opposites, rather than a relative range of colors understood as superficial. In other words, the difference of English and African

55. Jordan D. Winthrop, *White Over Black: American Attitudes Toward the Negro, 1550–1812* (Chapel Hill, NC: University of North Carolina Press, 1968).

56. The dualism of darkness and light is found in many cultures and in Christianity early took on the connotations of goodness versus evil, God versus the Devil, although without reference to skin color).

qua white and black was understood as defining their total being, locating Africans at the negative pole of a series of aesthetic, moral and ontological opposites.

However, the English and other Europeans from the first recognized that Africans were indeed human beings, although there was a recurrent tendency to demote them to the category of animal or beast, particularly as similar to apes.[57] Once acknowledged as human beings, Englishmen were forced by their religious tradition to recognize them as members of the same species as themselves. Although some nineteenth century social Darwinists would toy with notions of a plurality of ancestors for different races, with Africans descended from a different and more animal-like ancestor than Europeans, this idea remained heretical for orthodox Christians for whom all humans descended from the same pair of ancestors, Adam and Eve.

Once acknowledged to be members of the same species, descended from the same ancestors, Europeans felt compelled to explain the source of what were perceived to be such radical differences between themselves and Africans. One model for such change readily available to Christians was that of a fall or declension. Humans could be conceived as having been created 'white,' European in appearance, but deteriorating into different forms through some combination of difference of climate and adoption of bad habits. This model tacitly assumed that some humans were more 'fallen' and thus farther from God and salvation than others. This idea should not have been acceptable to Christians since Christianity asserted that all humans, descendents of Adam and Eve, were equally fallen and equally in need of divine grace.

Another model to explain human difference was also available and would become normative for social Darwinists, namely, betterment through growth or evolution. Humans could be conceived as having started out in an animal-like or ape-like condition and gradually improving, morally, intellectually, in physical beauty and skills, with some groups improving more than others. But many Christians would find (and still find) that idea of having been descended from ape-like animals difficult to accept.

Once the process of shaping differences was explained, human difference could then be arranged on the familiar hierarchy or 'chain

57. Jordan, *White Over Black*, pp. 29–32, 65, 235–39, 490–97.

of being' which Europeans inherited from Platonic philosophy. Ranging from pure Ideas to unformed matter, created beings were seen as ranging down a hierarchy from angels to humans to animals, plants and rocks. Already in Plato and Aristotle, Europeans had precedents for locating women in contrast to men, as well as different classes and races of humans (philosopher-king versus workers, civilized Greeks versus barbarians, free men versus slaves) in terms of a hierarchy which ranged from those closer to spirit and intellect to those closer to animals. This was understood as a hierarchy of power, as well as of ontology, i.e. rulers over ruled.[58] Whatever the model for explaining difference, what was unquestioned was that (upper class) Englishmen would always be located at the top of the hierarchy.[59]

At first the English could construe the African darkness of skin as manifesting a darkness of soul by identifying them as pagans or heathens. This, for English Christians, automatically put the African in the Devil's camp. But this raised the question, parallel to the question of relations to the Indians, of Christian responsibility to evangelize the African. Many slave-masters were reluctant to convert the African, both because this entailed some element of education, including the ability to read the scriptures, and because making the African a fellow Christian suggested claims to equality and freedom.

Churchmen quickly assured the slave master that freeing the African soul from sin need have no implications for freeing the African body. Indeed, Christianization would teach the slaves docility and obedience to their masters.[60] New Testament texts, such as Eph. 6:5: 'Slaves be obedient to those who are your earthly masters' and 1 Peter 2:18: 'Servants be submissive to your masters with all respect', came readily to mind for such a message.

By the mid-eighteenth century many slave masters allowed their slaves to be baptized and to attend church in the balcony of the master's church, where they would hear an edifying message of submission to their masters. The first great awakening of the 1740s

58. Plato, *The Republic, Phaedo*, Aristotle, *Politics*.
59. Jordan, *White Over Black*, pp. 223–28.
60. In 1727, the Bishop of London composed a public letter, *To the Masters and Mistresses of Families in the English Plantations Abroad* informing them that baptism in no way alters the Condition of servitude of a person, but makes them more diligent in their duties. Jordan, *White Over Black*, p. 191.

brought some Africans into more egalitarian churches, such as Baptists and Methodists. But by then slave masters had long mastered the contradiction of allowing slaves to be Christianized without being either emancipated or allowed to become literate.

The American Revolution brought a new challenge to the contradiction between holding slaves and the ideals of an equal humanity. The colonists freely used the metaphor of slavery to describe the evil condition imposed on them by the English king. The Declaration of Independence detailed the colonists' grievances, which justified their rebellion and freedom as 'a long train of abuses and usurpations, …evincing a design to reduce them under absolute despotism.' Moreover their declaration of independence was defined in terms of a universal 'rights of man' which made no distinction between races: 'all men are created equal.' If Africans were among such 'men,' then holding them in a much worse condition of slavery and despotism than the English king held the white colonists would surely be wrong and should equally justify their rebellion and assertion of their freedom and independence from their enslavers.[61]

Many Founding Fathers, including the author of the Declaration of Independence, Thomas Jefferson, were deeply troubled by this contradiction. Jefferson hated slavery, which he saw as corrupting the slave master (the effect on the slave was less compelling for him). But Jefferson was equally convinced of the inferiority of the African and their unfitness for free citizenship.[62] Moreover, Jefferson and others of the revolutionary generation were deeply opposed to intermarriage of white and black, which they believed would cause a 'deterioration' of the intellectual and moral quality of the American nation. They were convinced that freeing the African would lead quickly to a demand for marriage with whites and hence a 'mongrelization' of that very nation which they wanted to be a 'light to the nations,' especially to their fellow Englishmen. This fear, of course, ignored the fact that they (and possibly Jefferson himself[63]) had already done quite a bit of inter-racial reproduction without the benefit of marriage.

61. On the debate over slavery in the Revolutionary era, see Bailyn, *Ideological Origins*, pp. 232–46.

62. Jordan, *White Over Black*, pp. 429–81.

63. On the question of Jefferson's concubinage with the slave woman Sally Hemings, and fathering of her children, see Jordan, *White Over Black*, pp. 464–69. Also Peter S. Onuf and Jan E. Lewis, *Sally Hemings and Thomas Jefferson: History, Memory and Civic Culture* (Charlottesville, VA: University of Virginia Press, 1999).

Another compelling problem for the Founding Fathers was the forging of a united nation out of thirteen somewhat disparate colonies. The slavery question threatened to prevent a union as one nation under one Federal Constitution (and would eventually tear apart that union and necessitate a reunion by military force). Most of the anti-slavery sentiment came from leaders in the North, especially Quakers. Slave masters from the South were deeply opposed to any change in the status of slaves. Thus (apparently) the only way to forge a union was through compromise on the issue of slavery.

The right to property was assumed to be an integral part of the 'rights of man,' although the term property had not been so used in the Declaration. Thus it was agreed that the Constitution would make no change in the rights of the slave masters to their property qua slaves. Yet the Southern states, with a high percentage of slaves, also wanted them included in the population census for purposes of representation (by whites). Hence, the infamous 'compromise' in which slaves were included as 'three-fifths of other persons' (Constitution, Art.1, sec. 2).

Yet many of the delegates to the Constitutional Convention saw slavery as an evil that should best 'fade away.' It was agreed in 1787 that the slave trade should be abolished, although the implementation of this law on the Federal level was postponed for twenty-years (until 1808). Many Northern states banned the slave trade immediately. Some passed laws banning slavery as well, usually through some process of gradual emancipation. For example, Rhode Island ruled that all born to slave mothers after 1784 would be freed. Southern states passed laws allowing for private manumissions, although often with the requirement that the freed slave leave the state.

As a result slavery began to disappear in the North. But this began to sharpen the dichotomy between 'free' states and 'slave' states, states which allowed slavery and states which did not allow slavery. This conflict would shape U.S. American politics to the Civil War, particularly in regard to expansion of white settlement into the Northwest and Western territories, whether these territories would be admitted as 'free' or 'slave' states. After Congress opened territories west of the Mississippi to slavery with the Kansas-Nebraska Act of 1854, bloody struggles would be fought over whether these territories would be defined as free or slave. John

Brown would begin his anti-slavery crusade by striking back at
pro-slavery men in Kansas.[64] However, defining a territory or newly
admitted state as 'free' did not mean free blacks were encouraged
to come there. For many 'free soilers,' it meant whites only, no
slaves allowed, and free blacks not welcome.

Although many white intellectuals wanted slavery as an institution
to 'disappear,' very few of them could envision freed Africans
becoming equal citizens with themselves. This left two options. One
was to remove the freed Africans. The other was to free blacks, but
legally segregate and subordinate them to whites. In the first
decades of the eighteenth century some white Americans toyed
with the idea of creating a Western colony where freed blacks could
be removed and established as colonists under Federal supervision,
something like the reservations being set up for Indians. Others
thought perhaps blacks could be sent to the Caribbean or Latin
America. Still others preferred the idea of a colony in Africa to
which free blacks could be sent.

The American Colonization Society, founded in 1816, would focus
on this idea of sending blacks to Liberia.[65] A few black leaders also
affirmed, from a very different perspective, the idea of repatriation
of free Africans back to Africa. A northern free black, Paul Cuffee,
a wealthy ship owner and early black nationalist, embraced this
view and took thirty-eight freed men to Liberia in 1815.[66] But most
black leaders denounced the idea, claiming that America was now
their country and they should be not only freed but have equal
rights as citizens in it.

The wave of white anti-slavery sentiment of the Revolutionary
period, however, had largely faded by the early eighteenth century.
White anti-slavery feeling and organizations diminished for several
reasons. First, white anti-slavery groups had no alternative to slavery
acceptable to most whites. They themselves mostly could not
envision social and civil equality with free blacks and removal of
free blacks in sufficient numbers did not seem realistic. Secondly,

64. See W.E.B. DuBois, *John Brown* (New York: International, 1962).

65. Jordan, *White Over Black*, pp. 546–69. See also Philip J. Staudenraus, *The African
Colonization Movement, 1816–1865* (New York: Columbia University Press, 1961).

66. See Floyd Miller, *The Search for a Black Nationality: Black Colonization and Emigration,
1787–1863* (Urbana, IL: University of Illinois Press, 1975). Also Lamont D. Thomas,
The Rise to be a People: A Biography of Paul Cuffee (Urbana, IL: University of Illinois Press,
1986).

the invention of the cotton gin in 1792 by Eli Whitney made cotton plantations much more profitable, renewing the demand for slave labor, including a re-legalized or a covert slave trade.[67]

Another important factor in the fading of white anti-slavery sentiment was the anti-colonial rebellion of Santo Domingo in 1791 which finally drove out the French and won independence for the new nation of Haiti in 1804. This successful revolt struck fear into U.S. slave owners. News of the rebellion ran like wildfire through the U.S. slave community and inspired several slave rebellions, such as that led by the 'General' Gabriel in Richmond in 1800.[68] Even though the revolutionary leaders had eagerly imagined that their example of liberation from colonial rule would inspire like revolutions around the world, it quickly became evident that they had not envisioned that this might apply to Africans, much less to enslaved Africans in the Caribbean.

The immediate reaction for Southern slave states was to pass a series of 'Black Codes,' laws that defined tight control over and suppression of blacks, free or slave. Free blacks could not vote, hold office or property. They were excluded from more skilled professions. Slaves should not be taught to read or write, or even supplied with paper. Draconian measures were passed against even the slightest sign of resistance or independence.[69] In addition, white workers in Northern cities began to object to competition from free blacks. From the early eighteenth century many Northern states passed laws restricting the rights of free blacks, such as removing the right to vote, free movement within or into the state, restricting blacks from certain types of employment and denying access to public schools. White mobs burned black schools and gathering places where white and blacks mingled socially and/or for political interchange.[70] Such laws foreshadowed the Jim Crow laws that would be passed to prevent equality of free blacks with whites after the Civil War.

Most whites particularly objected to the possibility of inter-marriage of blacks and whites, as well as, to a lesser extent, of

67. South Carolina reopened its ports to the slave trade in 1803. See Jordan, *White Over Black*, pp. 316–19.

68. Jordan, *White Over Black*, pp. 375–402.

69. See Daniel S. Davies, *Struggle for Freedom: The History of Black Americans* (New York: Harcourt Brace Jovanovich, 1972), pp. 148–50.

70. See *Ebony Pictorial History of Black America: The African Past to the Civil War*, Intro. Lerone Bennett Jr. (Nashville, TN: The Southwestern Company, 1971), I, pp. 159–90.

whites with Indians or Asians. Laws against 'miscegenation' were passed already in the 1660s of the colonial period and lasted in American law to 1967, when they were ruled unconstitutional by the Supreme Court (Loving v. Virginia).[71] Even though white men had been the primary agents of such 'miscegenation' since the beginning of contact with blacks, they were obsessed with the fear that black men would take revenge by marrying or sexually 'using' white women. This obsession would continue to define race relations long into the twentieth century and to be central to the lynching of black males, which continued into the 1960s.[72]

The denial of the reality of white sex with blacks extended to the denial of civil rights to the offspring of such relations. Not only did slave status descend through the mother, assumed to be the black slave partner in such relations (even though white women sometimes did have black male partners, usually by choice), but white law defined as 'black' those with even a small amount of African ancestry. Unlike French and Spanish colonial laws and customs which allowed for gradations of 'mixtures' of ancestry, defining those with a half, a fourth or an eighth of African ancestry differently in terms of social status, U.S. Americans established the most rigid 'color bar,' applying legal codes against blacks to include anyone with 'one drop of black blood;' i.e., as long as black ancestry was in any way evident though physical appearance and personal claims of identity.[73]

This extreme definition of the 'color line' would bar even high-achieving light-skinned 'blacks' from equal access to housing, employment and political opportunity until recently. Even the term 'mulatto' has not been often used in the United States, since it implies

71. See Jacqueline Battalora, PhD dissertation, Northwestern University, 1999, *Toward a Critical White Racial Ethics: Construction of Whiteness in Antimiscegination Law*, see also Ian F. Haney Lopez, *White by Law: The Legal Construction of Race* (New York: New York University Press, 1996).

72. There are many studies of lynching as a tool of white terrorism of Blacks. For some studies written in the Jim Crow era, see the book by anti-lynching crusader, Ida B. Wells-Barnett, *On Lynching: Southern Horrors* (1891: reprint Salem, NH: Ayer Co., 1991), and James H. Chadbourn, *Lynching and the Law* (Chapel Hill, NC: University of North Carolina Press, 1933).

73. For the 'one-drop' rule, see F. James Davis, *Who Is Black: One Nation's Definition* (University Park, PA: Pennsylvania State University Press, 2001), pp. 4–6, 13–16, 54–58, 113–17, 189–200. On the difference of the United States from other countries where different status is defined according to the percentage of white ancestry, see Davis, *Who is Black*, pp. 81–113.

a distinction between those of African descent with little or no white ancestry and those with some or even much white ancestry.[74] Thus one has the oddity of even very light-skinned people with only a small percentage of African ancestry referred to in the United States as 'blacks.' This habit, ironically, has had the positive effect of keeping a certain sense of identity between all who share some African ancestry, rather than splitting them into different classes, as in French or Spanish regions of the Americas.

Although the limits of this chapter preclude any full discussion of African-American history in the United States, with its many remarkable achievements in all fields of culture,[75] a brief summary of this history will be attempted here primarily to indicate how this extreme pattern of racism would continue to shape relations between those Europeans culturally constructed as 'white' (itself a malleable category[76]) and those constructed as 'black;' i.e., those with any perceptible African ancestry, down to the present day.

The political and economic tensions between 'free' and 'slave' states in the 1850s burst into a succession of the 'slave' states from the Union in 1861 and the declaration of war by the Northern states to prevent this succession from the Union. At first Abraham Lincoln and other Northern leaders of the war sought to deny that the war had anything to do with abolishing slavery. Although hostile to slavery as an institution, Lincoln was himself a white supremacist who made his views on this matter clear in many statements.[77] Lincoln himself wished to narrowly define the goals of the war as 'saving the Union,' not freeing the slave. He even offered to pay slave owners for slaves freed in the District of Colombia.

However, as the war progressed Lincoln gradually accepted the necessity of the emancipation of the slaves. He issued the

74. See Jordan, *White Over Black*, pp. 167–68.

75. A good bibliographical guide to such history is found in Arvarh E. Strickland and Robert E. Weems, Jr, *The African American Experience: A Historiographical and Bibliographical Guide* (Westport, CT: Greenwood Press, 2001).

76. Much work has been done on American social history to show how groups originally discriminated against by English Protestants, such as Catholics, Irish, Jews, etc were assimilated into the category of 'white' as they became 'Americanized.' See, for example, Noel Ignatiev, *How the Irish Became White* (New York: Routledge, 1995); also Matthew F. Jacobson, *Whiteness as a Different Color: European Immigrants and the Alchemy of Race* (Cambridge, MA: Harvard University Press, 1999).

77. See William Douglas, *Mr. Lincoln and the Negroes: The Long Road to Equality* (New York: Athenaeum, l963), and Benjamin Quarles, *Lincoln of the Negro* (New York: Oxford University Press, 1962).

Emancipation Proclamation on January 1, 1863, although initially it applied only to those states 'still in rebellion,' not to those enslaved in areas that had remained or had become 'loyal' to the United States. Over Lincoln's dead body (literally) and the resistance of his Vice-President, Andrew Johnson, who became President after his assassination on April 14, 1865, white Republican radicals in Congress, such as Thaddeus Stevens of Pennsylvania and Charles Sumner of Massachusetts, insisted on pushing through congress a series of amendments to the Constitution: the thirteenth (ratified, 1865), the fourteenth (ratified, 1868) and the fifteenth (ratified, 1870).

These amendments abolished any form of slavery or involuntary servitude in the United States (except as punishment for crime), made all persons born or naturalized in the United States citizens, gave the vote to all male citizens twenty-one years or older (except those who had denied their loyalty to the United States through taking part in insurrection) and finally, declared that the vote should not be 'denied or abridged by the United States or by any state on account of race, color or previous condition of servitude.' With these three amendments the Radicals sought to lock in place full and equal citizenship for all (males), regardless of race.

For the first decade after the Civil War these Republican radicals continued to hold power in Congress, seeking to impeach President Johnson for his resistance to full equality for black people. They sought to effect a strict enforcement of the laws of Reconstruction and readmission of former Confederate states to the Union and of their leaders to citizenship. During this period of Reconstruction black people would be elected to the state legislatures, as well as the Federal Congress, from many former Confederate states. Progressive state constitutions were written in former Confederate states that sought to ensure political, social and economic equality for all. Some of these laws read like those of the 1960s, guaranteeing equal access of black people to all public services and facilities, abolishing property qualifications for voting and creating an integrated school system.

Influenced by white Southern views, this period of Reconstruction has gone down in many U.S. American history books still used in U.S. schools as an horrific period of chaos in which 'scalawags' (Southerners who sided with black rights) and 'carpetbaggers' (Northern immigrants to the South) dominated the legislatures, bringing into political power recently freed and ignorant blacks without any qualifications for government.[78] Critical study, however, has rejected this assessment, showing that the blacks elected to Southern State legislatures, as well as to the U.S. Congress, in this period were, in fact, highly qualified men who had achieved a good education and had excelled in law, business or other areas.[79]

If there was chaos in this period, it was primarily because white supremacists organized clandestine groups, such as the Ku Klux Klan, to terrorize blacks and their white allies.[80] There were also riots against blacks in Northern cities, led by whites that objected to competition from freed blacks. Such chaos reigned because Federal and local law enforcement refused to take strong measures to interdict it.

By 1877, the radical Republican generation in Congress was dead and Northern whites were increasingly disposed to let former Confederates and their descendents return to power in the South, rewriting the state constitutions and repealing the egalitarian laws written during Reconstruction. New Black Codes were passed disqualifying blacks from voting by various strategies (property qualifications, literacy tests, the grandfather clause that excluded anyone from the vote not descended from someone who voted in 1865). Blacks were again excluded from equal access to employment and education. There was a concerted effort to confine most blacks in the South to sharecrop labor in agriculture where they were kept in permanent indebtedness to white landowners. Outright slavery returned through imprisoning overly independent blacks for trivial offenses and the use of the prison chain gang for hard labor.[81]

By the 1890s these means of disenfranchising, subordinating and re-enslaving blacks by Black Codes, terrorism, imprisonment,

78. See, for example, Henry W. Bragdon, Samuel P. McCutchen and Donald A. Ritchie, *History of a Free Nation* (NY: McGraw-Hill, 1998), pp. 449–50. By contrast, Winthrop D. Jordan, Miriam Greenblatt and John S. Bowes, *The Americans: A History* (Evanston, Il: McDougal, Littell and Company, 1994), makes a point of refuting the stereotypes of Black elected officials during Reconstruction as ignorant and illiterate: pp. 393–94.

79. See *Ebony Pictorial History of Black America*, vol. II, pp. 22–42.

80. On the history of the KKK, see David M. Chalmers, *Hooded Americanism: The First Century of the KKK, 1865–1965* (Garden City, NY: Doubleday, 1965).

81. Davis, *Struggle for Freedom*, pp. 161–62. On the complex genesis of sharecropping as a form of southern Black labor, see Gerald D. Jaynes, *Branches without Roots: Genesis of the Black Working Class in the American South, 1862–1882* (New York: Oxford University Press, 1986).

economic marginalization and educational deprivation were supplemented by an elaborate system of Jim Crow Laws enforcing separation in all public facilities. Separate parks, schools, libraries, transportation or sections of these facilities became the rule. Blacks could not drink from the same water fountains, sit in the same seats, ride in the same elevators, walk up or down the same staircases and, in some cases, even look out of the same windows as whites. In 1896, the Supreme Court responded to concerted efforts of blacks and whites who sought to challenge these laws by ruling in Plessy vs. Ferguson that these laws were legal as long as the separate facilities were 'equal' (which was, of course, never the case).[82] Only in 1964 were Jim Crow Laws ruled inherently unequal and so illegal, in the Civil Rights Act of that year.

The hundred years from the end of the Civil War to the Civil Rights Act of 1964 would encompass a long determined struggle on the part of African-Americans to win the full legal rights and societal opportunities promised to them in Reconstruction Civil Rights Laws, stolen through Black Codes and Jim Crow Laws, and tacitly, if not actively, accepted by most of white America. This struggle represented not only a hard-won legal revolution, but also an effort to affect a revolution in the white consciousness so long shaped by black-white racist dualisms. During this century African-Americans would give evidence of their 'equal' human capacities in endless numbers of ways.

African-Americans would acquit themselves well in every U.S. war, from the Revolutionary War, the War of 1812, and the Civil War, to the Spanish American War, the First and the Second World Wars, not to mention all the wars since that time in which African-Americans find themselves now numbered among the generals, as well as a large percentage of the foot soldiers. African-Americans would found thousands of black schools from primary to college levels. They would pioneer outstanding achievements in music, the arts, literature, as well as the sciences and business. They would found their own churches, as well as becoming pastors and bishops in white denominations. Black preaching, liturgy and theology would come to define a distinctively African-American church that would rouse the whole nation in the 1960s. Yet, white stereotypes of blacks would remain largely unchanged by these achievements from the Civil War to the 1960s.

82. There are many histories of Jim Crow: See the classic study by C. Vann Woodward, *The Strange Career of Jim Crow* (New York: Oxford University Press, 1966).

In the first decades of the twentieth century thousands would vote with their feet by migrating from Southern fields to Northern cities, only to find there a different, more impersonal sort of segregation, not the fully open society that they hoped for. Having given their lives in the First World War African-Americans who survived service to their country returned to face white race riots against them in more than two dozen Northern cities in 1919.[83] The Depression would deepen African-American poverty, although some new opportunities would open to them in Roosevelt's New Deal, especially through the advocacy of Eleanor Roosevelt.[84]

By the time African-Americans found themselves giving their lives in the Second World War in a still segregated army, some black leaders became determined to make the demands for equal rights felt on the highest national level. A. Philip Randolph, militant labor leader since before World War I, founder of the Brotherhood of Sleeping Car Porters,[85] threatened President Roosevelt with a massive March on Washington in 1941, as the U.S. prepared to enter the war, if the President did not desegregate the army and the defense industries. Roosevelt agreed to desegregate defense industries and decree fair employment clauses in government contracts,[86] although the U.S. Army would not be desegregated until the Truman Administration in 1948. During the Second World War, African-Americans launched the 'double V' campaign, insisting that the 'V' for Victory over European anti-Semitism and fascism must be matched by a victory over anti-black racism at home.

The 1950s and 60s would be shaped by a continually growing effort to overcome Jim Crow in American law, as well as in American minds and hearts. An extraordinary generation of African-American leaders would arise, from preachers such as Dr Martin Luther King to black youth who shaped organizations such as the Student Non-Violent Coordinating Committee (SNCC),[87] the Black Power Movement and the Black Panthers. New voices, such as Malcolm X, would challenge the message of non-violence and easy

83. On the great migration, see Davis, *Struggle for Freedom*, pp. 186–203.
84. See Howard Sitkoff, *A New Deal for Blacks* (New York: Oxford University Press, 1978).
85. See Brailford R. Brazeal, *The Brotherhood of Sleeping Car Porters: Its Origins and Development* (New York: Harpers and Brothers, 1946).
86. Davis, *History of Black Americans*, pp. 209–10.
87. See Howard Zinn, *SNCC: The New Abolitionists* (Boston: Beacon, 1964).

inclusion of whites in the struggle with more militant messages.[88] Many blacks and whites would give their lives in the struggle for justice, including both King and Malcolm X. New laws were passed outlawing Jim Crow and decreeing equal access to all services, education and politics. A new generation of black politicians would come into office from local mayors to Congresses.[89] Edward Brooke, elected to the U.S. Congress in 1966, would be the first black elected to a full term in the U.S. Senate since Blanche K. Bruce entered the Senate from the state of Mississippi in 1875, ninety-one years earlier.

But the years since the 1970s would see new forms of backlash against the effort to match legal rights with affirmative action and investment in overcoming structural poverty. A new conservativism began to be shaped from the Reagan to the Bush Administrations from the 1970s to the twenty-first century. This would take the form not so much of overt racism, now seen as culturally discredited, but myriad ways to neutralize civil rights and anti-racism and sever their connection to broader efforts to overcome the growing disparities between wealth and poverty in America. Although African-Americans can now be found at the highest levels of wealth and power, with a black general (Colin Powell) and then a black woman (Condoleezza Rice) chosen as Secretary of State under President George W. Bush, these choices of black leaders would intentionally seek out those high achieving blacks willing to lend themselves to neo-conservative politics, at the expense of the vast majority of their own race. The two Bush presidents utilized a right-wing race-tokenism, appointing conservative blacks to undercut any progressive agenda of racial inclusion, while purporting to be supporters of 'color blind' policies.

In 2003 African Americans numbered 37 million, 12.8% of the American population. They were almost two and a half times as likely to be poor as whites. The white poor number 24.3 million (10.5% of whites), while African-Americans falling below (the unrealistically low) poverty line numbered 8.8 million or 24.4% of the total black population.[90] The class hierarchy in U.S. society

---

88. See Malcolm X, *The Autobiography of Malcolm X* (New York: Ballantine Books, 1973). Also Stokely Carmichael and Charles Hamilton, *Black Power: The Politics of Liberation in America* (New York: Vintage, 1967).

89. See Katherine Tate, *From Protest to Politics: The New Black Voters in American Elections* (Cambridge, MA: Harvard University Press, 1993).

90. *World Almanac, 2005* (New York: Media Co., 2005), p. 128.

continues to be, to a significant extent, a race hierarchy, with the two most excluded others, American Indians and African-Americans, disproportionately on the lower rungs.

These racist patterns were already deeply rooted in North America's English colonial origins. Reconfirmed rather than challenged in era of the founding of the United States in the 1770s–90s, the United States defined itself as an 'elect nation' essentially as a white Anglo-Saxon Protestant nation. What was inconceivable and still remains inconceivable to most white Americans is to value and rejoice in their people as a nation shaped by and enriched through *mestizaje* and *mullatez*, the amalgamation and mutual interchange between European, Indian and African cultures. In the next chapters we shall trace the fateful working out of this WASP definition of the United States' divine election and 'manifest destiny.'

Chapter Three

MANIFEST DESTINY AND ANGLO-SAXON RACISM — 1815–1875

In the mid-1830s to 1850s the United States saw a rapid territorial expansion across the continent. From thirteen colonies that hugged the Atlantic coast, in little more than a half century the nation had come to span the continent 'from sea to shining sea.' These developments shaped a new formulation of an American aggressive nationalism that drew on older elements of belief in divine election and the mandate to be democracy's 'light to the nations' with enlarged expansionist zeal. The term 'Manifest Destiny,' coined by New York journalist John Louis O'Sullivan in 1845, came to epitomize this new form of the vision of America's providential calling and mission.

Manifest Destiny and WASP Exclusivity

O'Sullivan coined the phrase first to justify the annexation of Texas as a state of the union. He advocated such annexation not only against opposition groups from within the U.S., but also from Mexico, who saw such annexation as a *causi belli*, and the efforts of the English to negotiate a sphere of influence for itself by maintaining the permanent independence of the Lone Star State. O'Sullivan later that year used the phrase again to argue for American expansion into the Oregon Territory against the British claims to the area. The superiority of the American claim to the Oregon Territory, O'Sullivan declared, was 'by the right of our manifest destiny to overspread and to possess the whole of the continent which Providence has given us for the development of the great experiment of liberty and federated self-government entrusted to us.'[1]

1. In the New York *Morning News*, 27 December, 1845: see Robert W. Johannsen, 'The Meaning of Manifest Destiny', in Sam W. Haynes and Christopher Morris (eds.), *Manifest Destiny and Empire: American Antebellum Expansionism* (College Station, TX: Texas A&M University Press, 1997), p. 9.

As is evident from O'Sullivan's rhetoric, the idea of 'Manifest Destiny' united various themes. There is, first of all, the claim that the continent itself provides a territorial mandate for expansion from the Atlantic to the Pacific coasts. Secondly, that this territorial expanse is a gift of divine providence to 'us,' the U.S. Americans. Thirdly, that this expansion is an expression of a unique mission entrusted by God to this American people to be the exponents of liberty and self-government under a federal system, presumably as an exemplar of such a superior form of government for the other nations of the world. Thus the concept of manifest destiny integrated faith in a divine mission given to the nation with its destiny to fill the continent from coast to coast.[2]

Albert Weinberg, in his magisterial 1935 study of the meaning of manifest destiny[3], delineates a number of themes that cluster under this term in the antebellum period. One of these is 'natural right,' the right to security and hence to expand to secure borders and to navigate waterways. Another is 'geographical predestinarianism,' that claims the continent itself is the natural borders of the nation. Such a claim leaves open-ended the north-south borders of the United States. Should such expansion include parts, if not all, of Canada, expansion into Mexico and perhaps farther South, to fill the whole of the two American continents? Aspirations of further expansion north and south would not be lacking in the nineteenth century.[4]

The notion that only those who till the soil have a right to it would also be used to dispossess the Indian, regardless of the fact that Indians did in fact till the soil, as we have seen in the previous chapter. These naturalistic claims were seen as giving Americans superior title that could override mere legal claims based on previous treaties or land titles. These notions of superior rights were combined with assertions of moral-political superiority, claims that

2. *Contra* Frederick Merk, *Manifest Destiny and Mission in American History: A Reinterpretation* (New York: Alfred A. Knopf, 1963) who argues for the separation of the ideas of manifest destiny and mission.

3. Albert K. Weinberg, *Manifest Destiny: A Study of Expansionism in American History* (Chicago: Quadrangle Books, 1935).

4. Claims to annex Canada into the US would be made periodically, often seeing in this the natural union of two Anglo-Saxon peoples: see John Dos Passos, *The Anglo-Saxon Century and the Unification of the English-Speaking People* (New York: C.P. Putnam's Sons, 1903). On the proposals to annex all of Mexico, see John D.P. Fuller, *The Movement for the Acquisition of all Mexico, 1846–8* (Baltimore, MD: The Johns Hopkins Press, 1936).

Americans were expanding the sphere of true freedom and democratic government. In so doing they were regenerating or uplifting previously depraved peoples and regions and hence engaged in a redemptive mission.

Although Weinberg uses primarily secular language, theological underpinning was never far from such claims. The placement of Americans in this particular continent was 'providential,' a gift of God, a promised land which then endowed its people with a redemptive mission. The themes of Americans as the New Israel, God's new elect nation, gifted with a promised land and called to redeem the nations, lurk behind such claims. With a little more rhetorical excess they easily come to suggest a millennial era to be gained for all humanity as the ultimate future of America's redemptive mission.[5]

However, the rhetoric of manifest destiny in the 1840s was closely connected with racial exclusivism. Not only is this mission given to a uniquely chosen nation, but also that nation comes to be identified with a particular race, Anglo-Saxons, as well as a particular religion, Protestant *Christianity*. Not only is this mission of expansion *qua* democratic uplift given uniquely to this racial-religious group, but it also comes to be assumed that only they are capable of its requisite virtues. Thus redemptive regeneration through democracy is not to be extended to either blacks or Indians since they are racially incapable of its duties. In the 1840s this same logic would be applied to Mexicans since as a debased 'mongrel race' that unites Spanish, Indians, blacks and Catholicism, they too are incapable of democracy.

This fusion of faith in America's democratic redemptive mission and Anglo-Saxon Protestant racism created some contradictions already in the era of the American constitution which would be aggravated as the nation expanded across the continent in the first half of the nineteenth century. If there are other races that are by nature incapable of democratic self-government, what does this mean for America's manifest destiny? The treatment of Indians and blacks became the models for how America should deal with other 'inferior races'; they should be either exterminated or enslaved. That is to say, they should be either viewed as new 'Indians,' in

5. See Ernest Lee Tuveson, 'When did Destiny become Manifest?' in *Redeemer Nation: The Idea of America's Millennial Role* (Chicago: University of Chicago Press, 1968), pp. 91–136.

which case they should 'disappear'; or they should be seen as new negroes, in which case they should be put into a form of servitude under white guardianship.

These options governed the debate about U.S. expansion into Mexican Territory in the 1830s to 50s, from the revolt of Texas from Mexico in 1835 and its annexation through the Mexican War of 1846–48. Most U.S. Americans assumed that the territory to be 'liberated' from Mexico should include not only Texas to the Rio Grande River, but also the whole of the New Mexico Territory and Alta California. Some hoped for larger claims: Baja California and the vast northern Mexican areas of Sonora, Chihuahua, Cohuila, some imagined occupying the whole of Mexico to the Yucatan.

But what should be done with so many Mexicans? If they were incapable of democratic 'uplift,' could they perhaps be made to 'disappear' like the Indians or put under servitude like the blacks? Other Americans who opposed such expansionism drew the opposite conclusion, while accepting the racist logic. If such inferior people could not be 'uplifted' to democratic government, then expansion and incorporation as a state of the union should be limited to those territories with relatively few Mexicans; i.e., Texas to California.[6]

As we have seen in the previous chapters, notions of a distinctive Anglo-Saxon Protestant identity of the American nation had deep roots in the colonial period and its English ancestry. Myths of an original pure Anglo-Saxon Church before corruption by Rome mingled with myths of the 'Norman yoke' that corrupted the original character of the Anglo-Saxons as uniquely apt for political freedom. The very notion that there existed such a thing as an 'Anglo-Saxon race' was itself dubious, and nineteenth century American ideological use of this term was always slippery, coming to be loosely equated with Western European Protestant whites. Those who used this term to laud a unique capacity for freedom and democratic self-government possessed by WASP Americans generally assumed that they represented the 'best' of Anglo-Saxon Germanic people in a unique expression under the conditions of freedom created in the U.S.

6. For the debate over Mexico in the mid-1840s see 'Race, Expansion and the Mexican War,' in Reginald Horsman, *Race and Manifest Destiny: The Origins of American Racial Anglo-Saxonism* (Cambridge, MA: Harvard University Press, 1981), pp. 229–48.

Such language was used vaguely in the late eighteenth century, often with the hope that other peoples could be uplifted and shaped by the influence of these superior characteristics exemplified by Americans. It was only after the 1830s that there emerged a more exclusivist claim to racial uniqueness that negated the assimilation of other peoples. This shift reflected both the hardening of the justifications of black servitude and the expulsion of Indians, as well as the new confrontation with Mexicans. But it was also justified by the assimilation of a new scientific racism, which sought to explain and classify the different 'races' of mankind in descending order, with 'whites' at the top.

These racial differences came to be seen as fixed unalterable characteristics that cannot be changed by education or amelioration of the social and material environment. Thus one of the leading physicians and professor of Natural History, Charles Caldwell, authored in 1830 the treatise *Thoughts on the Original Unity of the Human Race*, in which he argued against the theory that race differences had been created by environmental factors and so could be changed. Caldwell argued that God had created four distinct races: Caucasian, Mongolian, Indian and African, made the Caucasians the superior race and the others in descending order of inferiority. Only the Caucasians are capable of true civilization. 'To the Caucasian race is the world indebted for all the great and important discoveries, inventions and improvements that have been made in science and the arts.'[7] Such claims of unalterable racial differences increased rapidly after 1830.[8]

Thus the 1830s–40s, at the time of the heightening of confrontation with Mexico leading to the Mexican-American war, were also 'the decisive years in the creation of a new Anglo-Saxon political ideology.'[9] This ideology was continually in the mouths of politicians, journalists and leading intellectuals. Thus Horace Bushnell, prominent Protestant theologian, delivered an oration in August 1837 on the 'Principles of National Greatness'. Foundational to such greatness, for Bushnell, is the racial qualities of its settlers. 'Out of all the inhabitants of the world a select stock, the Saxon, and out of this the British family, the noblest of the stock, was

7. Charles Caldwell, *Thoughts on the Original Unity of the Human Race* (2nd edn; Cincinnati, OH: A. & U.P. James, 1852), p. 136.
8. Horsman, *Race*, pp. 177–38.
9. Horsman, *Race*, p. 208.

chosen to people our country.' Mexico, by contrast, was settled by inferior peoples. If such debased races had peopled Britain, they 'in five years would make their noble island a seat of poverty and desolation.'[10]

White Americans argued that inferior peoples, Indians and Mexicans, were innately incapable of making proper use of the land and so they, the superior race, had a God-given right to take the land from them. Thus T.J. Farnham, a traveler in California in 1840, describes the Californios (Spanish Californians) as a mixed breed incapable of energetic cultivation of the soil or good government:

> Thus much for the Spanish population of the Californias: in every way a poor apology of European extraction; as a general thing incapable of reading or writing, and knowing nothing of science or literature, nothing of government but its brutal force, nothing of virtue but the sanctions of the Church, nothing of religion but ceremonies of the national ritual. Destitute of industry themselves, they compel the poor Indian to labor for them, affording him a bare savage existence for his toil, upon their plantations and the fields of the Missions. In a word, the Californians are an imbecile, pusillanimous race of men, and unfit to control the destinies of that beautiful country.[11]

Farnham goes on to dilate on what he sees as the innate racial roots of this lack of weakness. Echoing the racial theories of the period, Farnham asserts that miscegenation with inferior races results in deterioration of the offspring, while the mingling of Caucasian peoples strengthens them.

> No one acquainted with the indolent, mixed race of California will ever believe that they will populate, much less, for any length of time, govern the country. The law of Nature which curses the mulatto here with a constitution less robust than that of either race from which he sprang, lays a similar penalty upon the mingling of Indian and white races in California and Mexico. They must fade away; while the mixing of different branches of the Caucasian family in the States will continue to produce a race of men who will enlarge from period to period the field of their industry and civil domination, until not only the Northern states of Mexico, but the Californias also, will open their glebe to the

10. Horace Bushnell, *An Oration, Pronounced before the Society of the Phy Beta Kappa, at New Haven, on the Principles of National Greatness* (August, 1937). See Horsman, *Race*, p. 209.

11. T.J. Farnham, *Life, Adventures and Travels in California* (New York: Nafis and Cornish, 1855), p. 363. Quoted from Robert F. Heizer and Alan J. Almquist, *The Other Californians: Prejudice and Discrimination under Spain, Mexico and the United States to 1920* (Berkeley, CA: University of California Press, 1971), p. 140.

pressure of the unconquered arm. The old Saxon blood must stride the continent, must command all the northern shores...and in its own unaided might, erect the altar of civil and religious freedom on the plains of California.[12]

A similar language that asserts the innate inferiority of the Mexicans as a 'mongrel race' of mingled Indian and Spanish, destined to 'fade away' before the superior Anglo-Saxon industry and might, pervades the statements of political leaders of the period. Wally Thompson of South Carolina, Minister for the Whig Administration in Mexico in 1842, in his *Recollections*, published in 1847, asserts the Mexicans are mostly Indians or of mixed Indian-white race and thus are destined to 'recede before us' just as the Indians in the United States have done. The general Mexican population he characterized as 'lazy, ignorant and, of course, vicious and dishonest.' The white race must inevitably push such inferior people aside: 'That our language and laws are destined to pervade the continent, I regard as more certain than any other event which is in the future. Our race has never yet put its foot on a soil which it has not only kept but advanced.'[13]

The Conquest of Texas and the War with Mexico

The conflict with Mexico was rooted in the desire of white Americans to expand across the continent. This expansion was impeded by the northern territories of the Spanish Empire, which stretched across the southwest from Texas to California. U.S. desire to acquire Texas began with the Louisiana Purchase in 1803, when Napoleon sold the vast territory from the Gulf of Mexico to the Canadian border to the United States, an area of 827,192 square miles that doubled the original territory of the United States. The question of the inclusion of Texas was raised at this time. In 1819 when the United States concluded a treaty with Spain for the acquisition of Florida, the United States relinquished claims to Texas.

In 1821, when Mexico declared its independence from Spain, talks between Mexico and the United States fixed the northern borders of Mexico as including the lands from the Red River (northern border of Texas) across parts of Colorado, Wyoming, through Utah

---

12. Farnham, *Life*, p. 413, from Heizer and Almquist, *The Other Californians*, p. 140.
13. Wally Thompson, *Recollections in Mexico* (1847), pp. 204, 238, from Horsman, *Race*, p. 212.

and Nevada to the California-Oregon border. In the late 1820s the U.S. twice offered to buy Texas, but these offers were rejected by Mexico. These areas were sparsely settled by Mexicans and raiding parties of Indians often depopulated such settlements that were established. Yet, Mexico regarded these lands as an integral part of its national territory based on Spanish exploration, confirmed by agreement with the United States.

In the last years of their rule in New Spain, the Spanish conceived the plan of inviting North Americans to settle in Texas to secure the area against the raiding Indians. The immigrants were required to pledge allegiance to Spain and adopt the Catholic religion. Stephen Austin was offered a vast land grant in Texas in 1821 and quickly led some 25,000 settlers into the region. These Anglo migrants to Texas had no contact with the Spanish culture of central Mexico, and only contempt for both the Catholic faith and the Indians and Mexicans they encountered in Texas. Although Mexico had abolished slavery under its new constitution of 1824, most of the Anglo settlers were Southern slaveholders who bought their slaves with them, registering them as contract labor. When the Texans declared their independence from Mexico in 1835, slavery was formally reestablished. Thus northern abolitionists and politicians from free states questioned expansion into these Mexican territories as opening new lands for slave states.

In 1830 the newly independent Mexico began to realize that these Anglo settlers outnumbered Mexicans four to one. Moreover, they had no Mexican identity and were quickly forming the basis for the independence of the territory. They then sought to end Anglo migration to Texas and to tax imports and exports from Texas to the U.S. In 1834, Antonio Lopez de Santa Anna became President of Mexico. He abolished the liberal constitution of 1824 and sought to strengthen the central government over the federalist movements for self-government by the regional Mexican states. This quickly led to a confrontation with the Texans who were using the federalist view to move toward independent self-government. Stephen Austin, who had sought to negotiate the conflict with Mexico, was imprisoned for treason, and returned to Texas on Christmas 1834 after a two-year confinement.

In 1836 Santa Anna, determined to reestablish control over Texas as a rebellious Mexican state, invaded Texas, overran the defenders of the Alamo Mission in San Antonio and shot more than 300 rebels who had surrendered the town of Goliad. The Anglo-Texans assembled a convention and issued a declaration of independence from Mexico as an independent republic on 2 March 1836. On 20 April 1836 they surprised Santa Anna asleep and quickly routed his army at San Jacinto. The captured Santa Anna was released only after signing the treaty of Valasco, granting Texan independence. But this treaty was repudiated by the Mexican Congress. Thus, despite Texan independence from 1836 and its annexation by the American Congress in 1845, from the Mexican point of view Texas remained a rebellious colony of Mexico that had no right to secede from the nation.

From 1846 to 1845 there were intermittent battles between Texans and Mexico as Mexico sought to reestablish control over Texas. An increasingly vociferous party in the United States began to call, not only for the annexation of Texas, but the occupation of the whole of the northern Mexican territories to California. This was opposed by northerners who saw this as a plot to vastly expand the slave states at their expense. England also saw an opportunity to establish its influence by negotiating a deal between Mexico and Texas whereby it would remain an independent republic and not be annexed into the United States. Since the U.S. was also seeking to take over the Oregon Territory claimed by Britain, some could see a renewed British effort to limit American expansion.

In 1844, James Polk was elected to the U.S. presidency on the platform of Western expansion, the acquisition of both the Oregon Territory and California. Outgoing President Tyler had already approved the resolution by Congress to annex Texas. It was admitted to the Union as a slave state on 29 December 1845, an act which the Mexicans regarded as a cause for war and which northerners regarded with alarm since it made slave states the majority in the senate. Polk first offered to buy all the lands from the Texas border to the Pacific from Mexico for $25 million, an offer that the Mexicans refused to consider, but he also began to prepare for war with Mexico.

As soon as he was inaugurated in March 1845 he ordered Zachary Taylor, General of American troops in Louisiana, to move his army to Texas to prepare to march south of the Nueces River, which the Mexicans regarded as the southern border of Texas. In February 1846 Taylor received orders to march to the northern bank of the Rio Grande, establishing a fortification across from the Mexican town of Matamoros. Since the Mexicans regarded this area from the Nueces to the Rio Grande as belonging to Mexico, the Mexican General, Mariano Ampudia, informed Taylor that he was encamped on Mexican territory and demanded that he withdraw to the Nueces River. At the same time the American navy was ordered to establish blockades on the Pacific and Atlantic coasts of Mexico. When the inevitable clash broke out between the American and Mexican armies at Matamoros on 25 April Polk then declared war, claiming that Mexico had 'invaded our territory and shed American blood upon American soil,' even though from the Mexican point of view the Americans had invaded Mexican soil by moving its troops to the Rio Grande. Congress voted for war three weeks later on 13 May 1846.

The war proceeded on three fronts. Zachary Taylor's army fought its way down the center of Mexico to Monterey. General Stephen Kearny proceeded from Santa Fe in September of 1846, arriving in California in December and declaring the conquest of this entire territory of northern Mexico. At the same time naval blockades surrounded Mexico on the East and West coasts. The Mexicans, however, still refused to capitulate. Polk then turned to General Winfield Scott to land an army at Veracruz and to march to Mexico City, having determined that the Mexicans would surrender only when they were defeated in their capital city.

On 9 March 1847 a fleet of 100 ships transported Scott and 12,000 men to Mexican shores a few miles south of Veracruz. Defenders of Veracruz were quickly overwhelmed, and Scott marched his army west, defeating the Mexicans at Cerro Gordo on 18 April and occupying the city of Puebla by 15 May. When further efforts to conclude a peace treaty with Mexico broke down, Scott advanced his army to the outskirts of Mexico City and finally took the capital itself in September of that year. Although the Mexican army had been repeatedly defeated, fighting was not entirely over and some leaders advocated continued resistance. Guerrilla groups formed and made attacks on the occupying American forces. This made prolonged occupation of Mexico by the U.S. army increasingly costly and helped close off the voices of those who advocated permanent take over of all Mexico.

As is typical in most wars, the Americans assumed that the Mexicans would be easily defeated by the U.S. army. They greatly underestimated the cost in American lives and dollars. Although

1,733 U.S. soldiers lost their lives in battle, another 11,550 died of wounds and disease. The army also suffered from continual manpower losses as more and more troops became deserters. It is estimated that about 10,000 deserted and another 10,000 were discharged on account of disabilities. Since many volunteers joined only for a year, and left when this year was up, it was also difficult to retain adequate numbers for the army as the war continued into its third year. Costs were also far higher than expected, some $50 million in war costs and another $64 million in veteran pensions.[14]

The costs for Mexicans were much higher. Figures suggest 12,000–15,000 soldiers died. This does not include the costs of civilian deaths and injuries. Several of her major cities had their productive industries smashed to rubble and so their international trade was destroyed. There was widespread hunger and disease. Even though American generals sought to curb atrocities committed by U.S. soldiers against Mexican civilians, these were a frequent occurrence, particularly from the less disciplined volunteer forces. The Texan Rangers were notable for their violence against Mexicans. When a U.S. soldier was shot by some guerrilla groups, the Americans would form posses that would invade local villages, pillaging, raping and taking dozens of lives. At times Mexican men or even women who happened to get in their path were shot, sometimes simply as target practice. Catholic churches were particular targets of pillage, reflecting the anti-Catholic hostility common in the army.[15]

The American army that fought the war was peculiar. Many soldiers were undisciplined volunteers who looked to their own group leaders, rather than the officers of the regular army, for their orders. The regular army was made up of a large number of recent immigrants who were subjected to humiliating discipline by their West Point trained officers. Social tensions were particularly high between these officers and Irish immigrants who joined the army because of their difficulties as Irish men in finding employment in eastern cities, such as New York and Boston. The officers looked down on these Irish men both for their religion and their ethnicity, which they saw as little better than the degraded Mexicans. The

---

14. K. Jack Bauer, *The Mexican War, 1846–8* (New York: Macmillan, 1974), p. 392.

15. See the chapter on 'Atrocity: the Wages of Manifest Destiny', in Paul Foos, *A Short, Offhand Killing Affair: Soldiers and Social Conflict during the Mexican-American War* (Chapel Hill, NC: University of North Carolina Press, 2002), pp. 113–37.

Irish were subjected to insults and sometimes forced to attend Protestant services, although later in the war the army leaders sought to ameliorate this conflict by hiring two Catholic chaplains.

This conflict with the Irish in the U.S. army was a source of one of the most notorious cases of U.S. soldiers who not only deserted, but also joined the Mexican side. As Taylor's army was encamped opposite the Mexican army at Matamoros, John Riley, an Irish sergeant and former artilleryman in the British army, swam across the river and joined the Mexican side, having become fed up with ill treatment by the officers and deciding that his sympathies lay more with the Mexicans as a Catholic people and as the weaker party unjustly invaded by the Americans. Eventually some 200 Irish and some Germans followed him into the Mexican army. They formed the Batallón de San Patricio (the Battalion of St. Patrick), fighting under a green flag decorated with a golden harp and the slogan 'Erin go Bragh' (Ireland Forever) on one side and a picture of St. Patrick on the other.

This battalion became notable for its fighting spirit, particularly in the battles at Buena Vista (northern Mexico near Saltillo), and at Cerro Gordo and Churubusco on route to Mexico City. At Churubusco they suffered 60 per cent casualties. After this battle seventy members of the San Patricios were captured and court martialed as deserters. Twenty, including Riley, were given 50 lashes and branded with a D on their cheeks. The fifty others were hanged. The San Patricios continue to be honored as national heroes of Mexico. There is a monument to them in Mexico City where officials of both Mexico and Ireland pay them homage twice yearly (on St. Patrick's day and on the anniversary of the battle of Churubusco).[16]

American historians of the war have often condemned the Mexican leaders for an absurd intransigence and an unrealistic assumption that their army could defeat that of the Americans. If they had accepted the American offer in 1845, the war could have been avoided. The Mexicans could perhaps have bargained for better terms than they finally received after their many defeats,

16. See Michael Hogan, *The Irish Soldiers of Mexico* (Guadalajara, Mexico: Fondo Editorial Universitario, 1996). Also Robert Ryal Miller, *Shamrock and Sword: The Saint Patrick's Battalion in the U.S.-Mexican War* (Norman, OK: University of Oklahoma Press, 1989).

culminating in the occupation of Mexico City.[17] It is certainly true that Mexico suffered from impoverishment, disorganization and quarrelling leadership during this period. Recently independent from Spain, its Criollo leaders had little experience in governing because the Peninsulares (Spanish born) had monopolized political leadership in the colonial period. The figure of Santa Anna was particularly dubious, as he, by turns, lost power and was expelled from Mexico and then managed to return to power, often making deals with the Americans themselves to betray his own people.[18]

But these judgments on the American side fail to reckon with two aspects of the Mexican view of the situation that made it all but impossible for any leader to accept the loss of their northern provinces without at least a major struggle. First, was the clear conviction shared by all Mexican parties that these territories were an integral part of the patrimony of the Mexican nation that had been recognized internationally, including by the U.S. itself. Secondly, the Mexican press and its political leaders were aware of the contempt with which Mexicans as a whole were held by U.S. opinion. The racist rhetoric of Manifest Destiny was translated and published in Mexico, and Mexican politicians experienced the sting of American contempt both when they went to Washington and when American representatives came to Mexico.

Thus public opinion (of the literate leadership class) became deeply offended by these hostile views and determined to resist the American assumption that they were rightless inferiors that should be swept aside. Some felt if they did not resist this U.S. takeover, their whole country would be occupied and their culture wiped out. Although some political leaders were aware that they were poorly prepared to fight the Americans and would probably be defeated, national honor demanded resistance. No leader could counsel capitulation without a fight and remain in power.[19]

17. See, for example, K. Jack Bauer, *The Mexican American War*: also the assessment of U.S. historians of the war in Cecil Robinson, *The View from Chapultepec: Mexican Writers on the Mexican-American War* (Tucson, AZ; University of Arizona Press, 1989), pp. xxxviii-xl.

18. For Santa Anna's secret negotiations with the Americans throughout the war, see 'The War and Secret Diplomacy', in Richard Griswold del Castillo, *The Treaty of Guadalupe Hidalgo: A Legacy of Conflict* (Norman, OK: University of Oklahoma Press, 1990), pp. 15–29.

19. See particularly Gene M. Brack, *Mexico Views Manifest Destiny, 1821–1846: An Essay on the Origins of the Mexican War* (Albuquerque, NM: University of New Mexico Press, 1975).

Mexican politicians, such as Manuel Crescencio Rejón, Minister of the Interior and Foreign Affairs in the war years, expressed this tragic sense of the weakness of Mexico, its need to resist the colonizing determination of the northern power and its fear of U.S. contempt for Mexicans, in his collected *Pensamiento Politico* (*Thoughts on Politics*),

> With the borders of our conquerors brought closer to the heart of our nation, with the whole line of the frontier occupied by them from sea to sea, with their highly developed merchant marine, and with them so versed in the system of colonization by which they attract great numbers of the working classes of the old world, what can we, who are so backward in everything, do to arrest them in their rapid conquests, their latest invasions? ...There they will develop their commerce and stockpile large quantities of merchandise from the upper states. They will inundate us with all this, and our own modicum of wealth, already so miserable and depleted, will in the future sink to insignificance and nothingness...[20]

Rejón urged resistance to the treaty of Guadalupe Hidalgo then being negotiated to end the war, with its acceptance the U.S. annexation of the northern provinces of Mexico, declaring 'what is proposed to us in this fatal treaty amounts to a sentence of death.' He saw the U.S., spurred by racist contempt for Indians, as embarked on a campaign to extinguish Mexico as a people:

> As almost all of us are descended from Indians, the North American people abominate us, their orators depreciating us even while recognizing the justice of our cause. Since they consider us unworthy of forming with them a single nation or society, they have manifested clearly that in their future conquests they will strip us of our land and thrust us aside. Has their conduct, in fact, been any other in their treatment of Indian tribes, former owners of the land, which now belongs to those same United States?[21]

Some American politicians who were opposed to the war did rise to sympathy for the Mexicans, seeing the war as unjust and its terms as ones that Americans would never accept if a foreign power had sought to impose them on themselves. Thus Thomas Corwin, Senator from Ohio, opposing new expenditures (in 1847) for the

20. Manuel Crescencio Rejón, 'Observaciones sobre los Tratatos de Guadalupe', *Pensamiento Politico* (Mexico, DF.: Universidad National Autónoma de Mexico, 1968), pp. 116–22: translated in Robinson, *The View from Chapultepec*, p. 97.
21. Robinson, *The View*, pp. 98, 100.

appropriation of territory from Mexico, declared that, when he had voted for earlier expenditures:

> I did hope, that with the two million then proposed, we might get peace and avoid the slaughter, the shame, the crime, of an aggressive, unprovoked war. But now you have overrun half of Mexico – you have exasperated and irritated her people – you claim indemnity for all expenses incurred in doing mischief and boldly ask her to give up New Mexico and California.

Corwin went on to claim that these territories were as dear to Mexicans as Bunker Hill was to Americans. If the situation were reversed, U.S. Americans would never have accepted the surrender of lands closely identified with their national history:

> What is the territory, Mister President, which you propose to wrest from Mexico? It is consecrated to the heart of the Mexican by many a well-fought battle with his old Castilian master. His Bunker Hills, and Saratogas and Yorktowns are there! The Mexican can say, "There I bled for liberty! and shall I surrender that consecrated home of my affections to the Anglo-Saxon invaders? What do they want with it? They have Texas already." …Sir, had one come and demanded Bunker Hill of the people of Massachusetts, had England's Lion showed himself there, is there a man over thirteen and under ninety who would not have been ready to meet him? …Is there a field but would have been piled high with the unburied bones of slaughtered Americans before these consecrated battle fields of liberty should have been wrested from us? But this same American goes to a sister Republic and says to poor, weak Mexico, "Give up your territory. You are unworthy to possess it; I have got one half already and all I ask of you is to give up the other."[22]

Satirizing the claim that America needed the land because it needed space for its future people, Corwin imagined what the American response would have been if England had asked for half of its land because it claimed it needed the extra space. He concluded with the ringing sentence, 'But you still say you want room for your people. This has been the plea of every robber chief from Nimrod to the present hour.'[23]

Abraham Lincoln, in 1847 a freshman Congressman from Illinois, also opposed the war and questioned whether the 'spot' where

22. Appendix to the Congressional Globe, 29th Congress, 2nd Session (Washington, DC, Blair and Rives, 11 February, 1847), pp. 216–17; excerpted in Michel Roth, *Issues in Western Expansion* (Westport, CT: Greenwood Press, 2002), pp. 73–74.

23. Roth, *Issues*, p. 75.

blood had been shed was actually U.S. soil, thereby challenging President Polk's rationale for the war. Outlining the history of the area by the Rio Grande to which American troops had been sent, Lincoln suggested by his queries that this territory had been continually a part of Mexico. General Taylor had been sent to this area, not to protect Texas, but to create a pretext for a war with Mexico.[24]

The Treaty of Guadalupe-Hidalgo

With General Scott's landing in Veracruz, Polk anticipated that he could now force Mexico to sign a treaty conceding the northern territories to the U.S. Polk sent Nicolas P. Trist, Acting Undersecretary of State under James Buchanan, to finalize the treaty. In a cabinet meeting held 13 April 1847, Polk and his advisors drew up the draft treaty, which Trist was to use as the basis of the negotiations. The draft treaty asked Mexico to concede not only the New Mexico and Utah territories, but Baja as well as Alta California and the rights of transit across the gulf of Tehuantepec (although he was instructed that Baja California and the rights of transit could be regarded as dispensable) and the Rio Grande as the border of Texas. America promised $15 million in exchange, as well as assuming up to $3 million in claims of American citizens against Mexico. The amount of money could also be negotiated, and it was permitted to add articles on the protection of Mexican citizens in the territories.

When the Mexican Congress refused to consider this treaty, Scott advanced his troops to the outskirts of Mexico City (after secret communication with Santa Anna proposing this move to force the Mexican government to negotiate).[25] Scott and Santa Anna then agreed to an armistice and entered into negotiation. But the Mexican negotiators were instructed only to give up Texas to the Nueces River and refuse to give up California and New Mexico. After various proposals and counter proposals that failed to meet U.S. terms, Scott cancelled the armistice and went ahead with plans to attack Chapultepec Castle and enter Mexico City. This took place between 12–14 September.

24. 'Abraham Lincoln's "Spot Resolution"', Roth, *Issues*, pp. 75–76.
25. Del Castillo, *Treaty of Guadalupe Hidalgo*, pp. 27–29.

From this position of dominance, negotiations were reopened with the Mexican government, which had fled the city and established a temporary seat of government at Querétaro, 100 miles north of Mexico City. Even though President Polk had ordered Trist to break off talks and return to Washington, Trist did not comply and continued with the negotiations. Manuel de la Peña y Peña, Presiding Justice of the Mexican Supreme Court, who favored the treaty, became President by the end of the year and negotiations were reopened 2 January. By 2 February 1848, a final draft of the treaty had been completed and signed by the negotiators that gave the United States its territorial demands, including the port of San Diego (but not Baja California). The indemnity was fixed at $15 million, plus the $3 million to cover US citizen claims.

The Mexican negotiators were particularly concerned to protect the civil and property rights of Mexican citizens in the territories. Articles VIII and IX were drafted to assure that Mexicans could elect to remain Mexican citizens if they did so within a year. Otherwise they would be admitted as soon as possible to U.S. citizenship with the enjoyment of all citizenship rights. 'In the meantime, they shall be maintained and protected in the enjoyment of their liberty, their property and the civil and religious rights now vested in them according to Mexican laws. With respect to political rights their condition shall be on an equality with the inhabitants of other territories of the United States.' Article IX also detailed the protection of religious liberty and church property for ecclesiastical corporations. Freedom of communication between church leaders in the territories and those residing in Mexico should also be guaranteed.

Article X protected the owners of Mexican land grants in the territories on the same terms of validity as if such grants had remained within Mexico. Since many land grant titles in the territory had not been completed at the time of the war, it allowed these holders of land titles to complete the process of perfecting their titles to the land within a stipulated period of time. This included land grants within Texas.[26]

Peña y Peña was willing to sign this treaty because he feared a worse situation would develop. In both the northern provinces south

26. For the original wording of articles IX and X of the Treaty of Guadalupe Hidalgo, see Del Castillo, *Treaty*, pp. 179–81.

of the new borders and Yucatan there were rebellions that threatened to fragment the nation, opening to way for the United States to snap up other parts of Mexico. Peña y Peña saw the treaty as necessary to salvage the nation. But the treaty still had to be ratified by the United States, an uncertain question given Trist's unofficial status. Despite his annoyance at Trist's defiance of his orders, President Polk decided to accept the treaty and ask Congress to ratify it. He was worried that Congress would not support further war appropriations and so a treaty as soon as possible was necessary. But he recommended the deletion of Article X on the acceptance of Mexican land grants.

In the Senate debate over the treaty, some opposed it because it did not give the U.S. more land. Senators, such as Sam Houston and Jefferson Davis, wanted more land. Houston wanted to annex the northern states of Mexico as far south as the state of Veracruz. Other Senators who had opposed the war objected to annexing as much land as the treaty proposed, which they feared would become slave states. The two factions ended stalemating each other, and the Senate ended by accepting the land acquisition basically as outlined in the treaty.

Article IX was also revised to make the civil and political rights of Mexican citizens less clear than intended by the original version and without the detailed language about the rights of the church. Article X on the validity of Mexican land grants was deleted. Article XI was changed to allow the U.S. to sell arms and ammunition of Indians, The Wilmot Proviso that would have ruled out slavery in the new territories was defeated. The U.S. Senate passed the treaty in this form on 10 March 1848 by a vote of 38–14, with most northerners opposing it.

The treaty then had to be ratified by the Mexican Congress. Many opposed it, led by Manuel Crescencio Rejón, who believed it would be the death knell of the Mexican nation. Others, such as Peña y Peña, believed it was the only way to salvage a reasonably intact nation, head-off local rebellions and end the occupation of Mexico by the Americans. The deletion of Article X on land grants and the revision of Article IX on the civil and political rights of Mexicans in the territories to be acquired by the U.S. were of grave concern. Luis de la Rosa, Minister of Foreign Relations, requested a meeting with the American commissioners, Nathan Clifford and Ambrose Sevier, to clarify the meaning of these changes. Two other

Mexican signatories of the treaty also attended, Bernardo Couto and Luis Cuervas.

A protocol was drafted and agreed by the two sides (the Protocol of Querétaro) which affirmed the changes in article IX 'did not intend to diminish in any way what was agreed upon by the aforesaid article.' On the deletion of article X, it said this 'did not in any way intend to annul the grants of land made by Mexico in the ceded territories. These grants, notwithstanding the suppression of the article of the Treaty, preserve the legal value which they possess and the grantees may cause the legitimate titles to be acknowledged before the American tribunals.'[27] The Mexicans regarded this protocol as a legally binding interpretation of the treaty and it was ratified by the Mexican Congress with this understanding. However, the American government did not accept the binding character of the Protocol, a difference of views that remains to this day.[28]

Boundary disputes also arose with the implementation of the treaty. Maps of the border between New Mexico (which included Arizona) proved to be in error in the placement of the Rio Grande and Gila rivers. The question of which side paid for the defense of the border from hostile Indians was also in dispute. The result was the sale to the United States of a strip of land on the south of the New Mexico territory for 10 million dollars (the Gadsden Treaty), and a release of the United States from the obligation of article XI in the treaty to police the border.

The Treaty of Guadalupe Hidalgo ended the war between Mexico and the United States, with the withdrawal of American troops from Mexico and promises that future disputes would be solved by negotiation, not war. This agreement has generally held, although there were to be brief occupations of Mexican territories by American troops during the Mexican Revolution of 1910–20. In 1914 American troops landed at Vera Cruz and in 1917 American troops entered northern Mexico in pursuit of Pancho Villa. But it did not solve at all the questions of the civil and political rights and protection

27. To compare the original language of articles IX and X of the treaty with the final version, see Del Castillo, *Treaty*, pp. 179–81 and 190. The Protocol of Querétaro is found in this same volume, pp. 181–82.

28. See Del Castillo, *Treaty*, pp. 54–55. For a detailed discussion, see Geofry Mawn, 'The Land Grant-Guarantee: The Treaty of Guadalupe Hidalgo or the Protocol of Querétaro?' *Journal of the West*, vol. 14, no. 4 (October 1975), pp. 49–63.

of land grants to former Mexican citizens within the ceded territories. On the contrary the contradictory history of the treaty in these areas has led to disputes about civil, political and property rights of former Mexican citizens and their descendents, which have lasted until this day.

Differences quickly arose between former Mexican citizens and American federal and territorial authorities over who was eligible for citizenship. Mexico had abolished slavery in 1824 and given citizenship to all, regardless of race. This did not mean that Mexico was an egalitarian non-racist society. Rather it was a caste society organized along lines of levels of 'mixture' of the races. During the colonial period the ruling class was the Spanish-born Spaniards (Peninsulares). Under them were the criollos, (American-born Spanish), then the mestizos, the mulattos, blacks and Indians. With independence, the Mexican constitution of 1824 gave citizenship and the vote to all residents of Mexico, including Indians, although nomadic Indians were excluded from the actual exercise of the franchise by property qualifications and occupation.

By contrast, the United States, at this time, forbade inter-marriage of the races and regarded white males (Western European) as the only full citizens. It sought to exclude from the franchise all the other races, including the mixed race people. This was particularly harsh toward those of any black ancestry (one drop rule). Indians, however 'civilized,' were excluded from citizenship. (All Indians received citizenship only in 1924). Free blacks were voters in some free states, but the general practice was an effort to exclude them from equal access to education and work. Women were excluded from autonomous civil status and suffrage in both societies, and there was no debate on the women's vote at this time.

Another major area of conflict with the U.S. takeover of the Mexican areas was Mexican property rights under land grants given by Mexico. Many of the titles to these grants were relatively recent and had not been finalized, due to the slowness of the Mexican bureaucracy in Mexico City. The Mexican negotiators of the treaty had tried to provide a means by which these titles could be completed under American laws, but the American authorities did not allow this. Moreover, holders of even completed titles had to prove this in American courts. Generally these Mexican land holders, even if rich in land, were poor in ready financial resources and had to sell land to pay for court expenses and lawyers in complicated legal processes which most of the Mexicans did not well understand, especially since litigation was conducted in English which many did not speak. Thus former Mexicans ended up losing most of the lands they had held under Mexican law. Within a generation even former large landholders were reduced to an impoverished state.

Betrayal of the Treaty: The Dispossession of Indians, Californios and Blacks

We will discuss this process of citizen and land rights of former Mexican citizens in the case of California. When news spread of the discovery of gold at Coloma in California on January 24, 1848, there was a rush of immigration to California, some from Mexico, Latin America and Europe, but mostly from the United States itself. One hundred thousand newcomers had arrived by April of 1849. This influx changed the ethnic population balance in California, swamping the earlier Hispanic population of 13,000. This large new Anglo population led to a demand to form a California state government and application to join the union. (By contrast whites were slow to enter the New Mexican territories, and the populations there remained predominately Indian and Hispanic. Statehood for New Mexico and Arizona took place only in 1912.)

In California the U.S. military issued a call for a convention to form a state constitution. Forty-eight delegates were elected from ten districts. The state constitutional convention was convened in Monterey from 1 September to 13 October 1849. Eight of the delegates were Spanish-speakers born in California. The rest were mainly Anglos who had lived in the state for an average of two years. Ten had lived in the state for less than a year.[29] The convention was conducted bilingually. The Federal Government had left the decision whether to be admitted as a free or a slave state up to the state conventions. The California constitutional convention opted to be a free state, but with severe restrictions on the citizenship of non-whites. There was extended debate in the convention about race and qualifications for citizenship and franchise.

29. Heizer and Almquist, *The Other Californians*, pp. 226–28. The ten districts that elected delegates were San Jose, Monterey, Los Angeles, San Luis Obispo, Sacramento, San Francisco, San Diego, San Joaquin, Santa Barbara and Sonoma.

An initial question for the delegates was whether the Treaty of Guadalupe Hidalgo was binding on their decisions about citizenship, compelling them to accept as citizens all who had been Mexican citizens who opted for U.S. citizenship, as called for in the Treaty. Most of the delegates thought this could be modified to conform to American law and practice, but were concerned that the Federal Government might reject the constitution if it too explicitly contradicted the treaty. The delegates were firm in their convictions that only white males should play any part in governing the state and sought to disenfranchise many who had held Mexican citizenship, which included some who had voted to elect them as delegates.

This led to a debate as to who was 'white.' One of the Californio delegates, Noriego de la Guerra, was concerned that it would be used to exclude dark-skinned Hispanics, such as themselves. Most of the Californio delegates were criollos, but one delegate, Manuel Dominguez, a wealthy landowner and banker, was part Indian and so would be excluded. Another delegate, Charles Botts, formerly from Virginia, replied that it did not mean skin color but race, excluding those of African and Indian race. Thus Dominguez' status was left ambiguous. Although he was allowed to sign the constitution, in 1857 he was excluded from testifying against a white man in court on the grounds that he was an Indian.[30]

The delegates debated whether Indians could be included in citizenship and the vote if they were settled property holders and paid taxes. Some would exclude only Indians who were not taxed, but most wanted to exclude all Indians. Although the question of whether those with some Indian ancestry could vote was not addressed, the delegates wished to exclude all Africans, including those with any African ancestry. This could have excluded the wealthy Californio Pico family who were of African, Indian and European (Spanish and Italian) ancestry, one of whom, Antonio Pico, was a delegate to the convention. Pio de Jesus Pico was the last Spanish governor of California in 1845–46 and a wealthy rancher and businessman after his return to California in 1848. (The African ancestry of the Picos does not seem to have been used to deny them voting status under U.S. California law.)[31]

30. Leonard Pitt, *The Decline of the Californios: A Social History of the Spanish-Speaking Californians, 1846–1890* (Berkeley, CA; University of California Press, 1998), p. 202.
   31. www.socialhistory.org/biographies/pico

Although California was to enter the union as a free state, most of the delegates wanted to exclude free blacks from entering the state. There was a fear that free blacks might flock to the state, and some southerners might bring their slaves under the guise of contract laborers or personal servants, allowing them to become free after a term of service. Strong racist statements were voiced by several delegates, claiming that blacks were inherently incapable of diligent labor, could only work under conditions of servitude and, when free, degraded the conditions of white labor. Delegate M.M. McCarver declared:

> No population that could be brought within the limits of our Territory could be more repugnant to the feelings of the people, or injurious to the prosperity of the community, than free Negroes. They are idle in their habits, difficult to be governed by the laws, thriftless and uneducated. It is a species of population that this country should be particularly guarded against.[32]

In the final votes, the question of the votes for Indians and for the exclusion of blacks from entering California were sidestepped, being left for clarification by the State Legislature. In 1852, the California Legislature acted to deprive any non-white person (Indian, black, or Oriental) from the right to testify against a white person. It further instituted a fugitive slave law that allowed any free black to be apprehended as a fugitive slave and removed by a former master unless he had a legal document proving that he was free. This law was abrogated with the 13th, 14th and 15th amendments after the Civil War, which gave blacks citizenship and the vote, although many found it difficult to exercise this franchise in practice. blacks were a small part of the California population in 1850–60, accounting for just 4,000.

The fate of Indians, Hispanics (criollo and mestizo) and Chinese in California will be briefly reviewed in the rest of this chapter. Indians numbered about 300,000 when the Spanish established the mission system in the mid-eighteenth century. The official Spanish view of the Indian was that he should be civilized and Christianized by the missionaries, but the severity of the treatment of Indians by the missionaries, punishing them for infractions by beatings, denial of food and imprisonment, and their vulnerability to white diseases, caused this population to fall in number to about 100,000 in 1834.

32. Heizer and Almquist, *The Other Californians*, p. 109.

The Anglo view of Indians from the outset of U.S. occupation caused an even further decline in the Indian population. Anglos saw Indians as a people to be exterminated or as destined to 'fade away' due to their incapacity for civilization. As we saw in chapter two, Governor Peter Burnett in his annual message in January 1851 declared it must be expected that a war of extermination would continue to be waged between whites and Indians until the 'Indian race becomes extinct.'[33]

Attacks on Indian villages by volunteer militias or regular army units and casual killings by whites were common until 1870. These were justified in various ways, on the grounds that Indians, often impelled by starvation, had stolen horses or livestock. When Indians killed a white man, often in retaliation for killing Indians, a posse of men would attack an entire village, killing a hundred or more, including women and children. There were numerous instances of such massacres in the 1850s. For example, in 1852 Indians killed a man named Anderson near Weaverville. They were followed and their whole village was attacked, killing 150, and taking three prisoners, a woman and two children.[34]

In the 1850s there was also a lively trade among whites in Indian slaves. Children whose parents had been killed or who were kidnapped were turned into indentured servants for ten or fifteen years, they were bought and sold. Indians walking in a white area might be defined as 'vagrant' or fined for some other infraction. Being unable to pay, they were enslaved. This was legalized in the Indenture Act of 1850 'for the Government and Protection of Indians.'[35]

In 1851–52 the Federal Government set aside tracts of land down the central area of California in treaties with a few Indians who they declared to be representative of the tribes, with the agreement that these tribes would be removed from much larger areas of land they had traditionally occupied. The California Legislature strongly objected to these reservations, on the grounds that whites had settled in some of these areas, and refused to accede to them. Some of the California senators wanted the Indians expelled from California altogether, although they were not clear to what land

33. Heizer and Almquist, *The Other Californians*, p. 26.
34. Heizer and Almquist, *The Other Californians*, p. 28.
35. Heizer and Almquist, *The Other Californians*, p. 46.

they were supposed to be expelled.[36] The population of Indians in California declined rapidly from 1850–70, being reduced to 58,000 in twenty years. By 1913, they numbered just 17,000. The 2000 U.S. Census listed Indians in California as 627,552, (including those who list themselves as Indian in combination with another race.)[37]

The Spanish-speaking population of Mexico did not suffer the same mass extermination as the Indians, although lynching of Mexicans was common. A few of the Californio elites, such as Mariano Vallejo and Pablo de la Guerra, were elected to the California Legislature. More held local leadership posts in areas with a Hispanic majority, but their political influence faded by the 1880s. Even the formerly land-rich suffered a systematic deprivation of their lands, merging descendents of former landowners into the population of more recent immigrants from Mexico who then all became defined in the mind of white Californians as 'foreigners.' For many Anglos they were all 'greasers.' In the words of Pio Pico, they had become 'strangers in their own land.'[38]

The large land grants held by Californios when the U.S. took over in 1846 were recent, and many of the titles were incomplete. Many of these land grants were given by the new Mexican government in the 1830s–40s with the secularization of the California missions. The chain of twenty-one California missions up the coast of Alta California from San Diego to Sonoma held millions of acres of land with great herds of livestock and profitable foreign trade. These missions were secularized between 1831 and 1845, abandoning 15,000 Indian wards of the missions. Many of these Indians went back to native villages. Some obtained land grants and started farms, while others simply squatted in the abandoned buildings.

The mission lands were quickly allotted to the Californio rancheros. About eight hundred of them carved up between them some eight million acres of land, with the largest tracts going to some 46 leading families. The herds of cattle declined rapidly,

36. Heizer and Almquist, *The Other Californians*, pp. 65–91.

37. Heizer and Almquist, *The Other Californians*, pp. 22, 58. *The World Almanac and Book of Facts, 2004*, p. 523. See also S.F. Cook, 'The Destruction of the California Indian', *California Monthly* (December 1968), pp. 15–19.

38. In an address at the time of the U.S. takeover Pio Pico warned against this, saying: 'What shall we do then? Shall we remain supine while these daring strangers are overrunning our fertile plains and gradually outnumbering and displacing us? Shall these incursions go unchecked, until we shall become strangers in our own land.' www.socialhistory.org/biographies/pico

slaughtered for the lucrative trade in hides and tallow. Many mission Indians were incorporated into the ranches as peon labor. A lively shipping trade that stopped at California ports brought finished products to the Californios in exchange for hides and tallow, affording them an elegant lifestyle. Some Anglos had come to the area in the 1830s and intermarried with the Californian elite families, learning Spanish. But this leisurely way of life would decline rapidly with the U.S. takeover in 1846–48.

For the new Anglo immigrants that flocked to California, particularly after the discovery of gold, the Hispanics were a 'defeated enemy' with no rights to the land or political power. A sign of this hostile attitude was the Bear Flag Rebellion on 6 June 1846. A band of armed men, led by John Fremont, raised a flag inscribed with a bear and proclaimed California a Yankee Republic, seeking to imitate the Texan example. Some then went to the home of General Mariano Vallejo, a leading Californio landowner and Mexican Comandante Militar del Frontera del Norte, in charge of the presidio in Sonoma, even though he was known to be friendly to the Americans. They took him, with his brother Salvador and son-in-law, Jacob Leese, prisoner, and delivered them to Fremont encamped at Fort Sutter (Sacramento) keeping them captive under oppressive and insulting conditions for two months.

The arrival of General Kearny in California in December, 1846 established more respectful relations with the Californio leadership class, and curbed for a while the usurped power of Fremont. The period 1847–49 saw fairly cordial relations between this leadership class and the American army, allowing the significant participation of men of the elite Spanish families in the state constitutional convention in Monterey in 1849. The convention was not only conducted bilingually, but the document was released in both languages. But this would be the last time Californios would participate as a group in California politics. The Bear Flag group represented a hostile view of all Hispanics, even the elites, as 'greasers' that would become typical of many of the new Anglo immigrants.

In the 1850s the land of the northern rancheros (Monterey to Sonoma) were largely decimated. The Land Law of 1851 established a three person (all Anglos) Board of Land Commissioners to examine Mexican land titles to affirm or reject their validity. Anglo squatters were given the right to occupy what was seen as 'vacant' land (actually grazing land) and to appropriate or buy cheaply land they had 'improved'. The Californios had difficulty establishing their titles to the satisfaction of these commissioners. The proceedings were conducted in English and the Californios often had to depend on unscrupulous lawyers to defend them and to sell land to pay for their legal expenses. By 1856, most of the great Mexican estates of northern Californian had been sold off or taken over by squatters.

Mariano Vallejo, who held half a million acres of land in the Petaluma and Soscol Ranchos (north of and in the area of San Francisco) in the 1840s had been reduced to a small farm of 200 acres around his country home, *Lachryma Montis*, near Sonoma by the time of his death in 1890.[39] Squatters were allowed to buy up his properties for as little as $1.25 an acre.[40]

The large landholdings of the Californios in the south lasted into the 1880s since these were more arid areas used mostly for cattle ranches, seen as less suitable for the agriculture prized by the Anglos. With the arrival of the railroad in the 1870s and 80s there was a land boom and large Hispanic landowners again found themselves bilked out of most of their property. Many had to mortgage their land to borrow money. Andres and Pio Pico, who once held hundreds of thousands of acres in what became Los Angeles and San Diego counties, lost most of their land by the 1880s through such inability to pay back loans. Pio Pico was several times fraudulently tricked into signing away land because of his inability to read English. In 1894, he died in poverty at his country home in what today is the Whittier area of Los Angeles.[41]

The Los Angeles county area also saw a virtual race war against Mexicans in the 1850s. Some Mexicans, smarting from the Anglo take-over and insulting behavior, became aggressive and successful bandits.[42] But this sparked a view of all Mexicans as thieves. Lynching of Mexicans became common as whites established vigilante groups and engaged in street 'justice' against any suspected Mexican. Throughout the state anti-Catholic and anti-Hispanic members of the Know-nothing Party were elected to office and added to the harassment of Mexicans.

39. Pitt, *The Decline of the Californios*, pp. 83–103.

40. See www.sfmuseum.net/bio/vallejo.html, from Zoeth Skinner Eldredge, *The Beginnings of San Francisco: From the Expedition of Anza, 1774, to the City Charter of April 15, 1850* (San Francisco: ZS Eldredge, 1912).

41. Eldredge, *The Beginnings of San Francisco*, p. 100. See also sfvhs.com/piopico.htlm

42. Eldredge, *The Beginnings of San Francisco*, pp. 167–80.

Laws were passed that were intentionally anti-Hispanic, such as forbidding horse races, theatre and other such entertainment on Sunday, common in the Hispanic community. The legislature refused to provide funds for translation of laws into Spanish, increasing the difficulty of Spanish-speakers to cope with legal struggles. In 1855, an anti-vagrancy law even referred to all Hispanics as 'greasers,' specifying 'all persons who are commonly known as "greasers" or the issue of Spanish or Indian blood…and who go armed and are not peaceable and quiet persons.' A year later this objectionable term was struck from the law, but it reflected the anti-Mexican hostility of Anglo popular culture. Hispanics found it increasingly difficult to be elected to state or local office.[43]

In the 1890s California's Hispanic heritage began to be romanticized by the Anglo city leaders, at a time when the Californios had largely lost any influence. This romantic view of the Spanish past was separated from the actual Mexican population of Los Angeles that was generally impoverished and despised.[44] The Mexican American population would continue to grow in California, reaching some 12 million or one third of California's population by the census of 2000. But this population has continued to be stigmatized as 'illegal' immigrants from Mexico, and has been under-represented politically and culturally. This situation began to change in the 1960s with the Chicano Movement. In 2005, Los Angeles elected its first Hispanic mayor, Antonio Villaraigosa, since Cristobal Aguilar in 1872.

One of the major sites of conflict between whites and other races took place in the gold mines in the 1850s. The discovery of gold brought a number of local Spanish Californians, as well as immigrants from Mexico (about 8000) and South America (about 5000) flocking to the Californian mines. Many Chinese also flocked to California, providing services in the gold mining towns, such as laundry and cooking, as well as building the railroads. The Anglo gold miners regarded gold mining as their exclusive right and quickly acted to exclude 'greasers' and 'coolies'. In 1850, Yankee gold miners forced most of the Hispanics out by imposing a 'foreign miner's tax' that was applied to all Spanish-speakers, including the California-born. The Chinese were also prohibited from obtaining

---

43. Pitt, *The Decline*, pp. 130–47; Heizer and Almquist, *The Other Californians*, p. 151.

licenses to mine gold. Mob violence was applied to the Hispanics and Chinese to hasten their departure.

Chinese Exclusion in California

The Chinese population expanded rapidly from 1850–1880, growing from 1,000 to 75,000. Anti-Chinese feeling also spread across California and the Northwest. In the 1860s anti-Coolie clubs were formed in San Francisco and other towns, which promoted political agitation and vigilante violence against the Chinese. It was claimed that the Chinese were by nature cunning, treacherous, immoral, vice-ridden, inhuman, incapable of responsible citizenship, degraded and undercutting the wages of white labor by taking low-paid employment.[45] The belief that the Chinese continued to be loyal to their emperor and sought to flood California with their people and take it over was promulgated under the slogan of 'the yellow peril.'[46]

The California Legislature passed numerous laws and statutes to prevent immigration of the Chinese and to hinder their ability to prosper. A police tax was imposed on all Chinese not working in agriculture. The immigration of Chinese women was limited by claiming that they came only for the purpose of prostitution. All Chinese were accused of running brothels and opium dens, making it difficult for the Chinese to obtain housing. Their children were segregated in the schools. This hostility spread to the national level. In 1876, F.M. Pixley, speaking on behalf of California before a joint congressional committee investigating Chinese immigration, declared:

> The Chinese are inferior to any race God ever made... I think that there are none so low... Their people have got the perfection of crimes of 4,000 years... The Divine Wisdom has said that He would divide

44. Pitt, *The Decline*, pp. 196–277: also see William Deverell, *Whitewashed Adobe: The Rise of Los Angeles and the Remaking of its Mexican Past* (Berkeley, CA: University of California Press, 2004).

45. Heizer and Almquist, *The Other Californians*, p. 157.

46. Heizer and Almquist, *The Other Californians*, p. 157. For the history of the Chinese in the U.S. and California, see G. Barth, *Bitter Strength: A History of the Chinese in the United States, 1850–1870*. (Cambridge, MA: Harvard University Press, 1964): also Alexander Saxton, *The Indispensible Enemy: Labor and the Anti-Chinese Movement in California* (Berkeley, CA: University of California Press, 1971).

this country and the world as a heritage of five great families... The Yellow races are to be confined to what the Almighty originally gave them, and as they are not a favored people, they are not to be permitted to steal from us what we have robbed the American savage of... I believe that the Chinese have no souls to save, and if they have, they are not worth saving.[47]

In 1882 the Federal government passed the Chinese Exclusion Act suspending Chinese immigration for ten years. Further exclusion acts were passed in 1902 and 1903 as a result of the lobbying of the California Oriental Exclusion League. Anti-Japanese sentiment was also growing in the West. In 1924 the United States passed the immigration Act that limited or excluded various races from immigration, including the Japanese.[48] This heritage of anti-Asian feeling in California would bear its most bitter fruit in the rounding up and internment of Japanese, including American citizens, in 1941 at the outset of the Second World War.[49] Ironically, Asians in 2000 are more than 10 per cent of the population of California and have become the 'model minority,' regularly outpacing whites in academic achievements and numbering more than 50 per cent of the students of the University of California at Berkeley.

47. J. tenBroek, E.N. Barnhart and F.W. Matson, *Prejudice, War and the Constitution* (Berkeley, CA: University of California Press, 1954 (3rd printing, 1968), p. 21: from Heizer and Almquist, *The Other Californians*, p. 167.

48. On prejudice against the Japanese in California, see Heizer and Almquist, *The Other Californians*, p. 178–94.

49. On the Japanese internment camps and their director, see Richard Drinnon, *Keeper of Concentration Camps: Dillon S. Meyer and American Racism* (Berkeley, CA: University of California Press, 1987).

Chapter Four

MANIFEST DESTINY AND AMERICAN EMPIRE: 1890–1934

The last decade of the nineteenth century saw key turning points in a number of trends in American society. The frontier was seen as closing, ending the era of free land to the West. The two excluded peoples, Indigenous Americans and African-Americans, experienced a low point in their mistreatment. The Dawes Act (1887) and the massacre at Wounded Knee (1890) sought to eliminate American Indians as a separate and resistant people to American expansion. The Supreme Court decision Plessy v. Ferguson (1896) confirmed the legality of Jim Crow segregation (see Chapter Two). At the same time immigrants from Eastern and Southern Europe poured into the United States, presenting a new ethnic and religious diversity that was seen as highly unwelcome by those who called themselves 'native' Americans; i.e., white Northern European Protestants.

From the 1870s there was rapid urbanization and industrialization. The railroads, electricity, motion pictures, cable cars and petroleum began to transform daily life. Huge fortunes were made by a few, while the vast majority labored long hours in oppressive conditions for just a few dimes an hour. A few hundred men held fortunes of over $1 million, while more than 80 per cent of the U.S. working population made less than $500 a year. Farmers saw a sharp decline in commodity prices, while the high prices charged by railroads and food corporations left them in chronic debt.

At the same time farmers and workers began to organize for better conditions. The Grange Movement, Northern and Southern Farmers Alliances and populist parties challenged tariffs and the gold standard that impoverished farmers. Labor unions led strikes for better wages and working conditions, often finding themselves shut out of factories by the armed militia of employers and the state. The Homestead Steel strike of 1892 and the Pullman strike of

1894 saw open warfare between workers and armed guards in which both were beaten and shot. The organized feminist movement also became increasingly visible in the 1880s, sparking a new rhetoric of anti-feminism that deplored declining fertility in the white middle-class and purported loss of virility in white males.

A new wave of imperialism saw the solution to these conflicts at home as the opening of new 'frontiers' to American expansion abroad. War was extolled as invigorating a threatened American (WASP) masculinity, while the conquest of new territories and opening of markets in the Pacific and Asia would deflect the 'over-production' of American factories and farms. This notion of a crisis of 'over-production' masked the real problem of low wages that denied many Americans adequate purchasing power. A racist language, often echoing the religious language of millennialism, envisioned an American world conquest and spurred imperialists into a war with Spain that quickly brought new colonies and protectorates in the Pacific (Guam, Hawaii and the Philippines) and in the Caribbean (Cuba and Puerto Rico). At the same time an anti-imperialist movement sought to raise the alarm against these new trends that it saw as destroying historic American republican values.[1]

Ideological Visions: Social Darwinism and the Social Gospel

Social Darwinism enjoyed a particular vogue in the United States in the era from 1870–1910. Social Darwinism appropriated Darwin's theories of evolution as the 'survival of the fittest' into a theory of winners and losers in social history. This theory was used to rationalize conservative views of laissez faire economics and hostility to any role of the state in social reform on behalf of the 'losers'. In the United States the class hierarchy of poor and rich was equated with racial assumptions about the 'natural superiority of Anglo-Saxons', against the poor, immigrant workers, Indians or blacks as the 'naturally unfit'.

Such racist views were nothing new in American thought. We have already seen their prevalence in earlier periods of American thought. But social Darwinism added a new 'scientific' veneer to old prejudices. It also made these prejudices appear unassailable.

1. A useful book that summarizes these trends in the 1890s is H.W. Brands, *The Reckless Decade: America in the 1890s* (New York: St. Martin's Press, 1995).

To dispute them was to be 'unscientific'. Christian thinkers who wanted to appear 'up to date', not reactionaries who rejected evolution on the grounds of a biblical literalism, but who were *au courant* with scientific theory, felt bound to take social Darwinism seriously.

The leading theoretician of social Darwinism was the British philosopher, Herbert Spencer, who expounded his views in a series of volumes, such as *First Principles* (1864), *The Man Versus the State* (1884), *The Principles of Sociology* (1876–97, 3 vols) and *The Principles of Ethics* (1895–98, 2 vols). Spencer synthesized conservative British thought of early industrialism, bringing together a Lamarckian idea of the inheritance of acquired characteristics, Malthusian views on population and the laissez faire ideology of the Anti-Corn Law League, all of which reinforced the view that the poor should not be helped by the state, but should be allowed to die off.[2]

Americans took to Spencer's thought in the 1890s with particular fervor. Major social philosophers, such as Henry James, Josiah Royce and John Dewey, felt they had to reckon with Spencer. But social Darwinism also deeply penetrated the thought of Christian Social Gospel spokesmen, such as Washington Gladden and Horace Bushnell, and particularly that of Josiah Strong. Social Darwinism also became current social wisdom continually cited in the media, among politicians and business leaders. Industrialist Andrew Carnegie was an enthusiastic adherent of social Darwinism and a personal friend of Spencer's.[3]

Social Darwinism resonated with traditional American conservative Calvinism, with its belief in the election and predestination of the few and the damnation of the many. Like Calvinism, it assumed that predestination was manifest through one's dedication to highly efficient hard work, rewarded by exemplary success. Both divine decree and the laws of nature assure that the hardworking are rewarded by wealth and the poor deserve their poverty because they are lazy and inefficient, views still widespread among Americans.

But social Darwinism added two elements lacking in traditional Calvinism. First, it claimed to be a purely rational, objective view based on natural necessity and hence universal, not dependent on

2. See Richard Hofstadter, *Social Darwinism in American Thought* (New York: George Braziller, 1959), p. 35.
    3. Hofstadter, *Social Darwinism*, p. 45.

any particular religious revelation. Thus it appealed to those, like Carnegie, seeking a substitute worldview for what he saw as a collapsed and obsolete Christianity. Secondly, it not only did not encourage, but forbade, social reform, or even charity, on behalf of the losers in the industrial capitalist system. Thus it blessed hard-heartedness as both morally right and biologically necessary for ultimate social progress.

The basic argument of social Darwinism was that the prosperity of the rich testifies to their essential 'fitness,' while the penury of the poor manifests their unfitness. Fitness and unfitness were assumed to be inherited biological characteristics, owing nothing to social context. The fit passed on their fitness to their descendents and the unfit their unfitness. So the argument for the survival of the fittest quickly became ethnic or racist, not just a judgment on individual prowess. Natural selection increases the fit and dooms the unfit to die out. Social progress thus is best served by aiding the process of natural selection of the fit, or at least by not impeding it by helping the unfit to survive.

For social Darwinists no social services or charitable help should be given to those who have not themselves earned these services by their own hard work (or presumably that of their families). Such help simply allows the unfit to survive and to pass down their feckless characteristics to their children, prolonging an inferior population that should disappear. Social Darwinists opposed public schools, public libraries, public sanitation, public health, even public postal systems or tariffs. Thus, social Darwinism advocated a totally privatized society in which services are available only to those who can pay. One should not read books, go to school, have medical services, eat, be clothed or have a roof over one's head if one cannot pay for it from one's own work. The role of the state was primarily negative. It should do nothing that interfered with the natural laws of competition. Its job was simply to maintain unfettered social and market freedom that allowed these laws to be played out freely.

Although social Darwinism was resolutely secular and presumably 'scientific,' this did not prevent Christian thinkers from integrating it into their religious visions of redemption. Indeed its own theories of competitive struggle through which inferiors are eliminated and the fittest survive lent itself to a secular millennialism of progressive improvement of the human species. Josiah Strong (1847–1916) is

one example of the synthesis of social Darwinism, Anglo-Saxon
Protestant racism and American imperialism and its integration into
Christian millennialism.

Strong was a clergyman who was the representative for Ohio of
the American Home Missionary Society in 1885 when he wrote his
most famous effort to state this vision of the unity of American
imperialist expansion and the triumph of Christ's Kingdom on earth,
Our Country: Its Possible Future and Present Crisis.[4] Like Christian
Socialists, such as Walter Rauschenbusch,[5] Strong rejected the
individualizing and spiritualizing of the Christian view of
redemption that understood the Kingdom of God as the heavenly
abode of the redeemed soul. For Strong, one of the major
advancements of Christian understanding of Jesus' teachings was
the recovery of the this-worldly, social meaning of Jesus' preaching
of the coming Kingdom of God. The Kingdom of God, for Jesus,
was not an otherworldly heaven, but the total redemption, material
and spiritual, of this world, bringing about a millennial perfection
of society.[6]

Strong believed that the millennial redemption of the earth was
no longer in the distant future, but the crucial turning point 'in the
world's salvation may depend on the next twenty years of United
States history,'[7] propelled by the expansion of American power.
Strong cites various proofs for what he sees as this coming
transformation of the earth. One of them is the rapid improvements
in technological progress, such as the stream engine; also increasing
scientific knowledge and individual liberty, manifest in such
developments as the abolition of slavery, women's education, the
increasing value of human life. The United States was the center of
these developments because it was uniquely favored in natural
resources, fertile soil, gold, silver, iron and coal. This gave it a vast
potential for agricultural and other development, capable of feeding
a much expanded population, up to 900 million in Strong's view.

4. Josiah Strong, *Our Country: Its Possible Future and Present Crisis* (New York: Baker
and Taylor, 1885).

5. Walter Rauschenbusch, *Christianity and the Social Crisis* (New York: Macmillan
Co., 1907) and *Christianizing the Social Order* (New York: Macmillan Co., 1912).

6. See Josiah Strong, *The Next Great Awakening* (New York: Baker and Taylor Company,
1902) and *The New Era or Coming Kingdom* (New York: Baker and Taylor Company,
1893).

7. Strong, *Our Country*, p. 15.

The expansion of American power went hand in hand with the Christianizing of the world. America is now the center of the church's mission to Christianize the world. Christianization also multiplies the desires for worldly goods of the earth's peoples, thus expanding markets for American products.

> The world is to be Christianized and civilized. There are about 1,000,000,000 of the world's inhabitants who do not enjoy a Christian civilization. Two hundred millions of these are to be lifted out of savagery. Much has been accomplished in this direction during the past seventy-five years, but much more will be done in the next fifty. And what is the process of civilizing but *the creation of more and higher wants.* Commerce follows the missionary... A Christian civilization performs the miracle of loaves and fishes and feeds its thousands in a desert. It multiples populations... And with these vast continents added to our market, with our natural advantages fully realized, what is to prevent the United States from becoming the mighty workshop of the world and our people "the hands of mankind?"

Strong draws on a favorite myth of American millennialism current since the eighteenth century; namely, the western movement of empire. The last stanza of Bishop George Berkeley's (1683–1753),'Verses on the Prospect of Planting Arts and Learning in America' contains the oft cited words,

> Westward the course of empire takes its way; the four first acts already past, A fifth shall close the drama with the day; times noblest offspring is the last.[8]

Strong cites Berkeley, as well as de Tocqueville, for what he takes as a truism of human history. 'Since prehistoric times populations have steadily moved westward, "as if driven by the mighty hand of God." And following their migration the course of empire, which Bishop Berkeley sang, has westward taken its way.'

Strong sees the 'world's scepter' as having passed from Persia to Greece to Italy to Great Britain. Today it is being passed to 'Greater Britain'; namely, the United States. This can only be the final and culminating empire since there is no further land to the west to which empire could pass; 'beyond is the Orient.' Strong then boldly compares this progress of empire from east to west, culminating in the United States, with the star from the east which traveled west to guide the three kings to the 'cradle of the young Christ.' The

8. Ernest Lee Tuveson, *Redeemer Nation: The Idea of America's Millennial Role* (Chicago: The University of Chicago Press, 1968), p. 94.

United States is thus the national equivalent of Christ. Although still a babe, it is destined to grow up to be the Messianic nation.

> The star of empire, rising in the East, has ever beckoned the wealth and power of the nations westward, until today it stands still over the cradle of the young empire of the West to which the nations are bringing their offerings.[9]

Strong, however, sees many dangers that may impede this messianic role of the United States. He cites eight key problems faced by the United States that threaten its redemptive mission: immigrants, Roman Catholicism, the secularization of public schools, Mormonism, intemperance, socialism and the concentration of wealth in the hands of the few, all of which find their seat of concentrated evil in the urban environment of big cities.

The current waves of immigrants are bad because they are drawn from the degraded peasant stock of Europe with low morals and inferior religious training. They are predominately Catholics, especially Irish, and tend toward socialism, drunkenness and disease. Roman Catholicism is, for Strong, incompatible with American values. This is a religion which demands the surrender of intellect and free conscience to the Pope. So Catholics in America are loyal to the Pope, and not to the American constitution. Mormonism is also bad for the same reasons. It harbors an ecclesiastic despotism and seeks to be a state within the state, ruled by all-powerful leaders. Polygamy is unacceptable also, but Strong thinks that this can be discarded, but the despotism will continue. (The President of the Church of Latter Day Saints in Salt Lake City had advised his followers to abide by the U.S. law against polygamy in 1890).

Intemperance, as well as the use of drugs (opium), are evils in themselves, but Strong is particularly concerned about what he sees as the 'liquor interests' which corrupt American urban politics. His argument against socialism is more complex since the Social Gospel did endorse a kind of Christian socialism. He condemns socialism as trying to regenerate society without regenerating the individual, although he admits that socialists might believe that the individual would be regenerated through regenerating society.

Strong polemicizes against socialists by conflating them with lawless anarchists of the sort that throw dynamite and caused the

9. Strong, *Our Country*, pp. 42–43.

Haymarket Massacre. In May 1886 in Haymarket Square in Chicago, during a rally of workers for the eight hour day, a bomb was thrown that precipitated a police massacre that was blamed on the Union leaders. Most historians now agree that the bomb that started the riot was probably thrown by the police themselves, but in the 1890s Haymarket was a by-word for 'anarchist violence,' much like the word 'terrorist' today.[10]

Strong also objects to the concentration of wealth in the hands of the few, creating an aristocracy of wealth and power, over against the poverty of the masses. But his solution to this seems to be a voluntary acceptance of cooperativism by the wealthy industrialists who would thereby share the wealth more equitably with their workers. Big cities are bad, for Strong, because they become the breeding ground for all these evils, the place where non-Protestant immigrants, addicted to drink and socialism, gather, creating rabble-rule under corrupt politicians sold out to liquor interests.

Strong is also concerned about the secularization of the public schools which he sees as institutions which should teach American Protestant morality foundational to the inculcation of the values of citizenship. Since such schools are key to Americanizing (and Protestantizing) immigrants, he is deeply opposed to Catholic parochial schools which had been founded on the grounds that the public schools were, in fact, Protestant institutions.[11] He argues that there is a common core of moral values in Protestantism, Catholicism and Judaism that can be taught in the public schools which should unite people of all three religions. But this ecumenical argument is at variance with his polemics against Roman Catholicism as incompatible with American values and his view that Protestantism is the true 'spiritual' Christianity and the basis for American values.

Strong then turns to his culminating vision in a chapter entitled 'The Anglo-Saxon and the World's Future.' The Anglo-Saxon unites two great ideas; civil liberty and pure spiritual Christianity. The union of these two ideas has been corrupted in England, but it has found its true home in the United States. 'Anglo-Saxons' are defined as the English-speaking people of the United States who have

10. For the social background of the labor leaders involved in the conflict, see Bruce C. Nelson, *Beyond the Martyrs: A Social History of Chicago's Anarchists, 1870–1900* (New Brunswick: Rutgers University Press, 1988).

11. See R.D. Cross, 'Origins of the Catholic Parochial School', in John Barnard, (ed.), *The American Experience of Education* (New York: New Viewpoint, 1976).

amalgamated through 'natural selection' the best of the white (Protestant) peoples of Northern and Western Europe. Thus he sees them as a 'finer breed' than the mere English. This American 'race' has uniquely united money-making capacity, excellent physique, aggressive energy to push into and settle new lands and a genius for colonizing lesser peoples. This is the missionary race which God has prepared to evangelize and colonize the rest of the world.

This unique breed of American 'Anglo-Saxons' is destined to spread down across Mexico and into all of Latin America, also into Asia and Africa. For Strong, American Anglo-Saxons will not only establish domination over these lesser peoples, but will outbreed them, populating these conquered continents with their own offspring. The religions and cultures of these people will disappear, overcome by the superior religion of Protestant Christianity and by American civic virtue, wealth and power. But Strong seems to think these non-white people themselves will disappear, through a process of 'natural selection' by which the 'less fit' will be eliminated. Americans will not actually have to exterminate them by war, since this disappearance of non-whites will happen by the natural processes of the 'survival of the fittest.' They will simply die off 'naturally.'

Strong exults in an enthusiastic vision of the advent of the messianic redemption of the world through Anglo-Saxon dominance.

> It seems to me that God, with infinite wisdom and skill, is training the Anglo-Saxon race for an hour sure to come in the world's future... Then will the world enter upon a new stage of its history – *the final competition of the races, for which the Anglo-Saxon is being schooled*...Then this race of unequaled energy, with all the majesty of numbers and the might of wealth behind it – the representative, let us hope, of the largest liberty, the purest Christianity, the highest civilization – having developed peculiarly aggressive traits calculated to impress its institutions upon mankind, will spread itself over the earth.[12]

Strong admits that there are some impediments to the fulfillment of this American millennial role, represented by Roman Catholicism and Mormonism, non-Protestant immigrants, liquor and socialism. However, he hopes these impediments can be eliminated by the Home Missionary Movement. Protestants, especially the wealthy, need to be converted to a view of their own wealth as belonging

---

12. Barnard, (ed.), *The American Experience of Education*, p. 222.

wholly to Jesus, to be used to uplift and convert their fellow citizens to true Christianity and American civic values. Thus America itself must be saved, in order to then become God's instrument for saving the world.

> Ours is the elect nation for the age to come. We are the chosen people. We cannot afford to wait, The plans of God will not wait. Those plans seem to have brought us to one of the closing stages of the world's career, in which we can not longer *drift* with safety to our destiny. We are shut up in a perilous alternative. Immeasurable opportunities surround and overshadow us. Such, as I read it, is the central fact in the philosophy of the American Home Missions.[13]

Threats to American Manhood and the Need for War

The 1890s were notable for a strident rhetoric of male gender anxiety. Women had, of course, been excluded from autonomous citizenship status from the beginning of the Republic, unable to vote, hold property in their own name, attend university or hold public office. American culture generally endorsed a 'cult of true womanhood'[14] that assigned women the auxiliary roles in the private spheres, while public leadership belonged to men. As public society became more secular, with the separation of church and state, piety and moral uplift were assigned to women in the private sphere, while men should be the protector and gainful laborer. Thus, the ideology of white racial superiority always had an implicit gender assumption. The normative Anglo-Saxon was male.

But the feminist movement that began in the 1830s and 40s, in alliance with the abolitionist movement, was making gains by the last decades of the century. Women won some access to property rights and entrance into higher education. In the Eastern U.S. this took the form of women's colleges that began to open in the 1870s–90s. In the West, state universities generally opened as coeducational from the beginning. Teaching at the primary school level in the public schools was readily opened to women who worked for lower wages than male teachers, but a few women began to teach at higher levels. Social work was also seen as an appropriate role for women.

---

13. Barnard, (ed.), *The American Experience of Education*, p. 264.

14. See Barbara Welter, 'The Cult of True Womanhood', in *Dimity Convictions: The American Woman in the Nineteenth Century* (Athens, OH: Ohio University Press, 1976), pp. 21–41.

Although this was first seen as volunteer charitable service appropriate for rich men's wives, it was becoming professionalized in the 1890s and led by single 'career' women. Settlement houses, such as Hull House in Chicago, founded by Jane Addams in 1889, set the pace for this more dynamic social work as social reform by college educated professional women.[15]

Women's suffrage was also making strides particularly on the state and local levels, and it seemed only a matter of time before women would gain the vote on the national level. Again western states, where women had been equal partners in pioneer settlements, took the lead in granting the vote to women. Wyoming as a territory opened the vote to women in 1869. Women in Wyoming were granted control over their own property at the same time. When Wyoming was admitted to the union in 1889, its state constitution gave women full suffrage. Utah as a territory also gave women the vote in 1870 and was admitted to the union with women's suffrage in 1896. But the work of winning the vote on the state level was slow and frustrating. Between 1870 and 1910 there were 480 campaigns in thirty-three states, only seventeen of which were able to bring the issue to a state vote. Only two of these were successful, Colorado in 1893 and Idaho in 1896.[16]

Women were not only targeting the male bastion of public political rights, but also that of war. Among the arguments of defenders of the exclusion of women from suffrage was the claim that citizenship was based on service in war. Since women did not bear arms, it followed that they also could not vote. (That women might someday be recognized as soldiers was at that time unthinkable, even though some women had actually fought in wars for millennia). Taking a page from theories of social evolution, women suffrage defenders and their male allies responded to this argument by claiming that war itself should be superseded. Settling differences between nations by war was itself a remnant of a barbaric state of human existence. Civilized human beings should abolish war and learn to settle disputes through arbitration.[17]

15. See Eleanor Stebner, *The Women of Hull House: A Study in Spirituality, Vocation and Friendship* (Albany, NY: SUNY Press, 1997); also Robyn Muncy, *Creating a Female Dominion in American Reform, 1890–1935* (New York: Oxford University Press, 1991).

16. Eleanor Flexner, *Century of Struggle: The Women's Rights Movement in the United States* (New York: Atheneum, 1972), p. 222.

17. An example of this argument is Jane Addams, *Newer Ideals of Peace* (NY: Macmillan, 1907).

On 11 January 1897 U.S. Secretary of State Richard Olney and British Ambassador Sir Julian Pauncefote signed a treaty committing both nations to settle disputes by arbitration for the next five years. This treaty followed a period of tension between the two nations over an 1895 British Guiana-Venezuela border dispute between Britain and Venezuela. This aroused great excitement in the United States, with some claiming Britain had violated the Monroe doctrine and calling for armed intervention. For U.S. pacifists this treaty was a harbinger of a new era when arbitration would replace war as a way of settling disputes between nations.

The organized feminist movement was highly visible in supporting the treaty. The Women's Christian Temperance Union, the largest women's organization at the time, had already created a department of Peace and International Arbitration in 1887 to promote arbitration as an alternative to war. The National Council of Women, the National-American Woman Suffrage Association and the General Federation of Women's Clubs, passed resolutions in support of the treaty.[18]

Supporters of a renewed American military and war-readiness responded to these calls to replace war with arbitration with cries of alarm. The United States had not fought a war since the Civil War in 1861–65 and its army had been greatly reduced, although in the 1880s there was a modernization of the American navy, seen as vital to compete with European colonial nations and with Japan for trade advantages in the Pacific.[19] Proponents of rebuilding the American military identified war with manly virtues necessary for the health and strength of American men. Ending war in human affairs would lead to male effeminacy and the degeneration of American power.

Theodore Roosevelt became the spokesman for this ideology of American virility through war. On April 29, 1896 he wrote to Senator Henry Cabot Lodge, also a leading advocate of militarism, of his

18. See Kristin L. Hoganson, *Fighting for American Manhood: How Gender Politics Provoked the Spanish-American and Philippine-American Wars* (New Haven, CT: Yale University Press, 1998), pp. 18 and 216 n. 7.

19. See Thomas Schoonover, *The War of 1809 and the Origins of Globalization* (Lexington, KY: University of Kentucky Press, 2003), p. 83. A major proponent of American power was Alfred T. Mahan. See his *The Influence of Sea Power upon History* (Boston: Little, Brown, 1890) and *The Interest of America in Sea Power, Present and Future* (Boston: Little, Brown, 1897).

views of the arbitration movement as threatening to produce 'a flabby, timid type of character which eats away the great fighting features of our race.'[20] In *The Strenuous Life* (1910), his paean to manly virtues, complemented by the housewifery and fertile maternity of 'true' women, Roosevelt lauds vigorous physical labor and war as the way to maintain a virile nation. When women no longer embrace abundant maternity, 'that nation is rotten to the core. When men fear work or fear righteous war, when women fear motherhood, they tremble on the brink of doom; and well it is that they should vanish from the earth, where they are fit subjects of scorn of all men and women who are themselves strong and brave and high-minded.'[21]

Roosevelt continually expressed his contempt for critics of American military development and expansion beyond U.S. borders as timid, lazy and 'over-civilized,' particularly the anti-imperialists who challenged the acquisition of American colonies in the Caribbean and Pacific after the Spanish-American war.

> The timid man, the lazy man, the man who distrusts his country, the over-civilized man, who has lost the great fighting, masterful virtues, the ignorant man and the man of dull mind, whose soul is incapable of feeling the mighty lift that thrills "stern men with empires in their brains" – all these, of course, shrink from seeing the nation undertake its new duties; shrink from seeing us build a navy and an army adequate to our needs; shrink from seeing us do our share of the world's work, by bringing order out of chaos in the great, fair tropic islands from which the valor of our soldiers and sailors has driven the Spanish flag. These are men who fear the strenuous life, who fear the only national life which is really worth leading.

Roosevelt played a key role in fixing what from the 1890s to the twenty-first century would become a typical trope of American political rhetoric: pacifists, critics of imperial wars, are effeminate wimps; aggressive militarists are manly.

This anxiety over the diminishment of American male virility was sparked not only by the thirty-year lack of war (other than Indian fighting), but also by the changing nature of elite male work. With industrialization and the development of large corporations

20. Hoganson, *Fighting for American Manhood*, p. 21: 29 April 1896, from *Selections from the Correspondence of Theodore Roosevelt and Henry Cabot Lodge*, I, p. 218.

21. Theodore Roosevelt, *The Strenuous Life* (New York: The Review of Reviews Company, 1910), p. 6.

fewer men did physical work and more were employed in managerial desk jobs. The increasingly sedentary nature of male elite work generated a fear that such men, particularly in the East, were becoming 'over-civilized,' incapable of vigorous physical activity. The growth of male sports clubs sought to compensate for this threat. Sojourns in remaining wilderness areas in the West, hunting and camping, became ways in which these 'over-civilized' men renewed their contact with an imagined earlier pioneer life.

Roosevelt made himself a paragon of these trends. A sickly, asthmatic child, he consciously strove to build his body as a young adult. In 1883, at the age of 25, he traveled west to live the life of a cowboy on two different cattle ranches and to commune with what he imagined was an earlier, more ideal life of the 'wild west.' His role as a conservationist in the setting aside of wilderness areas of America for permanent protection from development was also part of this fixation with renewed masculinity through vigorous outdoor life.[22]

When the Spanish-American war was declared, Roosevelt resigned as Secretary of the Navy in order to personally participate in the fighting. He enthusiastically organized his own volunteer cavalry regiment, consisting of cowboys and Indian fighters from the west and members of sports clubs from elite eastern universities. Traveling with his regiment to Cuba, he gloried in leading them on horseback in the charge up San Juan Hill, thus demonstrating his capacity and that of 'true Americans' to participate in manly warfare.[23] Needless to say his feats in the war boded well for his future political career, leading to his selection as Vice-President in the 1900 election (becoming President when McKinley was assassinated in 1901).

If Americans of Roosevelt's type were worried about the loss of manliness of American men, they were equally worried about the loss of femininity of American women, exemplified by suffragists who sought the vote, higher education, and professional employment. In the 1860s it was still common for white middle class American women to have families of 8 to 10 children. But family size among the white Protestant middle class fell rapidly in

22. See particularly the chapters on 'In Cowboy Lands' and 'The Natural Resources of the Nation', in Theodore Roosevelt, *An Autobiography* (New York: Charles Scribner's, 1925), pp. 93–128 and 393–422.

23. See Theodore Roosevelt, *The Rough Riders* (New York: Charles Scribner's, 1899).

the last half of the nineteenth century. College-educated leaders of the feminist movement, such as Jane Addams and Frances Willard, were choosing to remain single, living in communities of women with whom they shared vocations to social reform.

These trends were widely interpreted as threatening the ability of the WASP middle class to reproduce itself and maintain its dominance over the blacks and immigrants with larger families. Already in 1830 opinion makers, such as the Reverend John Todd, declared that education was bad for women's health.[24] Educator Edward Clarke, author of *Sex in Education, or a Fair Chance for the Girls* (1873), reiterated these views.[25] Women, Clarke said, had limited energy and most of it was needed to maintain their fertility. Education forced energy to the brain, making women sickly, nervous and sterile.

The fear that white women were becoming infertile also sparked the Comstock Law in 1873, that forbade the circulation or trade in 'obscene literature and articles for immoral use,' interpreted to include birth control literature or methods.[26] This was repealed only in 1936. As we have seen above, Theodore Roosevelt was among those whose fears of loss of masculinity of American men was paralleled by his fear that American women no longer wanted to devote their lives to the raising of large families, both of which he saw as leading to the destruction of the nation.

The Spanish-American War and the Curtailing of Cuban Independence

The Spanish-American war in 1898 became an arena for the acting out of these tropes of renewal of American masculinity through war, expansion and colonization. Such tropes were not so much the cause of these wars that led the United States into empire beyond the continental North America, as powerful forms of rhetoric to whip up enthusiasm and silence critics. The U.S. had long eyed

---

24. See G.J. Barker-Benfield, *The Horrors of the Half-Known Life: Male Attitudes Toward Women and Sexuality in Nineteenth Century America* (New York: Harper and Row, 1976), pp. 203–207.

25. Edward Clarke, *Sex in Education, or a Fair Chance for the Girls* (Boston, MA: J.R. Osgood, 1873).

26. David M. Kennedy, *Birth Control in America: The Career of Margaret Sanger* (New Haven, CT: Yale University Press, 1970), p. 218.

Cuba as a possible acquisition.[27] When other Central and Latin American areas became free of Spain in the wars of independence of the 1820s, Spain tightened its hold on Cuba and Puerto Rico, determined to hold on to this remnant of its American empire. Cuban independence movements were sternly suppressed from 1825–98. Native Cubans were excluded from political leadership.

But Cuban independence movements grew, with an increasingly organized guerrilla army of liberation and eloquent exile spokesmen, such as José Martí, then based in New York.[28] In 1895, a new wave of rebellion broke out, fought with destructive violence on both sides. The liberation army burned the sugar plantations of the elites, while the Spanish military commander, Valeriano Weyler, fought back with all-out war against the rebels and their peasant supporters. Weyler initiated a policy of *reconcentratos*. The peasantry was forced into controlled concentration camps, and the surrounding fields burned to deny the guerrillas food and hiding places. By 1898, the Cuba economy was in ruins. Some 300,000 Cubans, about 20 per cent of the population, had died in the struggle.[29]

The Cuban independence war brought cries in the United States for U.S. military intervention. Pro-intervention media and spokesmen in the U.S. portrayed the Cubans in romantic terms. The liberators were chivalric heroes, while Cuban women were pictured as damsels in distress longing for manly American men to save them. The Spanish were portrayed as cruel, corrupt fiends of a tottering regime whose day was done.[30] Democratic President Grover Cleveland, however, refused to intervene, and the efforts of the Cuban exiles to ship arms to their comrades were blocked.[31]

27. Benjamin Franklin, Thomas Jefferson and John Quincy Adams had all expressed interest in acquiring Cuba; see Olga Jiménez de Waggenheim, *Puerto Rico: An Interpretative History* (Princeton, NJ: Markus Wiener Publishers, 1998), p. 195 and José Trias Monge, *Puerto Rico: The Trials of the Oldest Colony in the World* (New Haven, CT: Yale University Press, 1997), pp. 21–22.

28. José Marti (1833–1895), the most revered of Cuba's revolutionary writers, was a leading poet and social philosopher. See *The America of José Marti: Selected Writings* (trans. Juan de Onís (New York: Noonday Press, 1953).

29. José M. Hernández, *Cuba and the United States: Intervention and Militarism, 1868–1933* (Austin. TX: University of Texas Press, 1993), p. 53.

30. See Hoganson, *Fighting for Manhood*, pp. 43–67.

31. Hernández, *Cuba and the United States*, p. 22. This detaining of the ships and confiscation of Cuban rebel war material took place on January 12, 1895. An account is found in José Marti, *Obras Completas*, (La Habana, Cuba: Editorial Nacional de Cuba, 1963–73, col. I, pt. 2), pp. 227–32.

His Republican successor, William McKinley, also sought a negotiated solution, despite rising war sentiment in the Congress. He was decried as spineless by Republican militarists. In Theodore Roosevelt's famous image, 'McKinley has no more backbone than a chocolate éclair.'[32]

The Spanish themselves recalled Weyler and sent a more conciliatory leader, Rámon Blanco, who offered the Cubans autonomy, but Spanish loyalists rioted in Havana in protest. McKinley decided to send the warship *Maine* to Havana, claiming that this was only a 'courtesy call.' But the gathering of the U.S. navy in the Caribbean seas suggested a readying for war. On the night of 15 February, the *Maine* exploded and sank, two-hundred and sixty men aboard died. The explosion was immediately attributed to a deliberate bombing by the Spanish. Subsequent studies have determined that it was almost certainly an accident caused by a coal bunker fire overheating a near-by powder magazine.[33]

War hysteria irrupted in the United States, and McKinley was under ferocious pressure to prove his 'manliness' by declaring war. American 'honor' demanded a military response. The Spanish offered to meet almost all American demands: reparations for the loss of the *Maine*, a military truce with the rebels and an autonomous government, already in place in Havana, that would decide on a permanent settlement.[34] Very likely, if the United States had responded by insisting on Cuban self-government, rather than military intervention (which the Cuban independence movement had never requested)[35], the Cubans would have won their independence on their own. But it quickly became evident that the U.S. agenda was primarily to sweep the Spanish from the Caribbean (and the Pacific), not to support Cuban independence.

On 11 April, McKinley called Congress to authorize war. The purpose of the intervention was defined as ending the civil war and securing a 'stable government.' Recognition of the Cuban insurrectionists was excluded as 'neither wise nor prudent.' The

32. Hernandez, *Cuba and the United States*.
33. Ivan Musicant, *The Banana Wars: A History of the United States Military Intervention in Latin America from the Spanish-American War to the Invasion of Panama* (New York: Macmillan, 1990), pp. 13 and 429 nn. 20 and 21.
34. Musicant, *The Banana Wars*, p. 15.
35. See Hernandez, *Cuba and the United States*, pp. 32 and 189 n. 15.

Congressional declaration of war on April 19 demanded that Spain accept the immediate abrogation of its sovereignty and government in Cuba. However, Colorado Senator Henry Teller managed to insert an amendment stating that the United States disclaimed any intention to exercise sovereignty over the island and that once the island was pacified, the government and control of Cuba would be left to its own people.[36] This amendment, passed almost unnoticed and without debate, would provide an impediment to subsequent desires of American militarists to outright annex Cuba, as they would shortly do with Puerto Rico.

The declaration of war evoked enormous enthusiasm. The depleted U.S. army was quickly expanded by 200,000 new recruits. The U.S. Navy swung into action to blockade and sink the Spanish navy in Cuba and seize the port of Guantánamo Bay. Meanwhile, on 1 May, Admiral Dewey steamed into Manila Bay and sank the Spanish fleet there, claiming control of the Philippines. While American war fervor had focused solely on the plight of Cuba, U.S. military strategists tacitly assumed that the goal was to take over the entire Spanish overseas empire in both the Caribbean and the Pacific. On 13–14 June army recruits were loaded onto transports to Cuba, often so poorly equipped for battle that they were sent off with wool uniforms to fight in the tropics in summer.

Singing the 'Star Spangled Banner' and shouting 'Viva Cuba libre (Long Live Free Cuba), the American troops landed with great enthusiasm. But their encounter with the Cuban Liberation army, presumably their allies on whose behalf they were coming, proved a shock. Not only was this army ragged and hungry, hoping for food and supplies from the Americans, but they were 80 per cent mulatto, a fact that American war propaganda had failed to mention. Quickly American racism asserted itself, and it became the reigning U.S. truism that Cubans were incapable of self-government. The rebel leaders were marginalized and ignored, while the Americans focused on fighting and then arranging the surrender with the Spanish.

Although the Americans lost only 345 soldiers in the few weeks of actual fighting, some ten times that number, 2,565, died of disease.

36. Musicant, *Banana Wars*, p. 16. It is likely that Teller was inspired to insert this amendment disclaiming any U.S. annexational intentions by personal acquaintance with exile Cuban liberation leaders, José Marti and Estrada Palma, in New York: see Hernandez, *Cuba and the United States*, pp. 32, 189 n. 13.

The U.S. soldiers were poorly prepared for the rainy summer weather, lacking rain gear and adequate tents, and often sleeping in the rain and mud. The trajectory of emotions experienced by American soldiers during the war is exemplified by a series of letters written by Lieutenant James Ord to his wife Rose between 15 May and 4 September 1898.[37] Ord and his two brothers, Garische and Edward, fought in Cuba. The first letter, addressed to his eight year old son, Jimmie, tells of the conditions in the camp in Tampa, Florida, where the army awaited the trip to Cuba:

> My dear son Jimmie:
> I have been intending writing you and Rebecca a letter for some time, so now I will do it. We are living in camp right in a big city. We live in tents and sleep on the ground and there are lots and lots of soldiers, thousands of them and the bands play and the bugles play all day long and they march and drill. They all have guns and pistols and the officers have swords. We are waiting for the order when we will go in big ships across the ocean to Cuba.
> Lots of people come out to the camp to see us and walk over our blankets and talk about us, but it is all very pleasant... There are lots of little boys here that talk Spanish, they are Cubanos. Their homes have been burned up and their poor mothers and fathers have died of starvation...

In Ord's letter to his wife of 1st June, still from Tampa, he tells her that the army will advance simultaneously on Santiago to Cuba and on 'Porto Rico' and only move on to Havana in late summer or Fall. That way there will be no danger of their suffering from yellow fever. He expects the Spanish army to be a relative 'push-over':

> You see, by going to Santiago and San Juan, we will be in little or no danger from fever and as far as the enemy is concerned, we will clean him out in great shape. So don't worry at all, there won't be any defeats to our troops...

As the U.S. troops loaded on boats for the trip to Cuba, Ord records their enthusiasm and his own eager expectations for battle:

---

37. James Thompson Ord was my grandfather on my mother's side. He and his two brothers, Garische Ord and Edward Otho Cresap Ord II, all fought in the Spanish-American war. The three young Lieutenants were sons of Civil War General, Edward Otho Cresap Ord. The letters were written to his wife, Rose Basavi Ord, then resident in Monterey, Mexico with the couple's small children, James Basevi, 8, Rebecca Cresap, 3 and Mary Mercer, 1. The twenty handwritten letters are unpublished and are in my possession.

Well, we are on board at last and will pull out some time this evening…
The port is a grand sight. There are over 30 great ocean ships, over ten
magnificent war ships and the glitter and splendor of the heavily
armed troops is something grand. We have loaded about 30,000 men
and we are going to make a glorious showing and I am right in it. And
Rose, old woman, if they give me half a chance, you will hear of me in
"general orders" and three head lines in a newspaper and that is
considered the height of glory now.

Everyone is wild with excitement and shouting like wild. The bands
are playing, crowds cheering and it looks like war, but I know what it
means when we land, just what I predicted to you.

By 27 June, when the troops landed under heavy fire, enthusiasm
is still high, but the realities had begun to set in. Ord writes to his
wife:

Campaigning in Cuba is no joke. All the troops are afoot. Cols. and
Generals are hoofing it on all sides as the horses have not been landed…

On 29 June he writes:

It rains most every day or night in heavy showers and we have been
wet continually, especially at night. I miss my slicker. I guess we all
will have chills and malarial fever before the moon grows old.

In an undated letter (probably 30 June), Ord writes grimly that
his brother, Garische, died in battle the day before:

My brother is dead. Garry died at the head of his men like a soldier,
after repeated acts of individual heroism. The battle yesterday was
very severe, our lost in killed and wounded is large but we drove the
enemy from all the entrenchments right into the city and captured all
the outlying outposts. Ed is safe. I saw him during and after the battle
yesterday…

By 4th July a truce had been declared and Ord turns his sorrow
at his brother's death into anger at what he now sees as mulatto
Cubans whose mixed race inferiority makes them unworthy of the
sacrifice of American life. Gone is his earlier sympathy for the little
'cubanos':

Rose, the Cubans are a miserable lot of mongrel mulattos. The cross
between the Spaniard and Mexican Indian is bad enough, but the worst
of degenerate Spain mixed with the foul African breed has produced a
race of vermin that crawl about robbing the dead and plundering the
wounded. To think the lives of our brave men have been sacrificed to
glorify this scum, rends my very heart.

Ord now speaks in praise of the Spanish troops, but by 27 July disease has begun to set in, weakening the American troops:

> The Spanish Army are a fine body of men full of vigor and fight, but we demoralized them by the intrepidity of our charges...
>
> We have a lot of sickness now and considerable fever, yellow, black, blue and several other colors and it is knocking the men out pretty badly. So far, I am fine as fiddle.

The next day, 28 July, he writes:

> This outfit is sick and getting sicker at the rate of 400 a day. There are nine kinds of fever, dysentery and a few other things which we get. A few days ago, I got a chill...

By 5th August, as his division prepares to returns home, he writes:

> Well dear, we are coming home and I have abandoned all military aspirations that mean to stay here. It is certain death from yellow fever or pernicious fever or dysentery or some other blame microbe. People are dying like sheep and our Grand Army is a big hospital camp and I am going to get out before I am laid out.

Ord soon after came down with malarial fever and almost died, but when his last letter was written to his wife on 4th September from the army camp on Long Island, he is on the mend and hopes soon to travel to Washington to check on his future in the army. President McKinley had the previous day come to the camp with a big entourage.

> I have been quite ill for the last few days, Cuban Malaria, but I am all right again today. It comes in spells, a chill, then high fever, then goes; but most of the men don't rally from the fever but become exhausted and die from sheer weakness.
>
> The President visited camp yesterday and drove up to the General's tent in a magnificent turn out, accompanied by various generals and their staff and other carriages containing Cabinet officers, Etc. He greeted (General) Shafter cordially, complimented him on his brilliant campaign. Then Shafter introduced his staff, your humble servant among the number. He shook hands with all of us and had something pleasant to say to each.

As suggested in Ord's letter, U.S. strategy was to seize Puerto Rico and Cuba at the same time. In late July General Miles landed in Puerto Rico and seized the city of Ponce and then the capital, San Juan. The Spanish then sued for peace. The U.S. responded with the following conditions: the Spanish must relinquish all claims to

Cuba and immediately evacuate. In lieu of a cash indemnity, they should cede Puerto Rico to the U.S., and an island in the Pacific Marianas (Guam). America should occupy the city and Bay of Manila in the Philippines, pending a final peace treaty. In the subsequent negotiations, the U.S. offered Spain $20 million for the Philippines. Spain acceded to the American terms and her maritime empire was handed over to the United States. In the same year Hawai'i, whose reigning Queen Liliuokalani, had been deposed in 1893 by a combination of American sugar planters, bankers and missionaries, was annexed to the United States.[38]

American military proconsuls were appointed to govern Cuba, pointedly ignoring the liberation army, the best organized group in Cuba outside the American army. General Leonard Wood, appointed governor of Santiago and a physician by training, quickly organized sanitation campaigns, schools and medical facilities, helping to eliminate yellow fever. General Brooke, having first commanded Puerto Rico, came to Havana as military governor. The liberation army was ordered to disband, and turn in their guns for $75 apiece. But the liberation army continued and occupied many areas, still hoping for recognition by the Americans. Wood and Brooke, however, preferred to appoint former Spanish administrators or elite Cubans to their government, suspicious that the Cuban insurrectionists represented both a demand for full independence and a social transformation of the class/race hierarchy of Cuba. Only gradually (by 1906) did they realize they had to include some of the insurrectionist leaders in the political process.[39]

Under American guidance a Cuban constitutional convention wrote the new laws for Cuba. To this constitution the U.S. governors added the Platt amendment, which prohibited Cuba from making any treaty or granting military or naval bases to any foreign government (i.e. any government other than the United States). The U.S. was to maintain a permanent naval base at Guantánamo. The U.S. could also intervene militarily at any time it saw American interests threatened.

38. The Congressional debate over the annexation of Hawai'i focused largely on the fear that it would bring a large number of non-whites into the Union. Statehood was in fact delayed until 1959 when the population had become one quarter white.

39. Hernández, *Cuba and the United States.*

Although this amendment curtailed any real sovereignty of Cuba, making it effectively a U.S. protectorate, the Cuban leaders reluctantly accepted it, feeling they had no choice. The U.S. threatened that it would continue the military occupation until it was accepted. As liberation army General José Miguel Gomez put it in his farewell to his troops, 'none of us thought that (peace) would be followed by a military occupation of the country by our allies, who treat us as a people incapable of acting for ourselves, and who have reduced us to obedience, to submission and to a tutelage imposed by force of circumstances.'[40]

That tutelage would continue in effect to 1934. During that time the U.S. intervened militarily twice in longer occupations, 1906–09 and 1917–22. The U.S. would also maintain until today a naval presence in Guantánamo and continual pressure to conform to government policies that suited U.S. business and geopolitical interests. This constant supervision by the U.S. military was superseded in 1934 by what would become the new U.S. strategy for control over resistant peoples of its empire – rule by U.S. supported strongmen. In Cuba Fulgencio Batista came to power in 1934. To repress increasing resistance Batista would institute a military dictatorship in 1952, staying in power until he was overthrown by the Cuban revolution of 1959.

Puerto Rico was ruled as a dependent territory of the U.S. until 1952, when the people voted to move to Commonwealth status. When Brooke was commander he officially changed its name to 'Porto Rico' and made English the language of government,[41] changes resisted by the Puerto Ricans. It remains in this status until today (2007), divided between some Puerto Ricans who would like it to become a state of the Union and others who demand the independence which it was denied when taken over by the United States in 1898.[42]

The Philippine-American War

In the 1870s the Philippines were experiencing the rise of a new generation of educated elite (*illustrados*) who sought liberalization of Filipino society and equality of *criollos* and *mestizos* with Spaniards.

40. Hernández, *Cuba and the United States*, p. 87.
41. Jiménez de Wagenheim, *Puerto Rico*, p. 213.
42. Jiménez de Wagenheim, *Puerto Rico*, pp. 136–40.

José Rizal was one of the leaders of this elite, seeking not independence, but simply full integration with Spain.[43] Other more radical independistas arose under the populist leader, Andres Bonifacio. Spain suppressed all these movements with a heavy hand, executing Rizal in 1896. The independence movement became increasingly organized, with Emilio Aguinaldo emerging as national leader, after a factional fight in which Bonifacio was executed. Aguinaldo proclaimed a Filipino Republic with himself a President and fought the Spaniards to a draw. In armistice negotiations late in 1897 he agreed to go into exile in Hong Kong.

In Hong Kong Aguinaldo devoted himself to raising arms for a new independence war. He also negotiated with the American consul for what he believed was an alliance in which the Americans would aid in removing the Spanish, allowing the Filipinos to establish an independent government. Aguinaldo was repeatedly assured by his American contacts that the United States sought no colonies. Colonies were completely contrary to American tradition. Aguinaldo claimed to be reassured, saying 'I have studied attentively the Constitution of the United States and I find in it no authority for colonies and I have no fear.'[44]

Meanwhile Admiral Dewey was being urgently advised by President McKinley to avoid any 'political alliance with the insurgents.'[45] Dewey in fact maintained a studied inconsistency with Aguinaldo. By turns he ignored him, then brought him back to the Philippines on a naval boat (19 May 1898), encouraging him to 'go ashore and organize your army,' while denying to the Navy Department that he had pledged 'to assist the insurgents by any act or promise.'[46] Aguinaldo meanwhile was determined to have a developed army and government in place so that the Americans would have no choice but to recognize them as the rightful national

43. José Rizal (1861–1896) wrote two novels that exposed the brutal intolerance of Spanish rule in the Philippines: *Noli Me Tangere* (1887) and *El Filibusterismo* (1891). For English translations, see *Noli Me Tangere*, translated *Ma Soledad Lacson* (Honolulu: University of Hawai'i Press, 1997) and *The Reign of Greed: El Filibusterismo*, Charles E. Derbyshire, (Manila: Philippine Education Company, 1939).

44. Stuart C. Miller, *'Benevolent Assimilation': The American Conquest of the Philippines, 1899–1903* (New Haven, CT: Yale University Press, 1982), p. 42.

45. Stanley Karnow, *In Our Image: America's Empire in the Philippines* (New York: Random House, 1986), p. 113.

46. Karnow, *In Our Image*, p. 115.

rulers. He set about with great energy to organize an army throughout Luzon, overrunning all the Spanish outlying garrisons, and digging fourteen miles of trenches around Manila, pinning the Spanish in the capital city.

Aguinaldo also had drafted a democratic constitution that guaranteed freedom of religion, speech and the press, gave equal rights to women and outlawed capital punishment except in war. On 12 June, 1898 he declared the independence of the Philippines from his home town of Cavite. The Declaration was witnessed by 97 Filipinos and one stray American retired colonel who happened to be present on business.[47] When the American army began arriving in July they found that the Spanish had already been displaced from any power in the countryside, were surrounded by Aguinaldo's troops in Manila and on the verge of surrender.

However, both the Spanish and the Americans were determined that the Spanish should surrender to the Americans, not to the Filipino insurgents. A mock battle was arranged between them for 13 August in which the Spanish then surrendered to the Americans. Aguinaldo's army was ignored, and he was barred from the surrender ceremony. False reports were sent back to the United States denying that the insurgents wanted independence and declaring that they favored annexation by the United States. This misinformation was gleaned by the American commander, Elwell Otis, talking only to a few conservative members of the Filipino elite in Manila and never going out to the countryside where Aguinaldo had overwhelming support from the populace.

However, the American army soon found that it too was pinned down within Manila, surrounded by Aguinaldo's army that controlled the countryside, including the trenches around the capital city. General Otis began a series of demands that Aguinaldo move his troops back from these trenches while he moved his troops forward, setting the stage for an inevitable 'incident' justifying the declaration of war. This incident took place on 4th February 1899, after Otis had moved a regiment forward into an area claimed by the insurgents. An American patrol fired on four unarmed Filipinos. The Filipino guarding the front line fired back, and the Americans then declared that the war to put down the Filipino 'insurrection' was 'on.'

47. Karnow, *In Our Image*, pp. 116, 117.

The Americans made it appear that the Filipinos were 'rebels' against an established American control (for which the U.S. had paid Spain $20 million in the December, 1898 Treaty of Paris). From the Filipino perspective the reality was otherwise. Aguinaldo's army controlled almost all of the country and had inaugurated a constitutional government. The Americans had embarked on a war of conquest. After the first shots were fired on February 4, the American army quickly fanned out. In twenty-four hours three thousand Filipino corpses littered the trenches and barricades ringing the city. Aguinaldo tried to arrange a truce, but Otis had determined that this would be a war of extermination of any insurgent forces.

Otis, however, continually underestimated, as well as misrepresented, the extent of Aguinaldo's support in the countryside. Aguinaldo quickly reorganized his forces for a prolonged guerrilla warfare, dividing them into small mobile groups that could continually move around, attacking the American forces and then fading into the bush. Otis founded he could win battles, but not maintain territory. After brief encounters, the Filipinos disappeared, and Otis moved his army back to their bases around Manila. Thus for more than a year there was little progress in actually securing a control over Luzon, much less the other islands, even though he continually announced to the press that Aguinaldo's army had 'almost' been destroyed and that the war was 'almost over.'

As the war dragged on the Americans began to use greater mass violence against the entire populace. Army commanders, who were themselves veterans of Indians fighting in the United States, began to conceive of the war as one of extermination. The Filipinos were variously dubbed 'niggers' and 'Injuns,' as well as uncivilized 'orientals'. Thus the language of inferiorization of three 'others' of the United States was heaped on the Filipinos. Above all, they were imaged as 'savages' without any capacity for 'self-government' who 'only understand force.'

In 1900 Otis was replaced as military commander by General Arthur MacArthur. William Howard Taft was sent as civilian governor. Taft was a firm paternalist who believed the Filipino's were 'incapable of self-government' and needed to be guided by the Americans, calling them 'our little brown brothers.' But he also believed that insurgents should be given no quarter. Prisoners should not be spared. Prisoners of war should be assumed to be murderers and executed. A policy of concentration camps was instituted, the very policy which the Americans had decried as barbaric when used by Spain in Cuba (but which they themselves had continually used against Indians)[48] Filipino peasants were herded into controlled areas, and their villages, crops and livestock destroyed. During the war 90 per cent of the water buffalo on which the peasants relied for their agricultural survival were destroyed.[49]

Atrocities multiplied on both sides. The Filipino army took to mutilating the bodies of slain American soldiers, cutting off their genitals and stuffing them in their mouths. This infuriated the Americans who responded with like atrocities, burning entire villages and massacring men, women and children. In September of 1901, a notable massacre of Americans took place at the town of Balangiga on the island of Samar. The Americans had established an outpost there, and when news of McKinley's assassination came, the commander called for a memorial mass to be held that Sunday at the church. From nowhere Filipino women appeared carrying small coffins which whey claimed held the bodies of children who had died in a cholera epidemic. But the women were actually men and the coffins held arms.

At six o'clock on the Sunday morning the armed Filipinos suddenly appeared, killing most of the seventy-four Americans in the company. General Jacob Smith was appointed to eradicate resistance from the island. Smith put marine major, Littleton Waller, in charge of the repression, ordering him to use utmost violence: 'I want no prisoners. I want you to kill and burn, the more you kill and burn the better you will please me. I want all persons killed who are capable of bearing arms in actual hostilities against the United States.' When Waller asked Smith the age limit of those deemed capable of bearing arms, Smith replied, 'Ten years. Persons of ten years or older are those designated as being capable of bearing arms.' In language taken from American Indian fighting, Smith declared that Samar should be turned into a 'howling wilderness.'[50] Waller proceeded to move systematically across Samar, destroying every village.

48. See Richard Slotkin, *Gunfighter Nation: The Myth of the Frontier in Twentieth-Century America* (New York: Atheneum, 1992), pp. 106–11.

49. Karnow, *In Our Image*, p. 194.

50. Karnow, *In Our Image*, p. 191.

As more and more stories of the army violence against civilians filtered back to the United States, there began to be an outcry of protest, although many journalists, soldiers and politicians insisting that this was the only way to deal with 'savages.' Waller was court-martialed for his indiscriminate violence, and he implicated Smith. Both were sent back to the United States, but remained heroes for many Americans.

The Anti-Imperialist League, organized by political and intellectual leaders opposed to the colonization of the Philippines, led the protest, claiming that this was exactly the kind of dehumanization of Filipinos and Americans themselves that could be expected when colonizing powers tried to suppress other people. The American presence in the Philippines began to appear less and less like a 'benevolent uplift' claimed by its proponents and more and more like unfettered destruction of the people and their land. George Hoar, the leading anti-imperialists in the Senate, evaluated the American record in the Philippines in the following words:

> We changed the Monroe doctrine from a doctrine of eternal righteousness and justice, resting on the consent of the governed, to a doctrine of brutal selfishness looking only to our own advantage. We crushed the only republic in Asia. We made war on the only Christian people in the East. We converted a war of glory into a war of shame. We vulgarized the American flag. We introduced perfidy into the practice of war. We inflicted torture on unarmed men to exhort confessions. We put children to death. We established reconcentrado camps. We devastated provinces. We baffled the aspirations of a people for liberty.[51]

In March 1901, Frederick Funston engineered an ingenious ruse to capture Aguinaldo. The ruse worked, and Aguinaldo, in American custody, swore allegiance to the United States and called on his followers to surrender.[52] Despite this blow, Filipino resistance did not immediately collapse. It continued into 1903, and pockets of resistance, particularly among the Moros of Mindanao, into 1912. Indeed the Moros have never accepted their pacification from the time of Spanish rule until now.

By 1903 Americans were tired of the Philippine war and wanted to forget about it. Hundred of teachers, missionaries, doctors and

51. See Robert L. Beisner, *Twelve against Empire: The Anti-Imperialists, 1898–1900* (New York: McGraw-Hill, 1968), p. 162.
52. Miller, *Benevolent Assimilation*, pp. 167–71.

sanitation workers arrived to deliver the promised 'uplift' and 'civilization' of the Philippines, and thus attempt to redeem the reality of four years of atrocity. Yet the carnage had been fearful. Records show 4,234 Americans had died in battle, 2,828 were wounded and thousands more died of disease. The destruction of the Filipino people was far greater. Hundreds of villages burned, with their livestock and crops; 20,000 Filipino soldiers and somewhere between 200,000 and 600,000 civilians had been killed.[53] The war had cost $600 million ($4 billion in 1989 currency).[54]

To the end most Americans leaders believed that their intentions were entirely benign, that there was no alternative to annexing the Philippines and repressing the independence movement with full force. President McKinley claimed that the decision to annex the whole of the Philippines had come to him as a personal revelation from God. Speaking to members of a Methodist missionary society visiting him at the White House in 1899, he confided in them that he himself had not actually wanted to take over the islands and had no idea what to do 'when they came to us a gift from the gods.' He had paced the floor of the White House nightly, even kneeling to beg 'Almighty God for light and guidance.'

Then one night, it all became clear to him. It would be 'cowardly and dishonorable' to restore them to Spain, and 'bad business and discreditable' to allow France or Germany to take them over. Nor could they be abandoned to the natives, 'who were unfit for self-government (and) would soon have anarchy and misrule.' His only choice therefore was to take the Philippines, and 'to educate the Filipinos and uplift and Christianize them, and by God's grace do the very best we could by them, as our fellow men for whom Christ died.'[55] That the Filipinos were already 95 per cent Catholic presented no impediment to McKinley's claim to the Methodists

53. General J. Franklin Bell estimated that one-sixth of the population of Luzon had died– 616,000 persons. But this seems to have been an exaggeration. Estimates based on army records suggested that there were 200,000 civilian deaths, but this also is a guess, since soldiers engaged in murderous sweeps through villages did not count the dead. See Slotkin, *Gunfighter Nation*, p. 119. Also Moorfield Storey, *et al., Secretary Root's Record: Marked Severities in the Philippine War: An Analysis of the Law and Facts Bearing on the Actions And Utterances of President Roosevelt and Secretary Root* (Boston, MA: G.H. Ellis, 1902).

54. Karnow, *In Our Image*, p. 194.

55. Karnow, *In Our Image*, pp. 127–28. This story is often cited. An early source for it is Charles S. Olcott, *The Life of William McKinley*. II. (Boston: Houghton Mifflin, 1916), pp. 110–11.

that they needed to be Christianized, since both assumed that th___ meant that they should be Protestantized.

Making Central America and the Caribbean America's Backyard: 1900–1934

Since 1823, when President James Monroe enunciated the Monroe Doctrine, the United States had regarded the exclusion of any European powers from intervention or settlement in the Western Hemisphere as a key article of its foreign policy. But at first this was mostly expressed in warnings which powerful imperial powers, such as Great Britain, felt at liberty to ignore. By the end of the nineteenth century, however, growing naval and international economic power allowed the U.S. to more actively enforce this principle. This took the form of President Theodore Roosevelt's 'Monroe Corollary.' This meant the U.S. was prepared to use its armed forces, particularly in Caribbean and Central American countries, when uprisings and financial bankruptcy threatened and European powers sought to land their forces in order to collect debts. These powers were to be forbidden to intervene, while the U.S, would take it upon itself to restore 'order' by armed force, appropriating control over the financial affairs of the country and organizing them to pay international creditors.

The first use of this policy was in 1904 in Santo Domingo when threatened bankruptcy and intervention by European powers brought military intervention by the U.S. (2 January–11 February). President Roosevelt negotiated an agreement with interim President Carlos Morelos under which the U.S. would take control of the custom's houses (where duties were collected), give forty-five percent to the Dominican government for operating expenses and put the rest in a New York bank to pay off the country's creditors.[56] These interventionist practices defined by the Corollary would guide U.S. policy in the Caribbean for the next thirty years.

Although space forbids detailed accounts of these events between 1904–34, major examples of such intervention will be mentioned briefly. Besides Cuba, the four major cases of such intervention, leading to longer occupations, were Panama, Nicaragua, Santo

---

56. The Corollary was aired by Secretary of War, Elihu Root, on 20 May 1904 on behalf of President Roosevelt: See Musicant, *Banana Wars*, pp. 242–43. See also Theodore Roosevelt, *An Autobiography*, pp. 507–10.

Domingo and Haiti. In addition, the U.S. Navy continually policed the Caribbean waters, with shorter interventions in Honduras, Guatemala and Mexico.[57] A central concern in all these interventions was the U.S. desire to control the building of a canal from the Caribbean Sea to the Pacific Ocean to shorten the journey from the east to the west coast of the U.S. and to Asia. Whoever controlled this canal would have a major role in controlling world trade.

Two major routes had been contemplated for this canal, across the isthmus of Panama (then a part of Columbia) and across Nicaragua (sailing west on the San Juan River, across Lake Nicaragua, then crossing the short coastal area that separated the lake from the Pacific ocean). The French sought to gain control of the Panama route, while the U.S. oscillated between both routes, seeking to control access to both regions, finally deciding on the Panamanian route. Having bought out French rights, the U.S. then focused on negotiating a treaty to pay Columbia $10 million for the rights, plus $250,000 annually. Since this was considerably less than Colombia was then collecting on railroad fees to cross the isthmus, the Columbian government vacillated.

President Roosevelt grew impatient and decided instead to facilitate a Panamanian revolution to secede from Colombia and declare itself an independent country.[58] The U.S. then immediately recognized Panama, and negotiated the treaty to build the canal on terms to its satisfaction. The Panamanians granted to the U.S. perpetual use, occupation and control of a ten miles zone on each side of the canal. U.S. troops would remain in Panama until 1914 to guide the building of the canal and would intervene periodically thereafter to quell 'unrest' that threatened U.S. lives and interests.[59]

Interventions in Nicaragua were originally related to efforts to control the area for a possible canal, and then to prevent Nicaragua from negotiating with another country to build a canal when the U.S. decided on the Panamanian route. The U.S. had continually

57. For a list of armed U.S. interventions between 1798 and 1945 see William Blum, *Killing Hope: U.S. Military and CIA Interventions since World War II* (Monroe, ME: Common Courage Press, 1995), pp. 444–52.

58. For Roosevelt's defense of his tactics in facilitating the revolution, see his *An Autobiography*, pp. 511–29. As Roosevelt puts it 'I did not lift a finger to incite the revolutionists… I simply ceased to stamp out the different revolutionary fuses that were already burning.' See especially p. 525.

59. For a detailed account of the Panamanian 'revolution' and the U.S. role in facilitating it, see Musicant, *Banana Wars*, pp. 79–136.

intervened in Nicaraguan affairs through the nineteenth century, even briefly supporting and then opposing an American adventurer, William Walker, who in 1855 seized the country and declared it a slave state with himself as President.[60] Nicaragua in the nineteenth and early twentieth centuries was rent by continual rivalry between two factions, Liberals, based in Leon, and Conservatives in Granada. In 1893, Liberal José Santos Zelaya was elected President. His rule gradually became more dictatorial, but U.S. objection to him was because he was a strong nationalist who sought to shape Nicaragua for an independent role in Central American politics. He also tried to negotiate with Germany an independent canal route across Nicaragua.

In 1909 the U.S. Marines landed and displaced Zelaya, putting Conservative leader, Juan Estrada in power. In 1912 they would intervene again to prop up the Conservatives, this time taking over and organizing Nicaraguan economic assets, and negotiating permanent naval bases in the Caribbean Corn Islands and the Pacific Gulf of Fonseca. A small Marine presence would remain until 1925, only to return again in 1926 when guerrilla war broke out, led by a nationalist leader, Augusto César Sandino. U.S. troops pursued Sandino for seven years, failing to apprehend him or to halt his movement.

Meanwhile the U.S. developed a different strategy for ongoing control of Nicaragua; namely, the building of a National Guard independent of either party to act as U.S. surrogate, choosing an upwardly mobile 'new man' fluent in English, Anastasio Somoza Garcia, to head it. As the U.S. forces withdrew, Somoza arranged an armistice with Sandino, then assassinated him and his key supporters after a supposed 'peace' meeting. Over the next few years Somoza tightened his control over the National Guard, making it a personal tool for his dictatorial rule and that of his two sons that would last for the next forty-five years.[61]

U.S. interventions and occupations of Dominican Republic and Haiti would follow similar patterns. After landing its armies, taking over the state finances and putting its own candidate in political power, the U.S. armies would then spend much of their time seeking to repress guerrilla rebellions against their rule. It would eventually

---

60. For Walker, see John A, Booth, *The End and the Beginning: The Nicaraguan Revolution* (Boulder, CO; Westview Press, 1985), pp. 18–20.

61. Booth, *The End and the Beginning*, pp. 46–95.

withdraw from direct occupation, after having dismantled the national army and organized an 'independent' national guard to suppress local dissent. In each country this national guard would become a tool of subsequent dictators who would rule with U.S. acquiescence.

As we have seen, in 1904 the U.S. had already intervened in Santo Domingo, putting its financial assets under U.S. receivership. It returned again in 1916, in part because of threatened German influence in the country's economic affairs. Having forced President Jiménez to resign, it declared martial law to prevent the election of Desidero Arias, who was poised to seize power. The U.S. then established a military government under its own control, ruling for the next eight years. During that time it would pursue and seek to destroy armed guerrillas that resisted U.S. rule (which the Americans insisted were simply 'bandits'). It would build miles of roads and organize sugar export firms, in both cases primarily to control U.S. interests in the country's economic assets.

In order to repress dissent and uprisings, the U.S. organized a national guard to which it would hand over power when it departed in 1924. Its chosen leader for this militia was one Raphael Trujillo, a wily petty criminal. Trujillo would strengthen his hold on the Guardia after the U.S. departure to make it a tool for a bloody and repressive dictatorship in which he would exercise absolute control of all assets of the society, with U.S. support, from 1930 to 1961 (when he was assassinated).[62]

U.S. occupation of Haiti would last almost twenty years, from 1915–34. Haiti's birth as an independent republic and its existence through the nineteenth century (and until today) has been torn by continual internal violence, partly due to continual foreign interventions and embargoes, and partly due to its own internal class structure, based on excessive exploitation of the peasantry by ruling elites.[63] The period 1911–15 had been a time of particular political chaos during which there were six different presidents, four of them killed in office. Although the U.S. claimed that this political upheaval and threatened economic insolvency demanded

---

62. See Howard J. Wiarda and Michael J. Kryzanek, *The Dominican Republic: A Caribbean Crucible* (Boulder, CO: Westview Press, 1992), pp. 34–38.

63. See the excellent analysis of Haiti's class structure in Michel-Rolph Trouillot, *Haiti: State against Nation: Origins and Legacy of Duvalierism* (New York: Monthly Review Press, 1990), pp. 59–108.

its armed intervention, the threat of German merchants taking control of Haitian affairs was a major consideration. In 1918 Haiti was pressured by the U.S. to declare war on Germany. German merchants were then imprisoned and their properties confiscated.[64]

The U.S. occupiers' first act was to install a puppet president, Philippe-Sudre Dartiguenave. They then took over the customs houses and national bank to organize Haitian public finances. The U.S. imposed a Convention giving it the right to police the country and control finances for ten years. Later it dissolved the Senate and extended the Convention to twenty years. Dissent was repressed and critical journalists were regularly jailed. The U.S. disbanded the Haitian army, which, despite its corruption, had a tradition of patriotic national independence from the revolutionary war era.[65] In its place it set up a national police force *Gendarmerie* (later called *Garde*), trained by the Marines primarily to suppress Haitian dissidents. Much of the rebellions in Haiti had stemmed from local militias in different sections of the country that represented a certain regional dispersal of power.[66] The Marines set out to destroy these regional armed groups (in the North called *Cacos*) descended from run-away slaves of colonial times.

The U.S. also revived an old law allowing forced (*corveé*) labor to build roads. This led to deepened resentment of the occupation by the peasantry. As the Marines crushed existing rebels, new rebel units formed, now on a national basis, seeing themselves as a national liberation movement. Charlemagne Péralte, landowner and officer of the disbanded army, emerged as a popular leader and thousands flocked to his banner. Late in 1919, through a paid informer, a trap was set for Péralte and he was shot in cold blood by a Marine captain. His body, tied to a door, was put on display to intimidate the populace, giving rise to the impression that he had been crucified. Leadership of the resistance was picked up by Benoit Betraville, but he was killed in an ambush in May, 1920. Marine campaigns against the rebels resulted in the killing of 6,000 peasants, plus another 5,500 who died in forced labor camps. The Marines gained the reputation of killing Haitians indiscriminately.

By 1930 there was increasing pressure in the United States for the Marines to leave Haiti. The whole policy of Marine intervention

64. Trouillot, *Haiti*, pp. 100, 104.
65. Trouillot, *Haiti*, p. 106.
66. Trouillot, *Haiti*, pp. 96–97.

and occupation was criticized. President Franklin Delano Roosevelt defined a 'Good Neighbor' policy that eschewed such intervention. Although the legacy of the twenty-year occupation of Haiti was not entirely negative – they did reduce the debt, stabilize the currency and temporarily end Presidential coups – but they also worsened many endemic problems. Economic dependence on coffee exports was increased, as well as the super-exploitation of the peasantry. They also destroyed the earlier patterns of regional diffusion of power, thus reinforcing centralization of all power in the executive in Port-au-Prince. In Michel-Rolph Trouillot's words, 'In the end, then, the U.S. occupation worsened all of Haiti's structural ills.'[67] The occupation also created a new and more dangerous militarism manifest in a national army mandated to repress dissident Haitians, rather than national defense. As in the Dominican Republic and Nicaragua, this national army became a tool of new dictatorial strongmen.

Most of all, the American occupation left Haiti with a bitter memory of American racism. Although not all military leaders were overt racists, all too many assumed that the darker the skin the less intelligent and competent the person. The occupiers habitually favored light-skinned presidents and administrators. The Americans had little appreciation for the distinctive traditions of Haiti, both on the popular level and the educated tradition that looked to France for its culture. All Haitians, even light-skinned mulattos, were assumed to be 'nigs' by virtue of African blood.

Such racism had the ironic effect of healing some of the chasm between light and dark-skinned Haitians, since all were regarded as inferior by the Americans. The experience of racism during the occupation also helped spark the 'noiriste' or 'Black Pride' movement in Haiti in the 1950s.[68] For many Haitians American arrogant ignorance of Haitian culture was summed up by a story told of Secretary of State, William Jennings Bryan. He had been briefed on Haitian history and culture by an American official in the Banque nationale. Bryan responded by commenting, 'Dear me, think of it, Niggers speaking French.'[69]

67. Trouillot, *Haiti*, p. 107.
68. Trouillot, *Haiti*, pp. 131–32.
69. See Lester D. Langley, *The Banana Wars: United States Intervention in the Caribbean, 1898–1934* (Lexington, KY: University Press of Kentucky, 1985), p. 123.

In the first third of the twentieth century the U.S. shaped a new system of imperial control over territories beyond the continental United States which, unlike earlier acquired territories, it did not intended to accept into the Union. Its purpose was 'to maintain unfettered access to labor, markets and resources' by putting or keeping in power local governing elites who would accept this subservient relation to the U.S. while repressing the protests of their own people, all the while claiming to be serving 'democracy.'[70] Marine General Smedley Butler, having led many such interventions, turned against this system after retirement in 1931 and denounced it in bitter words as a 'racket.'

> I spent thirty-three years and four months in active military service as a member of this country's most agile military force, the Marine Corps. I served in all commissioned ranks from Second Lieutenant to Major General. And during that period I spent most of my time being a high class muscle-man for Big Business, for Wall Street and for the Bankers. In short I was a racketeer, a gangster for capitalism... I helped make Mexico, especially Tampico, safe for American oil interests in 1914. I helped make Haiti and Cuba a decent place for the National City Bank boys to collect revenues in. I helped in the raping of half a dozen Central American Republics for the benefit of Wall Street. The record of racketeering is long. I helped purify Nicaragua for the international banking house of Brown Brothers in 1909–1912... I brought light to the Dominican Republic for American sugar interests in 1916. In China I helped to see to it that Standard Oil went its way unmolested.[71]

70. Saul Landau, *The Dangerous Doctrine: National Security and U.S. Foreign Policy* (Boulder, CO: Westview Press, 1988), p. 18.

71. Smedley Butler ran for Congress in 1933 and wrote a small book, *War is a Racket* (New York: Round Table Press, 1935). He was active with the League against War and Fascism, 1935–1937. These remarks, often quoted, appeared in a 1933 speech: www.fas.org/man/smedley.

Chapter Five

AMERICA'S GLOBAL MISSION: THE COLD WAR ERA, 1945–89

For more than forty years two rival empires, identified with two rival ideologies, confronted one another across bristling shields of deadly weapons capable of destroying the peoples of the earth many times over. Each defined themselves in messianic terms as saviors of the world's peoples against a deadly foe. The U.S. saw itself as the leader of the 'free world,' champion of freedom and democracy, against an evil system of totalitarian repression and slavery. The Soviets saw themselves as the leader of an 'inevitable' process of world transformation from capitalist exploitation of the workers to socialist equality, over against a United States that had taken up the banner of European imperialism at a time when that system was dying.

Stages in the Cold War

The period from 1945 to 1989 was not one of uniform hostility. It took several years after the end of the Second World War for the wartime alliance of the U.S. and Western Europe with the Soviet Union to be redefined as one of unrelenting antagonism. After the death of Stalin in 1953 until the late sixties there was some relaxing of tensions followed by renewed periods of hostility. The period from 1969–1979 was one of détente in which both sides pursued negotiations to resolve major issues of dispute, particularly the nuclear arms race. SALT I, (Strategic Arms Limitation Treaty) signed by President Nixon and Soviet leader Brezhnev in 1972, ended the race to develop defensive antiballistic missile systems (AMBs) and froze the number of nuclear missiles to 1,600 on the Soviet side and 1,054 on the U.S. side. This agreement actually left the U.S. two to one ahead, since the U.S. MIRVs (multiple independently targeted reentry vehicles) contained multiple warheads on one missile capable of hitting widely separated areas.[1]

The period from 1979–85 saw a rapid reversion to Cold War hostilities, sometimes called 'the second Cold War'.[2] In reaction to peace movements and a (mis)perceived belief that the U.S. was 'falling behind' in the arms race, there was a call from conservatives to reject détente and restore U.S. military superiority. A rhetoric of demonization of the USSR became typical of the new Reagan administration, discrediting the legitimacy and even the right to existence of the Soviet system. The second Cold War was accompanied by a roll back of social reforms in the U.S. and some European countries. A transfer of government spending from social programs to military budgets in the U.S. cut funds for alleviation of poverty and promotion of equality and sought to undermine the power of trade unions. The period of liberalization of the Civil Rights era, with the movements for equal rights for various minority groups (blacks, Hispanics, American Indians) and women was decried as one of libertine erosion of 'family values,' and there was a concerted effort to reestablish the legitimacy of traditional patterns of patriarchal authority.

From 1985 to 1989, this Cold War rhetoric was quickly and surprisingly dissipated by the rise of a new leader in the Soviet Union, Mikhail Gorbachev, who sought to reform the cumbersome Soviet bureaucracy (*perestroika*) and create a more open society (*glasnost*). This led to rising criticism of the Soviet system from within and awakened long repressed aspirations for national independence among member peoples of the USSR, such as Lithuanians, Latvians, Ukrainians, Georgians and others. By 1990, the Soviet Union was disintegrating and in December, 1991 ceased to exist. This deprived the U.S. of the 'enemy' against which it had defined itself for so many years, and opened up the possibility of entirely new ways of thinking of the world global order, a challenge which, as we will see in the following chapter, the U.S. leaders resolutely refused to allow, instead seeking new 'enemies' to bolster the military might and world dominance achieved during the Cold War era.

The reasons for the breakdown of the wartime alliance and the advent of the Cold War are disputed among historians. For historian Walter LaFeber, the struggle between the expanding U.S. and

1. Walter LaFeber, *America, Russia and the Cold War, 1945–1992* (New York: McGraw-Hill, 1993), p. 273.

2. Fred Halladay, *The Making of the Second Cold War* (London: Verso, 1986).

Russian Empires did not start in 1945 but goes back to the late-nineteenth century. Manifest Destiny had led the U.S. west across the American continent from which it reached out to control trade and resources in the Pacific and China, even as Russia completed an eastern expansion across Asia. The two expanding empires clashed in North China and Manchuria where the U.S. sought 'open doors' to trade, while the Russians tried to maintain a closed system controlled from the center under the Czarist bureaucracy.[3] In language that echoes Cold War hostility, Theodore Roosevelt condemned the Russians as 'utterly insincere and treacherous, they have no conception of truth ...no regard for others.'[4]

This hostility between the U.S. and Russia escalated at the end of World War I when the Czarist government was replaced by a Communist one. Woodrow Wilson sent 10,000 American soldiers in 1918–20 to aid a Western European effort to overthrow Lenin. In the 1919 Versailles peace conference the victors created a ring of buffer states in Eastern Europe to isolate the Soviets. Socialism was defined as the enemy of the American capitalist system. Already in World War I socialist dissenters against participation in 'imperialist wars,' such as Eugene Debs, were jailed as traitors.[5] The war was followed by a period of anticommunist hysteria in which communists and anarchists were deported. Government propagandists tried to convince the American people that all progressive movements, including feminist groups, were part of a 'spider web' of conspiracy masterminded by the Soviet Union to overthrow the American government.[6] FBI director, J. Edgar Hoover's anticommunist conspiracy theories were first honed during the 1920s.[7]

Although President Franklin Delano Roosevelt finally recognized the Soviet Union in 1933, relations continued to be hostile between

3. LaFeber, *America, Russia and the Cold War*, pp. 1–3.

4. LaFeber, *America, Russia and the Cold War*, p. 3, citing William Henry Harbough, *Power and Responsibility: The Life and Times of Theodore Roosevelt* (New York: Farrar, Straus and Cudahy, 1961), p. 277.

5. Eugene Debs was convicted of two counts of advocating refusal of duty in the arms forces under the Espionage Act of June 15, 1917 and sentenced ten years imprisonment on both counts. See www.law.umke.edu/faculty/projects/ftrials/conlaw/debs.html

6. See Saul Landau, *The Dangerous Doctrine: National Security and U.S. Foreign Policy* (Boulder, CO: Westview Press, 1988), p. 27; also Rosemary Ruether, *Christianity and the Making of the Modern Family* (Boston: Beacon Press, 2000), pp. 116 and 259 n. 37.

7. J. Edgar Hoover, *Masters of Deceit: The Story of Communism in America and How to Fight It* (New York: Holt, Rinehart and Winston, 1958).

the two countries in the 30s. Roosevelt refused to respond to Stalin's calls for help against Japan's invasion of Manchuria and for joint policies against Nazi Germany. When the English and French appeased Hitler in 1938 by giving Germany part of Czechoslovakia, Stalin perceived the West as seeking to destroy the Soviet Union by turning the German attack eastward. Stalin responded by signing a non-aggression pact with Germany in August 1939. Russia became an ally of the west only when the Nazis ignored the pact by invading Russia in June, 1941. Churchill and Roosevelt delayed opening a second front until mid-1944, leaving the Russians to defend Eastern Europe and Russia alone against the Nazi onslaught at tremendous cost. The defense of Russia against the Germans would destroy 1,700 towns, 70,000 villages, kill 20 million and leave 25 million homeless. 600,000 starved to death in the siege of Leningrad. Stalin and the Soviet leadership emerged from the war determined to protect themselves from another invasion from the West.[8]

At the end of the war the Red Army stood astride Eastern Europe, including the Eastern half of Germany. Despite the famous summitry of the three wartime leaders, Churchill, Stalin and Roosevelt (later Truman), misunderstanding quickly arose. Stalin was convinced that the Germans would quickly rebuild their country and wanted a permanently disarmed and neutral Germany, even if it meant surrendering control of Eastern Germany for a unified nation. The West wanted a rearmed Germany integrated into Western Europe, even if Eastern Germany remained communist. Determined to prevent another encirclement, Stalin roped off the Eastern European buffer states, pushing out non-communist national leaders and installing communist governments under Soviet control in Poland, Rumania, Bulgaria, Hungary and East Germany and Czechoslovakia. Yugoslavia resisted the trend of subjugation to the USSR led by an independent communist leader, Josip Tito. In a famous speech in 1946 Churchill described the division of Eastern from Western Europe as the 'iron curtain.'

The United States emerged from the war not only unscathed but with the world's strongest army and economy built through the war. In 1945, the U.S. controlled three-fourths of the world's invested capital and two-thirds of the global industrial capacity.[9]

8. LaFeber, *America, Russia and the Cold War*, p. 18.
9. Landau, *Dangerous Doctrine*, p. 34.

On August 6, 1945 the U.S. dropped an atomic bomb on Hiroshima, killing 100,000 people. Three days later a second bomb fell on Nagasaki. With this ultimate weapon in its hands, the U.S. saw itself as poised to dominate the world, taking over the role of the European empires that were tottering after the devastation of their mother countries.

The U.S. defined its hegemony as one where the resources and labor of the developed and developing nations would be open to U.S. exploitation, with U.S. military power as its ultimate sanction. The U.S. definition of the 'freedom' of the 'free world' was predominately one of 'free markets,' or access to global resources. Thus any socialist or independent nationalist regime which controlled access to a nation's resources and blocked U.S. access was by definition 'communist.' To ensure access to postwar markets, the U.S. met with other Western nations in Bretton Woods, New Hampshire, in 1944 to create the World Bank and the International Monetary Fund. The U.S., which controlled both these agencies through monopolizing their funding and decision-making, hoped to control postwar rebuilding of Europe and the less industrialized nations emerging from colonialism under the aegis of its economic system.

The American National Security State and Foreign Policy

By 1947 the U.S. began to define its foreign policy as one of active intervention to prevent the takeover of nations by nationalist or communist movements that would deny the U.S. this free access. The Soviet Union was seen as aggressively expansionist, seeking to take over nation after nation and subjugate them to its sphere of control. In a 12 March, 1947 speech that defined what became known as the Truman Doctrine, Truman described the world as split between two alternative ways of life, freedom versus totalitarian slavery. The American people must be ready to oppose totalitarian slavery and commit themselves to aiding people to 'freedom' anywhere in the world.

The timing of this declaration was significant. In 1947 Stalin had consolidated his hold on Eastern Europe, but showed no disposition to aid rising communist movements in other countries. The State Department had tacitly conceded to the Soviets their 'sphere of influence;' i.e., the Soviet Union and Eastern Europe. However in

Western Europe, in Greece, Italy, France, as well as the movements against colonialism in Africa and Asia, there were active communist and socialist parties that sought alternative ways of development from the dominant capitalist system controlled by the U.S. The Truman Doctrine of 'containment' of communism was actually aimed at preventing independent nationalist, socialist or communist groups from coming to power outside the Soviet sphere of influence, even while claiming that the 'threat' to these nations lay primarily in an expansionist drive of the Soviet Union. This misleading definition of the U.S. crusade against 'communism' would continue to define the Cold War through the Reagan years.

Two examples of the U.S. intervention to prevent leftist victories in Europe will illustrate the pattern that began to emerge in the late forties. In the 1946 election in Italy the Communist and Socialist parties together gained more votes than the Christian Democrats in the Constituent Assembly, but had run separate candidates and so were given only a few ministerial posts in a coalition government under a Christian Democratic premier. In 1948 the two parties united to form the Popular Democratic Front (PDF). Communists had been at the forefront of anti-fascist resistance during the war, while the Christian Democrats were filled with monarchists, old fascists and fascist collaborators. The Italian Communist and Socialist parties, by contrast, were based on an anti-Leninist Gramsci-ite tradition that was democratic and independent of Moscow.[10]

Nevertheless, the prospect of a victory of the Left in Italy aroused extreme alarm in Washington. A propaganda blitz was launched to convince Italians that the choice was between democracy and a communism that would submerge Italy under Soviet totalitarianism. Gifts of food and other aid poured into Italy from the U.S. with explicit warnings that food and monetary loans would be cut off if Italy 'went Communist.' A letter writing campaign was launched from Italian Americans to their relatives in Italy pleading to them not to vote for the PDF. They were told that food and aid from the U.S. government would be cut off, also that Italian Americans could no longer send money to their relatives in Italy or anyone who voted 'communist' would not be able to come to the United States. Propaganda films were shown throughout Italy showing the

10. Antonio Gramsci (1891–1937) developed an anti-Leninist form of Marxism. See *The Open Marxism of Antonio Gramsci* (trans. Carl Marzoni, New York: Cameron Associates, 1957).

miserable way of life of workers in the USSR with the implication that this would be the fate of Italians under the PDF. Stalin not only did not aid the Italian left, but even chose to reject the return of the port of Trieste to Italy five days before the election, thus delivering a body-blow to the Italian left. Nevertheless, the U.S. propaganda constantly sought to identify the PDF as a puppet of the Soviets. Under this intense barrage of propaganda, threats and intimidation, the PDF majority faded, with the Christian Democrats receiving 48 per cent of the vote to the PDF's 31 per cent.[11]

Another major U.S. intervention in the late 40s occurred in Greece. It was in the context of a request for appropriations for this intervention that Truman made his 'Truman Doctrine' speech on 12 March 1947. The 'communists' against which the U.S. was mobilizing its forces were the ELAS, People's Liberation Army that had been formed in 1941 to fight the Nazi occupation. ELAS, and its political wing, EAM, cut across the left political spectrum of Greek patriots from communists to democratic nationalists, numbering priests and bishops among its members. EAM was poised to become the leading political party at the war's end. But in October, 1944, when war still raged in Europe, the British, who had been routed by the Nazis from Greece in 1941, returned. They soon began to attack ELAS, while installing the Greek king back in power, surrounded by various conservatives, monarchists and former collaborators with the Nazis. Stalin did nothing to help, but rather ordered ELAS to lay down their arms, conceding Greece as the 'sphere of power' of the British, while assuming a similar acceptance of his sphere of power by the British and the U.S., as per his agreement with Churchill.

A succession of corrupt Greek governments followed which terrorized the left, tortured them in prison camps and did nothing to alleviate the misery of the Greek people. In the Fall of 1946 the Greek left broke with its subordination to Stalin's dictates and took to the hills as guerrillas. The British, however, could no longer continue to occupy Greece because of pressing needs at home and so handed over the task of defeating the Greek left and maintaining the corrupt regime in power to the Americans. Having engineered an invitation from the 'Greek government' written by the U.S. State Department, the U.S. army arrived in force in the Spring of 1947

11. See William Blum, *Killing Hope: U.S. Military and CIA interventions Since World War II* (Monroe, ME: Common Courage Press, 1995), pp. 27–34.

and conducted an intensive ground and air war against the guerrillas, even clearing large areas of the rural population in order to deprive ELAS of its local support. After three brutal years of warfare and tens of thousands of deaths, in October, 1949, ELAS declared a cease fire. Greece became virtually an American puppet state for the next two decades.[12]

The Truman doctrine promoted the shaping of the United States as a 'national security state' which significantly curtailed freedoms of speech, communication and organization and created a parallel secret government shielded from public scrutiny and congressional oversight.[13] The National Security Act of 1947 established the CIA, the National Security Council and related agencies of this secret government. Shortly after announcing his doctrine in March, 1947 Truman established the Federal Employees Loyalty Program which forced millions of government employees to undergo loyalty and security checks. Waves of repression went beyond government workers to critics of Cold War policies in the media, Hollywood, universities and trade unions. Members of the liberal-left-labor alliance of the New Deal era were targeted as disloyal. The Taft-Hartley Act forced union leaders to disavow not only affiliation with socialist parties, but any belief in socialist ideas, purging the more militant wing of the labor movement. The McCarthyite witch hunts against anyone 'soft on communism' that reigned in American national life from 1950–1955 only extended these purges into the corporate establishment. The results were a removal from American public life not only of more left leaning advocates, but also a whole generation of leaders with expertise on others areas of the world and desires for a more balanced and impartial view of world realities.

In the Fall of 1949, Mao was victorious in conquering all of China and the Soviet Union exploded its first atom bomb. These 'failures' were seen as further evidence of subversives within the U.S. itself that allowed the 'loss' of China and the 'leaking' of atomic secrets to the Russians. Early in 1950 Truman ordered the National Security Council to prepare a top secret document to reevaluate American security policy. This document, known as NSC-68, declassified accidentally only a quarter of a century later, would become the

12. Blum, *Killing Hope*, pp. 34–39; see also Stephen G. Xydis, *Greece and the Great Powers, 1944–47* (Institute for Balkan Studies, Thessalonika, Greece, 1963).

13. Blum, *Killing Hope*, especially 45–57.

blue print for waging the Cold War for the next 20 years. The Soviets were described as driven by a fanatic faith to dominate the Eurasian land mass and ultimately the whole world. The U.S. was defined as the leader in opposing this expansion and taking the 'lead in building a successfully functioning political and economic system in the free world.' [14] This job entailed not only economic pressure and other forms of non-military deterrence, but ultimately military action that could include use of nuclear weapons.

The NSC-68 document concluded with seven key recommendations. Negotiations with the Soviet Union were ruled out since such negotiations could not force the Kremlin to change its policies. The U.S. should develop the hydrogen bomb to offset Soviet atomic weapons. The U.S. should also rapidly expand its conventional military forces to fight limited non-nuclear wars. A large increase in taxes would be necessary to pay for this expanded military. There should also be a domestic propaganda war to create an American 'consensus' that unity and sacrifices for these goals were necessary. The U.S. should also create a strong alliance system in regions around the world to support its global role. Finally, the U.S. should take action to undermine the Soviet system itself.[15] In LaFeber's words, 'NSC-68 was a policy in search of an opportunity.'[16] That opportunity would arrive on 25 June 1950 with the invasion of South Korea by the North Korean army.

Korea had been occupied by the Soviet army in the North and the U.S. army in the South at the end of World War II, expelling the defeated Japanese who had occupied Korea since 1910 (with the connivance of the U.S.[17]). An informal demarcation line was set up on the 38th parallel, but neither side accepted the permanent division of Korea. For five years a civil war raged across this border between North and South with over 100,000 casualties. The U.S. was also determined to suppress the functioning popular government in the

14. LaFeber, *America, Russia and the Cold War*, p. 97.

15. LaFeber, *America, Russia and the Cold War*, pp. 97–98: see also Landau, *Dangerous Doctrine*, pp. 50–51 and 56–57 n. 22. The NSC–68 made available 25 years later is found in Thomas Etzold and John Lewis Gaddis (eds.) *Containment: Documents on American Policy and Strategy, 1945–50* (New York: Columbia University Press, 1978), pp. 385–442.

16. LaFeber, *America, Russia and the Cold War*, p. 98.

17. President William Howard Taft made a secret understanding with the Japanese in 1910 that if the Japanese acquiesced to American control of the Philippines, the U.S. would acquiesce to Japanese control of Korea.

South that had arisen out of resistance to the Japanese and to install its own leader, exile Syngman Rhee, who would be firmly under U.S. control. Japanese collaborators were kept in power, Japanese properties sold to these collaborators and land reform rebuffed.

By 1950 Rhee's government was discredited among South Koreans, so the American intervention rescued him from a unification that might have brought together Northern Korean and South Korean communist and non-communist nationalists. Without the American intervention, the northern regime would have won easily and the South Korean army and state would have 'collapsed in a few days.'[18] Kim Il-Sung, the North Korea leader, was a nationalist and communist. He was not under the thumb of either Mao or Stalin. Rather he bargained with both to gain support, but also to establish his own independence.

Truman quickly seized the opportunity to declare war unilaterally on North Korea, even while claiming to represent a 'UN action.' Although sixteen nations would eventually contribute to these forces, the U.S. and the South Koreans provided almost all the ground troops. Although originally claiming that the U.S. response would only reestablish the 38th parallel and not invade the North, General MacArthur in September pushed across the 38th parallel and approached the Yalu River (border with China). China then entered the war and routed the 'UN' troops, forcing them into rapid retreat. The war eventually stalemated at the 38th parallel which became the truce line in July, 1953. When MacArthur insisted on carrying the war into China, Truman finally sacked him (11 April 1951). The war devastated much of the infrastructure of South Korea, while three years of U.S. bombing leveled almost every modern building in North Korea. Estimates of casualties differ, but the best estimate seems to be about two and a half million dead. On the U.S. side, 36,568 (including 2,827 non-combatants) and 3,500 allies; South Korean military and civilians, 660,250; North Korean military and civilians, 1,316,600, and 460,000 Chinese.[19]

Truman and Dean Acheson used the war era to forward much of the design for global security under U.S. power of the NSC-68 document. Defense spending was escalated from $13 to $50 billion. Germany was rearmed under NATO, with more U.S. troops

18. According to Bruce Cumings. See his *Divided Korea: United Future?* (Ephrata, PA: Science Press, 1995), p. 35.

19. See users.erals.com/mwhite28/warstats.htm.

stationed in Europe. Commitments to the defense of Formosa (Taiwan) and Indochina were made, and tighter military ties negotiated with Japan through a new peace treaty that restored several islands to Japanese sovereignty. On the home front, Congress passed the McCarran Internal Security bill requiring Communist organizations and their members to register with the Attorney General (automatically making them liable for criminal indictment under the Smith Act of 1940 which forbade membership in any group presumed to be advocating the overthrow of the government). Immigrants who had been communists at any time could be deported and critics of American policy could be detained whether they were communists or not.[20]

Anti-Communism as the American Cold War Civil Religion

The Department of Defense would play a major role in this inculcation of an American civil religion centered in militant anti-communism that smeared even moderate liberals, such as the leadership of the National Council of Churches, as communist sympathizers. The American army had long taken the lead in inculcating the American Civil Religion that defined the United States as a chosen people and instrument of the will of God in world affairs.[21] But this role took on renewed power in the national security fears of the late forties. The end of the Second World War saw the emergence of a new, more politically involved movement of American evangelicals who organized the National Association of Evangelicals in 1942 as rivals to the liberal Federal Council of Churches (later the National Council of Churches of Christ).

In this period the military also professionalized the Chaplains Corps as an integral part of the military system. A generic military 'civil religion' emerged, intended to be non-denominational, to be served by these chaplains. Evangelicals sought to take over much of these appointments to the chaplaincy from what they perceived as undue influence from Catholics and liberal Protestants. The military came to be seen as a prime location for evangelical recruitment of the unchurched (who the army defined as 'atheists' and hence prone to 'communism'). Anyone who defined himself as

20. LaFeber, *America, Russia and the Cold War*, p. 112.
21. See Lori Lyn Bogle, *The Pentagon's Battle for the American Mind: The Early Cold War* (College Station, TX: Texas A&M University Press, 2004), pp. 21–47.

unchurched was encouraged to seek religious instruction and baptism. Under the influence of Cold War ideology a militant evangelical Christianity emerged that defined itself as an integral part of the American 'spiritual rearmament' to fight 'communism.' Communism itself was seen as amoral, and as a spiritual, as well as economic, political and military, 'threat' to American national identity.[22]

Truman already saw the usefulness of such an alliance of religion and Cold War anti-communism, but he sought an ecumenical alliance of Catholics, Protestants and Jews and promoted the appointment of a U.S. ambassador to the Vatican that was unacceptable to the evangelicals. For them, America as a chosen people was still to be understood as a Protestant nation. Dwight Eisenhower, by contrast, played into evangelical views (despite being himself an indifferent churchgoer), promoting the militant evangelist Billy Graham as his religious advisor. Graham claimed that American was 'losing' the Cold War because of its materialism and wickedness. Conversion to Christ went hand-in-hand with an enlarged army, military training for youth and aggressive foreign policy to win back God's favor and restore American might. Through his alliance with Graham. Eisenhower became both President and national High Priest, spearheading a moral rearmament.[23]

The fifties to early sixties saw a close alliance between leading military figures of a militant evangelical persuasion, such as Admiral Arthur Radford, Vice Admiral Robert Goldthwaite and Major General Edwin A. Walker, and right wing evangelicals, such as Dr. Billy James Hargis of the Christian Crusade and Fred C. Schwarz of the Christian Anti-Communist Crusade. Such active or retired military officers and extreme right evangelicals teamed together to bring the McCarthyite 'red scare' to the local community level, holding Cold War seminars in anti-communist indoctrination and fingering local teachers and community leaders as 'soft' on communism. New Deal democrats, Protestant liberals of the National Council of Churches and advocates of racial integration were smeared with the communist brush. When McCarthy went 'too far' and began to attack the military itself as 'soft,' the Department of Defense turned against the Cold War seminars and

22. Bogle, *The Pentagon's Battle*, pp. 59–76.
23. Bogle, *The Pentagon's Battle*, pp. 97–103.

began to rein in the participation of military leaders in it, but not before a decade of assault on liberals in many walks of life.[24]

Anti-communism also became a feature of American popular culture in the fifties in dime novels and popular films. In popular novels and films communists were portrayed as warped personalities, seeking to subvert good Americans through 'brainwashing,' and employing seductive female spies. But inevitably these female spies succumb to the superior sexual machismo and ideological militancy of American communist-fighters who win them over and rout the subversives who seek to 'infiltrate' American society. Macho hero, Michael Hammer, of Mickey Spillane's *One Lonely Night* (1951) bragged about all the bad guys he killed by saying, 'They were commies, Lee. They were red sons-of-bitches who should have died long ago... They never thought there were people like me in this country. They figured us all to be as soft as horse manure and just as stupid.'[25] Thus the rhetoric of fighting communism quickly fell into the familiar masculinist lines of a contest between 'softness ' and 'virility.'

Loyal party communists were seen as demonic figures lacking all natural feelings, having been turned into automatons of a totalitarian system. Fellow-travelers, by contrast, were portrayed as dupes, betrayed by a misguided idealism and lack of realism who can sometimes be won over to the American truth. The American way of life is portrayed as the champion of all human values of individualism and self-determination against a creeping menace that seeks to penetrate the American soul and to undermine these values. From 1948–54 Hollywood produced more than 40 films that played on various forms of the anticommunist theme.[26] The confessional narratives of anticommunist double agents, such Matt Cvetic's 'I posed as a Communist for the FBI' (1950) and Herbert Philbrick, *I Led Three Lives, Citizen, Communist, Counterspy* (1952) were readily transformed into newspaper serials, films and television series. 'I Led Three Lives' ran as a TV serial for 117 episodes from 1953–56 and reruns were popular until the mid-sixties.[27]

24. Bogle, *The Pentagon's Battle*, pp. 133–63.
25. Bogle, *The Pentagon's Battle*, p. 118. Also Cyndy Hendershot, *Anti-Communism and Popular Culture in Mid-Century America* (Jefferson, NC: McFarland and Co., Inc, 2003), pp. 9–12.
26. Hendershot, *Anti-Communism and Popular Culture*, p. 113.
27. Hendershot, *Anti-Communism and Popular Culture*, pp. 111–20.

The classic portrait of the American communist and their dupes was penned by the director of the FBI, *Masters of Deceit: The Story of Communism in America and How to Fight It* (1958).[28] The images of communists in American popular culture largely followed the lines that Hoover laid out. This image depended on the conflation of Communism with the demonic image of Nazism crafted during the Second World War. Communists were portrayed as simply the continuation of Nazism. Every possible evil is attributed to them, lawlessness, anarchy and immorality, above all hypocrisy and deceitfulness, at the same time the quest for total control of every aspect of American life by a small dictatorial elite. Communists are viewed as seeking every way to infiltrate American life in order to undermine it and make the United States a part of the Soviet system. For Hoover, it is an unquestioned article of faith that what Soviet communists seek is the ultimate goal— the overthrow of the American government and all the values 'for which it stands,' home, family, liberty and property. Even though at the time that Hoover published his book, membership in the U.S. Communist Party had fallen to less than 20,000, Hoover portrayed it as a growing threat insidiously surrounding Americans on all sides. Though committed party members were few, Hoover saw them as commanding an army of dupes who did their bidding.

For Hoover the ultimate basis of communism is atheism. Loss of religion is the prime pathway that leads people into communism. Having lost faith in the true God of the Judeo-Christian heritage, people seek an alternative faith and this makes them susceptible to ensnarement by deceitful communist propaganda. But such 'dupes' can be redeemed, for Hoover. Here the FBI agent is portrayed as a redeeming 'father confessor.' Those who begin to doubt communist propaganda should go at once to the FBI and make a confession of their mistakes, giving the FBI full information on their communist allies. Under the FBI sheltering care such wayward people can find themselves received back into the fold of 'loyal Americans.'

> ...loyal Americans must accept their sincere repentance as a return to the full scope of citizenship. All great religions teach that the sinner can always redeem himself. Who, then, can sit in judgment on the ex-communist? ... For our part, at the FBI, we have always sought to recognize the very real human and personal problems facing

28. J. Edgar Hoover, *Masters of Deceit: The Story of Communism in America and How to Fight It* (New York: Holt, Rinehart and Winston).

the ex-communists who have come to our offices to make such amends...[29]

In the 1950s alternative ways of relating to communism, and to those who sought an alternative to the capitalist way of life under the aegis of Marxist thought, had been largely stifled in American public culture. A dualism of good versus evil, God against demonic evil, dominated all levels of American culture, from sophisticated thinkers to popular culture. A few voices, such as that of social critic, Sidney Lens, continued to hold out for other ways of thinking about the relationship of the U.S. and the Soviet Union, capitalism and communism. In his *The Futile Crusade: Anti-communism as American Credo*,[30] Lens deplored the adoption of anti-communism as the central lens by which Americans viewed the world as a tragic mistake and a missed opportunity for the United States.

For Lens, the anticommunist crusade began in 1917 when the United States joined the western European nations in the encirclement and attempted destruction of the Russian Revolution. These attacks themselves led to the hardening of repressive leadership and facilitated the emergence of Stalin. Had there been nuanced support from the West, a recognition of the justice of the long bent up desire for liberation from Czarist feudalism, other forces within the revolution might have prevailed. For Lens, totalitarianism is not an inevitable expression of communism, but is a defensive response to western efforts to attack and destroy it. Moreover, with a different, less hostile policy, more democratic alternatives can emerge within the Soviet system today. Lens in no way condones blindness to the evils of Stalinism, but rather recognizes diverse potential within Russian society and fundamental values of justice within communist ideology that could be released if the West let up on its global crusade.

For Lens, the second great missed opportunity was at the end of the Second World War when Churchill was bent on reestablishing the European and especially the British Empire, while Roosevelt was ready to recognize the justice of the demands of the colonized peoples for independence. The United States might have forged a policy that supported the anti-colonial independence movements, while seeking a positive competitive co-existence with the Soviets.

29. Hoover, *Masters of Deceit*, p. 128.
30. Sidney Lens, *The Futile Crusade: Anti-communism as American Credo* (Chicago: Triangle Books, 1964).

Instead, with the 'Truman Doctrine,' U.S. policy turned to a two-bloc polarization. Third world independence movements that sought a socialist path were falsely identified with Soviet 'expansion' and 'takeover.' The U.S. allied with right wing anticommunist dictators, rather than supporting national independence movements that allowed the new nations to choose their own path of development. From this flowed a policy of remilitarization and continual U.S. intervention in the Middle East, Asia, Africa and Latin America to destroy what could have been positive national reformist and democratic socialist regimes. This is a perspective to which I will return later in this chapter.

Another critical thinker who might have warned against the slide into polarized 'good/evil' thinking was Reinhold Niebuhr, but instead he became the leading theologian of the Cold War. Unlike many Cold War thinkers Niebuhr knew Marxist thought and had some sympathy for the socialist desire for a more just society. In his critique of what he saw as the mistaken utopianism and pacifism of Social Gospel, however, he came to support all out war against the Nazis in the Second World War and then transferred this same hostility to the Soviets, even supporting the use of the atom bomb as an American instrument of war.

Niebuhr's anti-communism was based on his theological analysis of the limits of human capacity to create just conditions on earth within the finite conditions of history. Human sinfulness and finitude ever prevent the full realization of just, redeemed societies in history. For Niebuhr, the evils of communism spring directly from its utopianism. In its efforts to claim that they are bringing about the classless society, the Communists in power must repress dissent and assert absolute control in order to deny the ambiguity of their actual achievements. Hence, they become demonically totalitarian.

Niebuhr recognized that American ideology also contains a strong messianic strain that claims to bring about redemptive conditions on earth. But for Niebuhr the American system contains a pragmatism, a checks and balances, that prevents absolute power claims from emerging. Thus, American messianism remains restrained, doing some good, but accepting its inability to create utopian conditions. In his critique of the two ideologies, Communist and American messianisms, in his 1954 *The Irony of American History*, Niebuhr takes a forgiving 'ironic' stance toward American tendencies to run to extremes, while the Communist version of messianism is condemned as totally demonic.[31] Thus, Niebuhr failed to sound a note of alarm and warning toward American claims to represent the forces of God and goodness, while condoning total hostility toward Communism, failing to imagine that there might be potential for more pragmatic, humane and pluralistic approaches in their ideology as well.

Decolonization and Counter-Revolution

At the end of the Second World War in 1945, European colonial empires still controlled almost a fourth of the land surface of the world. The British Empire alone covered a fifth of the land mass of the world and a fourth of the world's population. In addition to Metropolitan Britain and the Commonwealth (Canada, Australia, New Zealand, South Africa and Ireland) this included several islands in the Caribbean and British Honduras, much of Southern and East Africa (Northern and Southern Rhodesia, Bechuanaland, Tanzania, Somaliland, Kenya, Uganda and the Sudan, and parts of West Africa, Nigeria, Ghana, Gambia and Sierra-Leone. In the Eastern Mediterranean, Britain controlled Cyprus, Egypt, Palestine, the Transjordan, Iraq, Kuwait and the Gulf States; in South and South East Asia: India, Ceylon, Burma, Nepal, Malaya, Hong Kong and Singapore.

The French held the next largest empire which included most of West and Central equatorial Africa, and Madagascar; Morocco, Tunis, Algeria, Syria and Lebanon in the Mediterranean and Middle East; Indochina in South East Asia. The Dutch still clung to major colonies in a trading empire of the East and West Indies. This included the Dutch East Indies, Indonesia (Sumatra, Java and Borneo) and New Guinea, as well as a few islands in the Caribbean and Dutch Guyana. The Belgians had one colony, the very large territory of the Congo and the mandated territories of Ruanda-Urundi in Central Africa. The Portuguese lost its major American colony, Brazil, in 1822 (although ruled by a Portuguese dynasty until 1889). But it clung to several African territories (Cape Verde Islands, Sao Tome and Principle Islands, Guinea, Angola and

---

31. Reinhold Niebuhr, *The Irony of American History* (New York: Charles Scribner's Sons, 1954).

Mozambique, as well as Goa, Macao and a part of Timor in South Asia. The Spanish also had lost their American colonies in the nineteenth century to nationalist revolutions and to the Americans in the Spanish-American War, including the Philippines. In 1945, it held only some areas on the coast of North-West Africa (Spanish Guinea, Morocco and Sahara). Italy had come late to empire, having been unified as a nation only in 1871. Italy had acquired several African colonies in the thirties (Libya, Eritrea and Italian Somaliland) but as a defeated power in World War II it was slated to lose these areas to the allies who had captured them during the war.[32]

During the war France, Holland and Belgium had been occupied by Germany, and Britain had been heavily bombed. Thus, the ability of these metropolitan areas to hold on to their empires was greatly diminished. Both Portugal and Spain were under fascist dictators (Antonio Salazar and Francisco Franco) and had remained neutral during the war. The leaders of these six nations were not ready to let go of their empires in 1945, but would be gradually forced to do so over the next twenty years. National independence movements had begun in some colonized areas, such as India, already in the 20s and 30s, and these were renewed after the war, often by leaders of national liberation movements who envisioned some kind of social transformation that would distribute national resources more equitably.

After initial resistance and the jailing of independence leaders, the colonial powers came to recognize the inevitable and began a process of negotiating transfer of power to national leaders, typically seeking to install a leader that the colonial power could control and who would leave their economic holdings (land, mines, industries) largely intact. The struggle for independence often became more protracted and bloody where there was a sizable population of white settlers who clung to power and refused to hand it over to indigenous leaders and when the indigenous leaders sought deeper social and economic change, such as land reform, nationalization of mines and industry.

In 1960, the right of national independence of all colonized areas was officially recognized by the United Nations. This Declaration (14 December, 1960) stated that 'The subjection of people to alien

---

32. For a survey of the colonies of these six European empires in 1945, see Muriel E. Chamberlain, *European Decolonisation in the Twentieth Century* (New York: Longman, 1998), pp. 3–12.

subjugation, domination and exploitation constitutes a denial of fundamental human rights, is contrary to the Charter of the United Nations and is an impediment to the promotion of World peace and cooperation,' that 'all people have a right to self-determination,' and 'all armed action or repressive measures of all kinds directed against dependent people shall cease in order to enable them to exercise peacefully and freely their right to complete independence.' Immediate steps were to be taken to transfer the power of self-government to the people in all territories not yet granted independence, and no attempt to break up the national territory into separate areas is to be allowed. This Declaration was passed by 89 members of the United Nations, with most of the European colonial nations (Belgium, France, Portugal, Spain and Britain), as well as the United States, abstaining.[33]

U.S. American policies toward the emerging nations were to be a continual violation of the principles of this Declaration. Since detailed exploration of the national independence movements for each of these colonized areas goes beyond the limits of this study, I will mention three cases in Africa, Ghana, Kenya and the Belgium Congo. I will then turn to issues of American intervention in Latin America in the 50s to 70s, in South Asia (Indochina) from 1945–75, and then to a discussion of intervention in Central America during the Reagan years.

Ghana (the Gold Coast) was one of the first African colonies of Britain to gain independence.[34] Movements for independence had begun already in the 1920s, and Africans were gradually incorporated into government under the British. J.P. Danquah, a lawyer representing the business classes, was seen as the likely leader. He called nationalist leader, Kwame Nkrumah, then in London, to join the independence party. However, Nkrumah had a much more radical vision of African independence, calling for an anti-imperialist pan-African alliance to join with other new nations to form a non-aligned movement of nations in the Cold War. Jailed by the British from 1948–51 Nkrumah continued to exercise leadership from prison.

33. The nine nations that abstained from the Declaration also included Australia, the Dominican Republic (under the control of the United States) and the Union of South Africa. See Chamberlain, *European Decolonisation*, pp. 26–27.

34. For an outline of the stages of the Ghanaian independence movement, see Chamberlain, *European Decolonisation*, pp. 66–70.

Independence was gradually negotiated, and in 1956 Nkrumah's party won the majority vote for independence which was granted in 1957. In 1960, Ghana became a Republic with Nkrumah as President. Nkrumah declared himself a socialist and leader of a non-aligned movement, seeking aid from China and the USSR, as well as the West, but became increasingly dictatorial at home. In 1965, he published his book, *Neo-Colonialism: The Last Stage of Imperialism*,[35] detailing his vision for an Africa freed of Western neo-colonial control. The U.S. quickly protested and denied Ghana $35 million in aid. Four months later in February, 1966, Nkrumah was overthrown by an army coup backed and funded by the CIA.[36] Ghana thereafter has alternated between military governments tied to the west and brief efforts to restore civilian rule.

The struggle for Kenyan independence was exacerbated by the presence of a larger settler population (65,000 whites and 200,000 Asians in 1945).[37] White settlers organized already in 1911 seeking dominion status with a whites-only franchise. The Kikuyu, a major African people of the region, also organized and sought African rule. Jomo Kenyatta became its leader in the 1940s. From 1950–55 a guerrilla (Mau Mau) movement of Kikuyu killed some white settlers (and many more Africans) and this led to a panic among whites. Kikuyu were rounded up into detention camps and many were killed. Although not in charge of the Mau Mau, Kenyatta was jailed. In the 60s independence was negotiated, with Kenyatta winning the majority vote. He became Prime Minister of an independent Kenya in 1963 and President of a Republic in 1964. Kenya was ruled by Kenyatta and then by his successor Daniel Moi as a one party state until 1992 (Moi continued to rule until 2002). In the 1970s, Asians who had not taken out Kenyan citizenship were expelled. Kenya is ranked among the top most corrupt countries of the world.

The Belgian Congo is another African nation that has been plagued by civil war and corrupt, dictatorial government.[38] It was ruled as a personal fief of the Belgian King Leopold from the 1880s–1908,

35. Nkrumah, Kwane, *Neo-Colonialism: The Last Stage of Imperialism* (New York: International, 1966).

36. The CIA's role in the 1966 coup in Ghana was revealed by former CIA officer, John Stockwell, in his book, *In Search of Enemies* (New York: W.W. Norton, 1978). See also Blum, *Killing Hope*, pp. 198–200.

37. For an outline of the Kenyan struggle for independence to 1964 see Chamberlain, *Decolonisation*, pp. 78–84.

38. See Chamberlain, *Decolonisation*, pp. 194–96.

who extracted a vast fortune though slave labor. Then put under the jurisdiction of the Belgian Parliament, there was little effort to develop education or participation in government for Africans to provide a transition to independence. Agitation for independence developed in 1955–58. Belgium announced a plan for national independence in 1960 with little preparation, and power was transferred in June, 1960, with two national leaders, Joseph Kasavubu as President and Patrice Lumumba as Prime Minister. Civil war quickly broke out, with Moise Tshombe leading a movement for the succession of the rich Katanga province where most of the mining wealth was located.

The Belgians, who sought to control this wealth, supported the succession, as did the U.S. initially. A UN force was sent to replace the Belgian paratroopers. Lumumba came to be seen by the Europeans and U.S. as a dangerous nationalist ready to appeal for help from the USSR. The CIA formulated an elaborate scheme to assassinate him with a lethal virus. General Joseph Mobutu became the choice of the western powers to control the Congo and make its wealth accessible.[39] Lumumba was taken into custody by Mobutu in December, 1960 and handed over to Tshombe who promptly assassinated him. Between 1963–65 Tshombe gained control of the whole country, but in 1965 Mobutu led an army coup that overthrew Tshombe and took control. With the continual covert U.S. funding, Mobutu ruled until 1997, despite his corruption, dictatorial violence and repression of all dissent.[40]

Counter-revolution in Latin America

Although Latin America had become independent of Spain and Portugal in the nineteenth century, the U.S. had long regarded it as its exclusive 'backyard,' and reacted quickly and negatively to any effort at economic reform and independence from U.S. neocolonial control. One of the first to feel this repressive hand after World War II was Guatemala. From 1898, Guatemala had been ruled by oppressive dictators, Manuel Estrada Cabrera and then Jorge Ubico, representing the big landowners. The U.S.-owned United Fruit Company was virtually a state within the state. It owned vast

39. On the CIA role, see Stockwell, *In Search of Enemies*, pp. 105, 137, 236–37.
40. See the sections on the assassination of Lumumba and the CIA support to Mobutu in Blum, *Killing Hope*, pp. 156–63 and 257–263.

plantations linked to its own railroads, ports and power companies, gave starvation wages to its workers and paid little taxes. In 1944, a reform movement developed, modeled on the American New Deal (not Marxism). Ubico was overthrown and a democratic constitution brought the rights to unionize, votes for women, social security and expanded education.

Under the new constitution, reformers Juan José Arévalo (1945–51) and Jacobo Arbenz (1951–54) were elected. Arbenz initiated a land reform program, much needed in a country in which 2.2 per cent of the landowners owned 70per cent of the arable land, and peasants who labored on the plantations were virtual slave laborers kept in continual debt by the owners. Arbenz expropriated large tracts of uncultivated land and distributed it to 100,000 landless peasants. Much of this uncultivated land was owned by United Fruit, who demanded payment of $16 million. The government offered to pay $525,000, which was United Fruit's own declared valuation for tax purposes.[41] Arbenz supported unionization by industrial and farm workers. Some communists, representing the Guatemalan Labor Party, held a few seats in Congress. But communists by no means dominated Arbenz's coalition, nor were they in any way linked to the USSR, which ignored Guatemala.

Nevertheless, in Washington, at the urging of United Fruit, a major propaganda war was organized, labeling Guatemala as 'communist' and a tool of the Soviet Union. In 1952, Truman approved a CIA plan to topple Arbenz which was shelved by Secretary of State Acheson, but then revived by the Eisenhower Administration in 1953, with John Foster Dulles as Secretary of State (both he and his brother, Allan Dulles, head of the CIA, had ties to United Fruit). The Guatemalan and Latin American press were flooded with stories of the 'communist danger,' while plans were developed for an invasion led by army colonel Carlos Castillo Armas. A campaign of disinformation was accompanied by plants of arms from the Soviet Union, cutting off of foreign credit to Guatemala and continual bombing of ports, the international airport, military barracks, radio stations, schools and the national palace. U.S.-sponsored Nicaragua dictator, Somoza, provided the main base for the military and air attack. By late June, the Guatemalan army

41. Thomas P. McCann, *An American Company: The Tragedy of United Fruit* (New York: Crown Publishers, 1976), p. 49.

was convinced that they had no choice but to capitulate, to force Arbenz to resign and to accept Armas as national leader.[42]

Armas quickly initiated a purge of reform leaders. Thousands were rounded up, tortured and killed. A law was passed allowing the government to declare anyone a communist with no right of appeal. The agrarian reform law was cancelled and the land returned to United Fruit. Opposition newspapers were shut down. Three-fourths of Guatemalan voters were disenfranchised by barring illiterates from the polls. Political parties, labor unions and peasant organizations were outlawed. A reign of terror against any dissidents was inaugurated that would continue in renewed waves into the 1990s. The Guatemalan army became virtually a state within the state, with its own banks and schools, controlling the government and making and breaking presidents.[43] In the forty year civil war, some 200,000 were killed, mostly on the side of reformers and peasants, more than 450 villages were destroyed and 1.5 million were driven from the countryside into army controlled labor camps, refugee camps in Mexico or squatter areas on the edge of cities.

But the major confrontation between the U.S. and a revolutionary government in the Caribbean was yet to come. On New Year's Day, 1959, a guerrilla army led by Fidel Castro took over the Cuban government and the American-sponsored dictator, Fulgencio Batista, fled. Even before Castro had defined himself as a communist or sought aid from the USSR, the U.S. began making plans to overthrow the new revolutionary leader and his government and to restore the former status quo of American control. Bombing attacks on Cuban cane fields and sugar mills by planes based in the U.S. started as early as October, 1959. Plans were made under the Eisenhower Administration to invade Cuba, which were inherited by John F. Kennedy. In April, 1961 a CIA organized group of Cuban exiles landed at the Bay of Pigs in Cuba. The presumed uprising of the Cuban people failed to happen. Over 100 exiles died in the attack and some 1,200 others were taken prisoner.

The Kennedy Administration was acutely embarrassed by the fiasco, but responded by intensifying a vendetta of sabotage, trade

42. The best account of the coup is Stephen Schlesinger and Stephen Kinzer, *Bitter Fruit: The Untold Story of the American Coup in Guatemala* (New York: Doubleday, 1982).

43. For the ongoing repression in Guatemala, see Blum, *Killing Hope*, pp. 72–83, 147–48 and 229–39. Also Susanne Jonas, *The Battle For Guatemala* (Boulder: Westview Press, 1991); Thomas and Marjorie Melville, *Whose Heaven Whose Earth* (New York: Knopf, 1971) and Eduardo Galeano, *Guatemala, Occupied Country* (New York: Monthly Review Press, 1969).

and credit denial, economic trade embargo and dirty tricks against the Castro regime, seeking to prevent it from achieving economic success that might become a model for other Latin American countries.[44] This effort to isolate and undermine Cuba continues to this day. When Castro turned to the Soviet Union for aid and trade to alleviate the embargo, that only confirmed the U.S. view that Cuba was a beachhead for a Soviet 'take over' of Latin America.

The U.S. effort to destroy the Cuban revolution led to a major crisis with the Soviet Union in 1962. Soviet Premier, Nikita Khrushchev, agreed with Castro to install nuclear missiles on Cuba capable of reaching the U.S. Khrushchev's purpose was to deter any further U.S. invasions of Cuba, as well as to pressure the U.S. to dismantle nuclear missiles surrounding the USSR, such as in Turkey. He also thought the U.S. needed a taste of its own medicine, to feel what it was like to be surrounded by nuclear missiles aimed at one's heartland. The discovery of these missiles led to a major world crisis in which, for a few days, it appeared as if the U.S. and USSR were on the brink of nuclear war.

But Khrushchev backed down in the face of the American threat 'to require a full retaliatory response on the Soviet Union' in response to any nuclear missile launched from Cuba against any nation in the Western Hemisphere. He agreed to dismantle the missile sites, in return for an American promise not to invade Cuba (a promise which the U.S. never officially confirmed).[45] This crisis, in which the world stood on the brink of a major exchange of nuclear weapons between the U.S. and USSR, continued to reverberate for a generation, leading to renewed efforts to curb nuclear weapons. Mutually Assured Destruction (MAD) came to define the relationship of the two powers' nuclear weapons, each assured that the other would not actually use nuclear weapons for fear of a retaliation that would bring total destruction.

Kennedy launched the Alliance for Progress in March, 1961, intended to be a major aid program to convince Latin Americans that better economic development could occur under American-style capitalism than under communism. But subversion, including

44. For U.S. sponsored dirty tricks against Castro, seeking to injure or kill him and undermine the Cuba economy, see Warren Hinckle and William W. Turner, *The Fish is Red: The Story of the Secret War against Castro* (New York: Harper and Row, 1981).

45. See the account of the crisis in LaFeber, *America, Russia and the Cold War*, pp. 224–29.

armed invasion, continued to be the major U.S. policy for deterring reform or revolutionary movements in Latin America. Either with direct CIA planning or U.S. funding, Latin America fell under a series of military dictatorships that repressed any movements for change, while delivering their countries economic assets to U.S. exploitation. One of the most longstanding of these dictatorships was that of Alfredo Stroessner in Paraguay. Stroessner reigned for 35 years (1954–89) with continuous U.S. support, despite his torture and murder of thousands of political opponents. In Brazil, reform movements were growing under presidents Kubitscheck and Goulart (1954–64). The CIA organized a major campaign of anticommunist propaganda and destabilization of the economy, leading to a military coup in 1964. As in Guatemala, a reign of terror followed in which tens of thousands were arrested, tortured and killed, left publications were shut down, political parties banned (except two, officially representing the government), peasant and workers unions forbidden, and popular education (reflecting the method of Paulo Freire[46]) repressed. Brazil would emerge from this repression only twenty years later in 1985. Uruguay, Bolivia and Argentina also fell under repressive regimes during the sixties into the eighties, with CIA sponsorship and ongoing support.

A major example of a U.S. organized coup against an elected reformer president occurred in Chile in 1973. When Salvador Allende, a committed Marxist, came within 3 per cent of winning the Chilean presidency in 1958, the U.S. determined that the next election in 1964 should not be left to the free choice of the Chilean people. A campaign of pressure, funding of opposition groups and propaganda was launched, resulting in the election of Christian Democrat Eduardo Frei. Despite ongoing CIA activity against Allende and other leftist candidates from 1964–70, Allende's Socialist Party won the election in September, 1970. The U.S. then began an intensified campaign of subversion, undermining Allende's reform efforts and wooing anti-reform elements in the military and ruling classes.

Despite this campaign Allende's party increased its plurality in congress from 36 per cent to 44 per cent in elections in March, 1973. By September of that year plans for a direct military coup were

46. Paulo Freire was a Brazilian educator who pioneered methods of teaching literacy through consciousness raising. See his *Pedagogy of the Oppressed* (New York: Herder and Herder, 1970).

carried out. Allende died in a military assault on the presidential palace, and a junta, headed by Army Chief of Staff Augusto Pinochet, took power. A brutal campaign to destroy all reformist activity was instituted, banning political activity, and rounding up and killing reformers.[47] Only in 1993, were some democratic conditions reinstated. In 1998, Pinochet was arrested and detained in England on an extradition order from Spain charging him with causing the execution of Spanish citizens. Although the extradition order was denied and Pinochet returned to Chile, continuing charges against him have become a way in which Chileans seek to reckon with the dark night of repression that reigned in their country for twenty years.

U.S. Interventions in Southeast Asia

The biggest fiasco of U.S. Cold War interventions in the independence struggles of nations emerging from colonialism was in Indochina (Vietnam, Cambodia and Laos). France had taken over the area in the 1880s, but resistance to French rule began to develop already in the 1920s and 30s. In 1919, the Ho Chi Minh had written to the U.S. Secretary of State asking for help in achieving civil liberties and better living conditions in the French colonies. In 1930, Ho Chi Minh organized the Indochinese communist party and in 1941 founded the Vietminh to work for Vietnamese independence. In 1945–6, Ho Chi Minh appealed to President Truman to aid Vietnamese independence from the French. As in 1919, his appeal was ignored. Ho Chi Minh was an admirer of the Americans and modeled his own Vietnamese Declaration of Independence after the American one. The Japanese, who occupied Indochina during the war, transferred power to the Vietminh when they departed in August of 1945. But the British landed in Saigon in September and returned power to the French.

France was determined to hold on to control of the region, although willing to grant self-rule within the French Union. But Ho Chi Minh resisted and in 1950 declared that the Democratic Republic of Vietnam was the only legal government. His government was recognized by both the USSR and China. The United States quickly began funding the French effort to reconquer Vietnam and by 1953

47. On the Chilean coup see Blum, pp. 205–15. Also Gary MacEoin, *No Peaceful Way: Chile's Struggle for Dignity* (New York: Sheed and Ward, 1974).

was supplying most of the French arms. But the French nevertheless lost to the Vietminh in the disastrous battle of Dien Bien Phu (March, 1954). The U.S. offered to use atomic bombs to destroy the Vietminh and the countryside they occupied, but the French pointed out that their troops would die as well.[48]

In July, 1954 an agreement was reached in Geneva to cease hostilities throughout Indochina, and to divide Vietnam into North and South, pending a national election to be held in 1956, with preparatory negotiations through 1955 between the two regions. The U.S., however, refused to sign the agreement and was determined to continue the war to defeat the Vietminh. Eisenhower himself was well aware that if national elections had been held in 1956, Ho Chi Minh would have won by 80 per cent.[49] In 1955, the CIA rigged a coup in which Bao Dai, the heir to the Vietnamese throne who had been installed by the French, was overthrown and the pro-U.S. strong man, Ngo Dinh Diem, installed in power.

From 1954–63 U.S. covert support for Diem's regime expanded, with Diem consolidating an increasingly repressive and dictatorial rule. Local communists in South Vietnam (VietCong) expanded their organized resistance. In 1963, the Americans decided that Diem was useless to them and arranged his overthrow by his Generals who then murdered him and his powerful brother, Ngo Dinh Nhu. On 2nd August 1964 the Americans created a phony incident in the Gulf of Tonkin in which the American destroyer *Maddox* was attacked.[50] President Johnson used this incident to call for escalated funding for the war. North Vietnam was bombed and American troops began to land.

Although the U.S. leaders assumed that the Vietminh would quickly crumble once the full might of the American military was brought to bear,[51] massive bombing proved inept against determined guerrilla fighters on jungle trails. Between January to February, 1968, the Vietcong launched the Tet offensive of

48. See Bernard Fall, *Hell in a Very Small Place: The Siege of Dien Bien Phu* (Philadelphia: Lippincott, 1967), p. 307.

49. Dwight D. Eisenhower, *The White House Years: Mandate for Change, 1953–1956* (New York, Doubleday, 1963), p. 372.

50. See Joseph C. Goulden, *Truth is the First Casualty: The Gulf of Tonkin Affair – Illusion and Reality* (New York: Rand McNally, 1969).

51. On American confidence in its hegemonic military power in its move to war in Vietnam, see Gareth Porter, *Perils of Dominance: Imbalance of Power and the Road to Vietnam* (Berkeley, CA: University of California Press, 2005).

coordinated attacks on dozens of targets. Although it was defeated, it made evident how little the U.S. had succeeded in suppressing resistance within South Vietnam, despite the Phoenix Program which had rounded up, tortured and killed tens of thousands of suspected Vietcong (which continued until May, 1971). Protests against the war escalated within the U.S. By 1970 the American leaders were seeking a way out.

North Vietnam, however, was reluctant to accept negotiations that would leave the country divided and the South under U.S. control (as in Korea). The U.S. (to its embarrassment) finally had to appeal to the USSR and China to bring the North Vietnamese to the negotiating table. A peace agreement was concluded and the last U.S. combat troops left in 1973. In 1975, North Vietnam overran South Vietnam and unified the country under its power. The war had cost 1.3 million Vietnamese and 58,000 U.S. lives, destroyed vast areas of the Vietnamese countryside, leaving it littered with antipersonnel weapons and toxic herbicides that continue to cause injuries and high rates of cancer to the present day. When the U.S. left, they promised to provide $3.25 billion for reconstruction of the damage that had been done, but this aid is still not forthcoming. Instead, until 1994 the U.S. imposed an embargo on Vietnam to stifle its trade and development.[52]

The war spilled over Vietnam's western borders into Laos and Cambodia. Both areas had attempted to remain neutral, but soon found themselves war zones with both Vietnamese and U.S. encampments. In Cambodia the royal heir, Norodom Sihanouk, had negotiated the independence of the country from the French in 1955. In 1970, the U.S., frustrated by his insistence on neutrality, arranged for his overthrow and replacement by a U.S. controlled strongman, General Lon Nol. The U.S. conducted numerous bombing raids to destroy Vietnamese bases, which also destroyed much of the countryside. The U.S. was determined to prevent Vietnamese control. When they departed, they tacitly blessed the anti-Vietnamese Khmer Rouge guerrillas who took over in 1975. Under their leader Pol Pot, the Khmer Rouge conduced a genocidal war from 1975–9 killing 1–2 million Cambodians. The Vietnamese then intervened in 1979, ousting the Khmer Rouge for a pro-Hanoi government led by Heng Samrin.[53]

52. See Blum, *Killing Hope*, pp. 122–33.
53. See Blum, *Killing Hope*, pp. 133–40.

Laos also fell victim to the war. It was offered independence by the French in 1950 under the French Union, led by its traditional royal family, One member of the royal family, Prince Souphanouvong, in 1951 organized the Pathet Lao, an independent communist party. Although the Geneva Conference of 1954 divided Laos into a northern Pathet Lao area and a southern area under royal control, by 1957 the two areas had arranged a coalition government that sought to remain neutral. This was unacceptable to the U.S. which arranged its overthrow in 1959. Civil war ensued, with the Pathet Loa winning large areas of the countryside. The U.S. conducted continual bombing of Pathet Lao areas between 1965–73, virtually demolishing the infrastructure of the countryside, killing or wounding hundreds of thousands of people, mostly civilian peasants.[54]

A ceasefire was arranged in 1973 and fighting gradually ceased, with the Pathet Lao, led by its royal founder, Souphanouvong, taking over as President in 1975.[55] Thus, the American efforts to control the region and suppress nationalist communist movements for independence ended with the U.S.A's worse fears realized. All three areas in 1975 were under communist control, but only after a vast destruction of social infrastructures, poisoning of land, and carnage of human life. All this could have been avoided if the U.S. has accepted the Geneva Peace Settlement of 1954, which would have allowed nationalist and communist forces to work out their own governments, and to remain neutral in the Cold War, with alliances to both the west and to USSR and China.

The Second Cold War and Renewed Intervention in Central America

As mentioned earlier in this chapter, anticommunist rhetoric was renewed with the election of Ronald Reagan in November of 1980. Roll back of social programs, neo-liberal (what the U.S. would call 'conservative') economic policies and expanded military spending were all part of Reagan's second Cold War. In July, 1979 the Sandinista National Liberation Front, which had been struggling against the U.S. supported dictators, Luis and Anastasio Somoza, since 1965, swept to victory. Samoza fled with most of the national

54. On the U.S. bombing of Laos, see Fred Branfman, *Voices from the Plain of Jars: Life Under an Air War* (New York: Harper and Row, 1972).
55. On U.S. intervention in Laos, see Blum, *Killing Hope*, pp. 140–45.

treasury, leaving the country with $1.6 billion in debt. Records show 35,000 had died in the revolutionary struggle, mostly young people.

The Sandinistas defined their government as a mixed economy, a third remaining private, a third state-owned and a third to be allocated for peasant cooperatives. The huge Samoza estates, largely unused, were to be confiscated to carry out such land redistribution to the peasants. The FSLN intentionally allied with the European Socialist International (to which the British Labour Party, as well as other western European Socialist parties, belonged), not the Communist International. Openness to a plurality of parties, democracy and a reformed constitution to assure free elections were key elements of their platform. A literacy campaign involving thousands of university students, coordinated by Jesuit Fernando Cardenal, a member of the Sandinista government, brought popular education centers to the poorest areas of the country and reduced illiteracy dramatically in just 12 months. A parallel health campaign built popular health centers to bring free medical services to the poor. Labor, peasant and women's unions sought to expand the popular base of the revolution.

President Carter had cut Nicaraguan funding and sought to funnel aid to non-Sandinista forces, including the notorious National Guard[56]. When Reagan came to power in January, 1981 he became obsessed with destroying the Sandinista Revolution, insisting on seeing it as a 'communist' beachhead of Soviet control that would soon spread across Central America and even 'invade Texas', if not stopped. The Sandinistas were accused of 'exporting revolution' by sending arms to the guerrillas in El Salvador, although most of the evidence for these charges were fabrications that were hardly believed by the CIA themselves. By 1982, Reagan was providing major funding to the 'Contras' (counter-revolutionaries, at first made up of National Guardsmen who has fled to Honduras and were engaging in petty sabotage on the northern border of Nicaragua).

Providing them with vast funding, arms, and air support allowed the Contras to greatly expand their numbers and carry out much more intensive sabotage of Nicaraguan efforts to develop the impoverished country. Schools, health clinics, agricultural cooperatives and popular education centers were attacked and roads mined to blow up trucks bringing produce to market.

56. Blum, *Killing Hope*, pp. 290–91.

Nicaraguan ports were also mined and the fishing industry decimated. Cutting off aid and embargoing trade, the U.S. sought to strangle the Nicaraguan economy, preventing oil for fuel and spare parts for machinery from being imported. All the resources of the country were to be turned from social and economic development to self-defense. In 1980, more than half of the government budget was spent on health and education and only 18 per cent of it was spent on the military. By 1987, this had been reversed with the military consuming more than half of the budget and health and education less than 20 per cent.

Nicaragua's Latin American neighbors sought to negotiate a peace process that would end this U.S. intervention, first the Contadora group (Panama, Mexico, Colombia and Venezuela) and then President Oscar Arias of Costa Rica's 'Central American Peace Accord.' But the U.S. blocked all these efforts. The Nicaraguans also took their case of sabotage by the U.S. to the World Court, where they won and were awarded $17 billion in damages (which the U.S. refused to pay). When the U.S. Congress forbade funding for the Contras in the later 1980s, Reagan arranged for such funds to be sent through covert channels, under the notorious Oliver North.[57] The U.S. insisted that Nicaragua was a totalitarian state that prevented free elections, even though the Sandinistas were elected by a 2 to 1 vote in 1984 that was certified as both allowing multi-party candidates and being free and fair.[58]

In February, 1990 a second national election was scheduled to be held. The U.S. confected a coalition party, UNO, led by Violeta Chamorro, the widow of popular conservative party journalist, Pedro Joaquin Chamorro (assassinated by Samoza in 1977). Unlimited funding and propaganda materials were channeled to this opposition party, while President Bush pointedly made clear that the Contra War and the embargo would continue unless the Nicaraguan people voted the Sandinistas out of power. Exhausted by the war, the strangling of the economy and the carnage of young people in the fighting, Nicaraguans, particularly women, voted UNO. UNO, to the surprise of most Nicaraguans, won 60 per cent

57. See Lawrence Walsh, *Firewall: The Iran Contra Conspiracy and Cover-up* (New York: Norton, 1997); Also *Iran Contra: The Final Report* (New York: Times Books, 1994); Jonathan Marshall, Peter Dale Scott and Jane Hunter, *The Iran Contra Connection: Secret Teams and Covert Operations in The Reagan Era* (Boston: South End Press, 1987).
    58. Walsh, *Firewall*, p. 299.

of the vote, although the Sandinistas remained the largest party in the national assembly.

Contrary to U.S. myths of Sandinista totalitarianism, the FSLN bowed to the decision of the people and their own democratic constitution and allowed Violeta to take office. But since the FSLN remained the major party and soon began to negotiate coalition governments with other parties, the U.S. remained unsatisfied with its victory. It delivered little of the promised aid, and continues today to exercise pressure to undo the gains of the revolution and to funnel money to opposition parties, particularly to prevent Daniel Ortega from winning subsequent elections for President.[59] Nevertheless, in 2006 Ortega was again elected President of Nicaragua, although no longer with the revolutionary agenda of the 80s.

Struggle for reform turned into revolutionary civil war in the 1980s in El Salvador, not because of aid for the FMLN guerrillas coming from Nicaragua, but as an expression of long pent-up frustration with poverty and the blocking of all efforts to make change from the oppression exercised by the ruling families and their military henchmen. The frustration was summed up by reform President José Duarte in a *New York Times* interview in December, 1980: 'Fifty years of lies, fifty years of injustice, fifty years of frustration. This is the history of a people starving to death, living in misery. For fifty years the same people have had all the power, all the money, all the jobs, all the education, all the opportunities.'[60]

The fifty years to which Duarte referred recalled the efforts of labor leader Agustin Farabundo Marti to organize workers and peasants in the 1930s. When the unions called a General Strike in 1932 they were rounded up and 30,000 massacred. Marti was executed. Farabundo Marti became the icon of the liberation struggle in El Salvador, parallel to Sandino in Nicaragua. The guerrillas named themselves the Farabundo Marti Front for National Liberation (FMLN) in his memory. General Maximiliano Hernández Martinez ruled as dictator from 1932–44. After the Second World War new efforts at political reform were resisted. The coffee

59. In a January, 2005 visit to Nicaragua which included a visit with former Secretary of State, Miguel d'Escoto, the elaborate pressure brought to bear by the U.S. to prevent a threatened victory by Ortega was described to me.

60. Raymond Bonner, *Weakness and Deceit: U.S. Policy and El Salvador* (New York: Times Books, 1984), p. 24.

oligarchy (often called the 'fourteen families' for the richest and most powerful group[61]) institutionalized military rule and organized ORDEN, an arm of the military, to spy on leftists and assassinate their leaders.[62] U.S. aid began to flow to the El Salvador military in the 1950s, but it turned into a gush during the 1980s, when more than $6 billion is estimated to have come from the U.S. to prop up the oligarchy and its army.[63]

Some sectors of the Catholic Church, inspired by Medellin (the progressive statements of the Latin American Bishop's conference in 1968) and liberation theology, began to organize base communities and cooperatives to promote peasant leadership. The oligarchy responded by stepped up attacks on priests and church leaders. 'Be a patriot — kill a priest' was the slogan of one death squad, as well as leaflets dropped around El Salvador.[64] Rutilio Grande, a popular parish priest dedicated to the poor, was gunned down with his driver and a young boy on his way to take the sacraments to the sick on 12 March 1977. These murders radicalized the Bishop of San Salvador, Oscar Arnulfo Romero, who began to speak out insistently in his sermons and radio broadcasts against the repression. He called upon President Carter, 'Christian to Christian,' to stop the military aid. In his last sermon he addressed the El Salvador army with the words, 'I beseech you, I beg you, I order you, in the name of God, stop the repression.'[65] The next day an assassin, sent by Roberto d'Aubuisson (founder of the rightist ARENA party), stepped into the center aisle of the church where Romero was saying mass and fired a bullet into his heart. In December of that same year four North American church women were raped and massacred.

Under Reagan the U.S. went all out to prevent the victory of the guerrillas who the president insisted on seeing as another beachhead of communist 'infiltration,' not only from Nicaragua, but from Cuba and the Soviet Union, which, if not stopped, would soon take over not only South but North America as well.[66] With the latest high-

61. See Jenny Pearce, *Under the Eagle: U.S. Intervention in Central America and the Caribbean* (Boston: South End Press, 1982), p. 221.

62. See Clifford Kraus, *Inside Central America: Its People, Politics and History* (New York: Summit Books, 1991), p. 66.

63. See Blum, *Killing Hope*, p. 357.

64. Blum, *Killing Hope*, p. 354, also Kraus, *Inside Central America*, p. 70.

65. Oscar Arnulfo Romero, *Voice of the Voiceless: Four Pastoral Letters and Other Statements*, Introduction: Ignacio Martin-Baro and Jon Sobrino (Maryknoll, NY: Orbis, Books 1985).

tech military equipment and air power, the countryside was continually bombed, entire villages were rounded up and massacred, and survivors fled to refugee camps in Honduras. An estimated 75,000, mostly civilians, died during the twelve-year civil war.

Despite the carnage, the FMLN grew stronger. In November, 1989 they planned a major offensive which they hoped would wrest power from the oligarchy. Although they failed, the strength of the offensive made clear to American military advisors that all the U.S. money and stepped up repression was not ending the civil war. A shocking event of this period was the killing of six Jesuit priests who were intellectual leaders of progressive Catholicism. The leading theologian, Ignacio Ellacuría, had recently returned from Spain on an invitation from the junta to help negotiate peace with the FMLN. Instead, they were actually plotting his assassination. On 16 November 1989 members of the Atlacatl battalion broke into the Jesuit residence at the Central American University in San Salvador, dragged five of the Jesuits into their garden and blew their brains out at close range. Another Jesuit, their housekeeper and her daughter were shot in the rooms where they were sleeping. These murders horrified the world and led to an insistence on peace negotiations which even the U.S. had to heed.

But it wasn't until early 1992 that the war finally came to an official end, when a UN commission negotiated a cease-fire between the two sides. The FMLN were to lay down their arms and become a political party. A UN Truth Commission issued its report on the war in March, 1993 confirming that the main perpetrators of the massacres during the war were the government, not the FMLN, although they were charged with some crimes, including killing several mayors. The commission called for the dismissal of forty high ranking military personnel and a number of government officials charged with approving the violence.[67] Although 'peace' has officially come to El Salvador, poverty has been little changed. Moreover, the U.S. continues to fund the ARENA party as its chosen agents to deliver the resources of El Salvador to U.S. exploitation, including the passage of CAFTA (Central American Free Trade Agreement) While the FMLN has become a political party, the U.S. continues to apply its funding and political pressure to prevent it

66. *New York Times*, 7 March, 1981, p. 10, cited in Blum, *Killing Hope*, p. 352.
67. Blum, *Killing Hope*, pp. 365–66.

winning the top office in the national elections.[68] It has, however, won office in many local municipalities, which have been credited with being the best run cities in El Salvador.[69]

The End of the Cold War: An Opportunity Betrayed

As noted at the beginning of this chapter, in the mid-1980s Mikhail Gorbachev came to power in the USSR and initiated movements to open up and restructure Soviet society. He also made clear to the leaders of the Soviet satellite states that the USSR would no longer intervene militarily to prop up their power if they could not hold on to their power through popular acceptance. In a remarkably short period of time, this led to popular revolts of these states and the disintegration of the Soviet Union. The U.S. military and political establishment, to its surprise and consternation, lost its familiar bogeyman and with it the rationale for its huge military establishment designed to 'contain' the threat of communism. The rapid disappearance of the USSR has also thrown a question mark over the U.S. Cold War worldview. Was there not from the beginning of the 'Truman Doctrine' in the 1940s through to the Reagan years a continual exaggeration of both Soviet power and its aggressive intentions (and capacities)?

For many in the U.S. the end of the Cold War was a welcome opportunity to scale down the huge military budget of over $300 billion a year and turn some of this vast expenditure to the renewal of the infrastructures and social services of American society, which had been deeply de-funded in the 80s. Speaking hopefully of a 'peace dividend,' reformers hoped to rebuild bridges, roads, schools, and libraries, make new investments in environmental protection and restore spending for the alleviation of poverty and for health and education. But the American military had no intention of reducing their military budgets and soon began searching for new 'enemies'

---

68. See Blum's account of the U.S. tactics to prevent the FMLN from winning the March, 1994 election, *Killing Hope*, pp. 267–69. In January, 2005 during a trip to El Salvador, I was told of the intense propaganda used by the U.S. to prevent an FMLN national victory, including threats to withdraw aid, and a telephone campaign paid for by the U.S. through ARENA to get Salvadoreans in the U.S. to telephone their relatives and tell them that their remittances from the U.S. would be denied if they voted for the FMLN.

69. This is the result of a study reported to me in El Salvador in January, 2005.

to justify their vast expenditures. They insisted that they needed to be able to fight 'two wars at once' and defined the still dangerous states as Cuba, Iran, Iraq, North Korea and even Libya, despite the unconvincing global danger of any of these states. 'Star Wars,' Ronald Reagan's fantasy of a counter-missile system that could shoot down any entering missile, continued to be lavishly funded.

As Gorbachev lost power, he quickly faded from American consciousness, yet he himself continued to define a vision of an alternative world that might open up as the Cold War ended. It is worth considering his vision to assess how great was the opportunity that was betrayed at this crucial period. An essay published in English in 1995, *The Search for a New Beginning: Developing a New Civilization*,[70] expressed his hopes. In this essay Gorbachev criticized the Soviet system as a mistaken effort to impose 'artificially constructed utopian schemes' from above, which ended in creating a repressive society where people felt like a 'cog in a machine.' Yet he was also critical of American individualism and consumerism which lacks a social vision. The dichotomy of capitalism versus socialism needs to be transcended in a new synthesis in which the values of both systems are integrated in a new vision of both social justice and democracy.

Gorbachev sees a need for a renewal of world religions, as well as the world's humanist traditions, to envision and promote a more just and loving world, one which recognizes that personal, inner change must go hand in hand with social change. Unless people are converted from a competitive world view that sees their own advantage through the weakening of their neighbor to one that truly cares for others as much as for oneself, there can be little real change.

For Gorbachev, industrialization worldwide is on the brink of crisis because it has been built on a pattern of mutual antagonism between human groups and exploitation of the environment which is inherently destructive. The Cold War epitomized this antagonistic worldview in both economic and military terms, threatening the whole world with mutual destruction. The end of the Cold War signaled the shattering of this vicious circle, and opened up the hope for an alternative vision. He warned that it must not be seen

70. Produced and edited by the Gorbachev Foundation and published in English by Harper San Francisco. Mikhail Gorbachev, *The Search for a New Beginning: Developing a New Civilization* (San Francisco, CA: Harper San Francisco, 1995).

as a victory for one side (the U.S.) at the expense of the other side (the USSR), but as an opportunity to move from a win/lose to a win/win vision of the global relationships. The environmental crisis which knows no national boundaries should make clear the need to think in terms of the global welfare of all peoples in their interdependence with one another, not the victory of some through the destruction of others.

Gorbachev also saw new dangers arising with the end of the Cold War and the disintegration of the USSR. He recognized a growing nationalism and separatism which was taking the form of renewed antagonisms between ethnic communities. He also saw globally a growing gap of rich and poor that was leading to increasing anger by the have-nots against the haves. This was being expressed in mistaken outbursts of terrorism of those who saw themselves and their people as the losers in this world race for wealth. Such actions renew the cycle of violence and prevent the emergence of a global vision of mutual concern for all peoples. The new civilization he envisioned is one that would recognize the rich diversity of cultures, but also seek for the common values that could relate this diversity to cooperation and mutual help. The 'greening' of politics, which affirms the unity of humanity in the ecological system of the globe, must be the base for this new civilization of mutual respect. 'Honoring diversity and honoring the earth creates the basis for genuine unity' he concludes.[71]

Reading this hopeful little book ten years later underlines the gravity of the opportunity which was betrayed, especially by the U.S. military and political leaders, in the transition to a post-Cold War world. But it also points to the need to renew a version of this vision in the twenty-first century, if the human project is to survive on earth. The last chapter of this book will return to an effort to define that alternative vision. But meanwhile we must look at the disastrous course that would be pursued by the U.S., which saw the end of the Cold War, not as the end of a win/lose world, but rather as the final victory and vindication of the American system of capitalism, buttressed by its military, over all forms of socialism, which then opens up the vistas of ultimate hegemony of that U.S. system over the whole world.

71. Gorbachev, *The Search for a New Beginning*, p. 65.

Chapter Six

AMERICAN EMPIRE AND ITS DENOUEMENT: 1990–2007

For military and political leaders shaped by forty years of Cold War with its polarization of the world into the spheres of 'freedom' and 'tyranny,' the collapse of the Soviet Union was both unsettling and unwelcome, despite the rapidity with which they claimed an American 'victory' won through unrelenting economic and military pressure on the 'enemy.' In order to avert the 'threat' of a 'peace dividend,' with its demands for a scaling down of the American military in favor of rebuilding social services at home and responding to social needs abroad, new enemies needed to be found that could be defined as equally dangerous to that of the former USSR and hence demanding equivalent global American military and police power. In a revelatory moment, Chairman of the Joint Chief of Staffs Colin Powell quipped, 'I'm running out of demons. I'm running out of villains. I'm down to Castro and Kim Il Sung.'[1]

New Demands for Military Expansion

During the George H.W. Bush Administration in the early 1990s military planners were at work crafting a new rationale for U.S. military expansion post-Cold War. Early in 1992, Paul Wolfowitz, then undersecretary of Defense for Policy, circulated a draft of the current Defense Planning Guide which frankly acknowledged that America was now the sole superpower and should shape its defense planning to assure its permanent preeminence over the entire globe, not only defeating existing competitors for global power, but projecting such overwhelming power that any potential competitors

---

1. From an interview in the *Army Times*, 5 April 1991; see James Mann, *Rise of the Vulcans: The History of Bush's War Cabinet* (New York: Viking, 2004), p. 203.

would be convinced that 'they need not aspire to a greater role or pursue a more aggressive posture to protect their legitimate interests.' This preeminence included not only potential adversaries, such as China, but also 'advanced industrial nations' (such as Europe and Japan).[2] The draft, leaked to the press in March, 1992, aroused a furor.[3] Here for the first time American power is projected, not as deterrence of an adversary on behalf of the U.S. and its allies, but for imperial dominance over all other nations. Although the Bush Administration disowned the policy guide, writing it off as unofficial speculation, it was claimed by Richard Cheney, then Secretary of Defense, and a sanitized version of it appeared later in the year.[4]

During the presidency of William Clinton over the next eight years, there were some rhetorical gestures in the direction of downsizing the military budget, but very little real cuts. By 1996, Republican conservatives out of power and leaders of right wing think tanks, such as the Heritage Foundation and the American Enterprise Institute, became convinced that America was in danger of losing its global dominance through a declining military power. In 1997, they established the Project for the New American Century designed to counteract this decline, chaired by leading neo-conservative Irving Kristol. In their September 2000 Report: *Rebuilding America's Defenses*, they project a major transformation and expansion of the American military.[5]

The report calls for a realignment of American military power, from deterrence against a Soviet invasion of Western Europe to a Pax Americana whose military bases positioned throughout the world would maintain American preeminence in all regions of the globe. Four core 'missions' are defined: 1) defending the American homeland, 2) the ability to fight and win multiple, simultaneous major theatre wars, 3) perform 'constabulary' duties worldwide wherever there are threats to American interests and 4) radically upgrade American forces to take advantage of new technology,

2. See Andrew J. Bacevich, *American Empire: The Reality and Consequences of U.S. Diplomacy* (Cambridge, MA: Harvard University Press, 2002), pp. 43–45 on what he calls the 'Wolfowitz indiscretion.'

3. Patrick E. Tyler, 'U.S. Strategy Plan Calls for Insuring No Rivals Develop', *New York Times*, 8 March 1992, p. 11.

4. See Mann, *Rise of the Vulcans*, pp. 211–13.

5. Available online, Project for the New American Century.

including the militarization of space and cyberspace. Active duty strength should be expanded to 1.6 million and defense spending should continually expand to reach 3.5 to 3.8 per cent of GDP. The 1990s are said to have been a time of 'defense neglect.' The next president must greatly expand military spending and revolutionize weaponry to maintain America's position as 'the world's sole superpower and the final guarantee of security, democratic freedom and individual political rights.'[6] The authors of the report foresee a long struggle of several decades to carry out this revolutionizing and expansion of the American military, 'absent some catastrophic and catalyzing event — like a new Pearl Harbor.'[7]

On September 11, 2001 a 'new Pearl Harbor,'[8] occurred, ominously suggested in this report as the 'catalyzing event' that would hasten the needed American military transformation. Islamic terrorists, armed with box cutters, seized four American commercial airlines and crashed them into the World Trade Centre buildings in New York and the Pentagon, with the fourth, possibly headed for the White House or the Capitol, crashing in a field in Pennsylvania. A new Republican President had come to power by judicial fiat after the contested election in November 2000. George W. Bush installed in office all the leading neo-conservatives who had been pushing for an expanded U.S. military role for a decade. Dick Cheney, leading hawk and G.H.W. Bush's Secretary of Defense, became Vice President. Donald Rumsfeld, Secretary of Defense under President Ford, became again Secretary of Defense, with Paul Wolfowitz as Under-secretary of Defense. Colin Powell, former chair of the Joint Chiefs of Staff and popular war hero, was awarded the role of Secretary of State (while being carefully blocked from any power in the Pentagon)[9]. Bush's appointments were notable for its promoters of military power, while strikingly lacking in leaders with experience in diplomacy and international institutions.[10]

6. *Rebuilding America's Defenses*, September, 2000, p. 4.

7. *Rebuilding America's Defenses*, p. 51.

8. The use of this term by the PNAC document, as well as many unanswered questions about the lack of government response to warnings about a coming terrorist attack has suggested to some that 9/11 was, if not planned, at least 'facilitated' by the Bush Administration in order to achieve their goal of an expanded military: see especially David Griffin, *The New Pearl Harbor: Disturbing Questions about the Bush Administration and 9/11* (Northampton, MA: Olive Branch Press, 2004).

9. See chapter 8, 'Who runs the Pentagon?' in Mann, *Rise of the Vulcans*, pp. 261–76.

10. Mann, *Rise of the Vulcans*, p. 274.

Although George W. Bush had not distinguished himself as an advocate of expanded military power in eight months of his administration, disappointing the neo-conservative hawks with his maintenance of Clinton's military budget,[11] and showed little interest in terrorism, all that would change radically with 9/11. The advocates of American global preeminence through expanded military power, advocated by Wolfowitz and the Project for the New American Century, would seize control of government policy, and George W. Bush would become their primary spokesman.

On 17 September 2002 the Bush White House released the 'National Security Strategy of the United States of America,' to epitomize the new defense doctrine. The document declares the United States to be the preeminent nation that epitomizes the 'single sustainable model for national success, freedom, democracy and free enterprise.' Only nations who follow this model will be able to 'unleash the potential of their people and assure their future prosperity.' American values are universally applicable: 'right and true for every person, in every society — and the duty of protecting these values against their enemies is the common calling of freedom-loving people across the globe and across the ages.' These values are seen as threatened by terrorists who oppose all these values. Although intelligence, law enforcement and cutting off terrorist financing are seen as tools of fighting terrorists, the primary tool is presumed to be military power.

Central to the document is the new 'Bush Doctrine' of preemptive war. Terrorists are constantly portrayed as seeking 'weapons of mass destruction,' especially nuclear weapons, even though the primary terrorist acts of 9/11 were carried out by men armed only with box cutters. The document declares the intention of the United States to attack such terrorists 'before they [their threats] are fully formed;' i.e., to act preemptively with massive military assault against threats that may be impending, but not actually imminent. This 'doctrine' violates the basic principle that has underlain the United Nations and international law since their foundation; namely, that aggressive war can be carried out only in response to an actual attack or one that is clearly imminent.[12]

---

11. See Gary Dorrien, *Imperial Designs: Neoconservatism and the New Pax Americana* (New York: Routledge, 2004), p. 144. Also Mann, *Rise of the Vulcans*, pp. 291–93.
12. Dorrien, *Imperial Designs*, Mann, *Rise of the Vulcans*, p. 328.

Since such massive military technology has been shaped for wars between nation states, not for attacks on stateless terrorists, there is a basic disconnect between this declaration of readiness for preemptive war and the adversaries thus defined as America's new global enemies. This disconnect is glossed over by claiming that 'we make no distinction between terrorists and those who knowingly harbor or provide aid to them' (p. 5). This rejection of any 'distinction' allows the document to claim the right to attack nations or states, such as Afghanistan, defined as responsible for 'harboring' terrorists. This would be used to include Iraq, even no such proof of 'harboring' terrorists could be proved or confirmed. The hijacking of the 9/11 terrorist attack and its use of a doctrine of preemptive war within a worldview of promotion of U.S. global predominance on every level, military, political and economic, thus turns on this basic disconnect between fighting stateless terrorists, and making war on 'rogue states' seen as challenging U.S. world predominance, a disconnect that has never been seriously discussed in American public discourse since this 'doctrine' has been declared. Once such a doctrine has been enshrined, the 'hit list' of nations seen as potential 'threats' that can be 'preemptively' attacked is endless. Iran, Syria, North Korea, Lebanon and Libya appeared to be on most of the neo-cons' short list, after Iraq.[13]

War as a Tool of Foreign Policy

Although Bush II would adopt a 'doctrine' of preemptive war, during the previous two administrations of Bush I and Clinton the military was resorted to continually as a tool of foreign policy. During the 90s there were some two dozen military campaigns of various sorts, far more than during the forty years of the Cold War. The first major post-Cold War military campaign (where communism was no longer the rationale for war) took place in Panama on 20 December 1989, within weeks of the fall of the Berlin Wall. The target of this campaign was Manuel Noriega, who had been on the CIA and Defense Department's payroll for two decades, but in the late 1980s began to operate far too independently of U.S. control for their liking, turning the region into a hub of drug trafficking. After several efforts to remove Noriega by political

13. See Dorrien, *Imperial Designs*, p. 243.

means, including an attempted coup in October, the U.S. invaded with 26,000 troops and a display of high-tech weaponry. Within hours Noriega was deposed (although he eluded capture for some weeks). Twenty-three American soldiers, and several hundred Panamanians, including a large number of civilians, died[14].

The Panamanian invasion was the first major use of the American military since the end of Vietnam, and corresponded to the 'Weinberger-Powell doctrine' that had emerged as the 'lessons' of the military establishment from that conflict. These were: use the military as a last resort, and only when the goals are clear and limited, when there is major public support, a clear exit strategy, and when overwhelming force is used to secure the goals rapidly and with few American casualties.[15] These limits would not always please political leaders who wanted a far more open-ended use of the military.

The major war under the Bush I Administration, in 1991, was to turn back the invasion of Kuwait by Iraqi leader, Saddam Hussein. This also was a case of the U.S. cutting down a thuggish dictator who had long been on the U.S. payroll, but who began to aspire to being an independent power in the region. From the time of British colonization of the Middle East after World War I, British and then American foreign policy in the region had been shaped by the control of oil. A series of small states around the Persian Gulf (Kuwait, Bahrain, Qatar, Oman and the Arab Emirates) had been created by the British as bases for oil extraction and transportation. The concern of the British, and then the Americans, was to keep these regions as dependencies, even if granted nominal political independence.

In 1953, an independent nationalist, Mohammed Mossadegh, came to power in Iran and sought to nationalize Iranian oil. The British and Americans collaborated in ousting him, restoring the young Shah, Mohammed Reza Pahlavi, whose reign Mossadegh had interrupted.[16] From 1953 to 1979, support for the Shah, with his modernizing but repressive regime, would be the centerpiece of

14. The standard account of the Panama invasion is Thomas Donnelly, Margaret Roth and Caleb Baker, *Operation Just Cause: The Storming of Panama* (New York: Lexington Books, 1991).

15. Mann, *Rise of the Vulcans*, pp. 43–44, 119–20. Also Andrew J. Bacevich, *The New American Militarism: How Americans are Seduced by War* (New York: Oxford University Press, 2005), pp. 48–49.

16. See William Blum, *Killing Hope*, pp. 64–71.

U.S. control of the region. This policy would bear bitter fruit of anti-Americanism when the Shah was overthrown by a militant Islamic regime in 1979. Militant Islam in Iran signaled a new expression of independence of the Islamic world against Western colonialism, now led by the United States.

In 1963 in Iraq the CIA supported the anti-communist Ba'ath party to take power against a left-leaning regime led by General Abdel-Karim Kassem. A young Saddam Hussein with other Ba'ath activists gunned down Kassem and many others on a list the CIA provided. In 1968, the CIA fomented another revolt to eliminate rivals to the Ba'ath party. In 1979, Hussein became president and the U.S. began to see him as a counter-weight to the new militant Islamic regime in Iran. In 1980, Hussein invaded Iran to counter Iranian influence on Iraqi Shiites. When he began to lose, the U.S. intervened to arm and aid him, including giving him satellite intelligence on Iran's deployments.

Between 19–20 December 1983, President Reagan sent Donald Rumsfeld as his envoy to the Middle East to meet with the Iraqi Deputy Minister and Saddam Hussein to assure him of U.S. support.[17] Iraq continued to receive arms from the U.S. funneled through various covert channels until 1989, including bacterial cultures to make weapons-grade anthrax and equipment to repair rockets. In December, 2002 Iraq was required to submit to the UN Security Council an 11,800 page dossier on the history of its weapons program. Officials of the Bush Administration rushed to New York to take possession of it, excising some 8,000 pages from it to conceal the weapons the U.S. and other Western countries had sold to Iraq before 1991.[18]

Saddam Hussein soon began to look on himself as destined to become a regional power, an aspiration which aroused the concern of Israel. In 1990, Hussein revived Iraq's old territorial claims on Kuwait (which had been a province of Iraq before the British carved it into a separate state). After first consulting with the U.S. State Department representative in Baghdad, April Glaspie, who appeared to give him the green light, Hussein invaded Kuwait on

17. Mann, *Rise of the Vulcans*, pp. 123–25.

18. See Tony Paterson, 'Leaked Report says German and U.S. Firms Supplied Arms to Saddam,' *Independent*, 20 December 2002; also Chalmers Johnson, *The Sorrows of Empire: Militarism, Secrecy and the End of the Republic* (New York: Henry Holt Co., 2004), p. 224.

1st August 1990.[19] Once this invasion had taken place, U.S. rhetoric quickly shifted to portraying Hussein as a demonic figure, a veritable Hitler. Rebuffing all efforts of other Middle East nations and the UN to resolve the issue peacefully, Bush I assembled a 'coalition' force (out of 600,000, 573,000 were U.S.) to launch Operation Desert Storm to 'liberate' Kuwait (16 January–28th February 1991). The U.S. flew some 110,000 sorties, dropping 88,500 tons of bombs, including cluster bombs and depleted uranium devices. It largely destroyed the infrastructure of Iraq, water purification plants, food processing plants, electric power stations, hospitals, schools, telephone exchanges, bridges and roads. As Iraqis, including many civilians, fled back to Iraq, the U.S. military carpet-bombed them, killing thousands in what pilots called a 'turkey shoot'.[20]

But the war ended, not with ousting Saddam, but simply weakening him and his army. While giving the green light to Shiites and Kurds to rise up against him, Bush I then stood by while Hussein slaughtered them, fearing that Iraq would erupt into civil war without the central government that he represented. For the next ten years the U.S. and Britain would carry out a complex cat and mouse game with Hussein. Fencing him off with sanctions, they insisted that he must give proof of complete disarmament before the sanctions could be lifted.[21] Claiming that he was cheating on the sanctions and hiding weapons, they maintained continual bombing sorties to enforce 'no fly zones,' while at the same time using the international disarmament forces to spy on Hussein and undermine the success of the disarmament program. By claiming that Hussein had not fully disarmed, U.S. policy makers held out the option of another invasion to force a 'regime change.'[22] The Iraqi people were the victims of these maneuvers, with some 500 children estimated as dying each month from malnutrition and curable diseases.[23]

19. See 'April Glaspie Transcript,' in www.whatreallyhappened.com/articles.April
20. See 'April Glaspie Transcript,' p. 226.
21. See 'The Sanctions War,' www.geocities.com/iraqinfo/sanctions/sanctions and www.globalpolicy. org/security/sanctions.
22. On the double game played by the U.S. on disarmament, undermining its success, to maintain the option of regime change, see Scott Ritter, *Iraq Confidential: The Untold Story of the Intelligence Conspiracy to Undermine the UN and Overthrow Saddam Hussein* (New York: Nation Books, 2005).
23. For the effects of the sanctions on Iraqis, see the report of the International Committee of the Red Cross, *Iraq: A Decade of Sanctions* (14 December 1999), www.icrc.org

By 1997, leading neoconservatives, organized under the Project for the New American Century, began to openly call for the U.S. to intervene militarily to overthrow Hussein. On January 26, 1998, a group of 18 of them wrote a letter to President Clinton demanding that the U.S. give up the disarmament policy in favor of military intervention to overthrow Hussein. 'That now needs to become the aim of American foreign policy.' Among the signers of this letter were Elliot Abrams, John Bolton, Francis Fukayama, Robert Kagan, William Kristol, Richard Perle, Donald Rumsfeld, and Paul Wolfowitz, all leading neocons, many of whom would come to power under Bush II.[24]

While the Gulf War of 1991 would become the most fateful intervention with long-term consequences for American foreign policy, Bush I also initiated a military action in Somalia at the end of his term of office (December, 1992) that the next President would regret. The declared purpose of this intervention was to enable relief organizations to deliver food to the population. When William Clinton took office in January, 1993 25,000 U.S. soldiers were still in Somalia. Clinton expanded the mission, seeking to broker a solution to Somalia's long-standing civil war and rebuild civic institutions, handing over partial responsibility to UNISOM II, a UN peacekeeping force. This put the peacekeepers and U.S. forces in conflict with tribal leaders vying for control of the country.

As the U.S. forces were harassed by the populace, they became indiscriminate in using firepower on civilian crowds. Clinton added Special Forces' rangers in an effort to capture the rebel leader, Mohammed Farah Aidid. These efforts ended in disaster, with rebel militia shooting down U.S. helicopters. No fewer than 16 Americans died and 78 were wounded, with TV cameras broadcasting images of a mutilated GI being dragged through the streets. The Clinton Administration[25] quickly went into damage control, blaming the UN for the failure and terminating the U.S. presence. This incident became an example of what not to do with the U.S. military; i.e., trying to engage in 'nation building' in a civil war where U.S. high-tech weaponry would have little relevance. The failed intervention

---

24. The letter appears on the cover of Gary Dorrien's *Imperial Designs: Neoconservatism and the Pax Americana* (New York: Routledge, 2004).

25. On the failed intervention and the US military response, see Bacevich, *American Empire*, pp. 143–48.

violated all the carefully honed caveats of the 'Weinberger-Powell doctrine'.

To avoid the mistake of another Somalia, President Clinton, during the remainder of his two term Administration, adopted a policy of using the military as an instrument of American foreign policy that avoided putting U.S. troops on the ground, employing high altitude precision bombing out of the range of local anti-aircraft capacity. This 'Clinton Doctrine' Andrew Bacevich refers to as an updated American version of 'gunboats and Gurkas.'[26] Whenever the U.S. wanted to 'send a message' to a deviant political leader, the response of choice became high altitude precision bombing. This was employed continually against Saddam Hussein throughout the 1990s, but also in response to terrorist bombs which devastated American Embassies in Kenya and Tanzania in August, 1998. Clinton's response was to bomb reputed terrorist training camps in Afghanistan and a pharmaceutical factory in Khartoum in the Sudan. Although no terrorists apparently were killed in Afghanistan — non-terrorist locals were — and it turned out that the factory made medicines vital for Sudan and not weapons, there seemed to be little disposition to criticize these 'gestures.'[27]

High altitude bombing was at times combined with 'gurkas;' that is, the training and employment of proxy armies recruited from the locals involved in particular conflicts. This strategy was employed by the U.S. in drug wars in Latin America, in the East Timor conflict and also in the chronic conflicts in Bosnia and Kosevo racked by ethnic wars. Here, Clinton used both gunboats and Gurkas, recruiting locals to fight on the ground, while flying longer or shorter campaigns of high altitude bombing. Since American casualties were minimal and civilian casualties on the ground were largely unreported (and even more rarely photographed for U.S. audiences), this appeared to be a 'clean' way to use military force, while seemingly avoiding getting Americans into 'wars.'

Neocon writers David Frum and Richard Perle would refer to this Clinton use of the military contemptuously as ineffective 'pinpricks,' although as always, for victims on the ground who were killed or maimed and whose buildings were destroyed, these were hardly 'pinpricks.' Frum and Perle themselves preferred a far more

26. Bacevich, *American Empire*, pp. 140–66.

27. See 'The El Shifa Tragedy', Scott Loughrey, 1999, *Media-criticism*; also 'U.S. Faces Court Action over Sudan Bombing', Tony Karon, 28 July 2000, www.Tune.com.

aggressive use of the military, of the sort that would emerge with neocon dominance of the Bush II White House,[28] as we shall see later in this chapter.

Economic Globalization and U.S. Empire

Despite his use of military force. Clinton put his primary faith for the pursuit of U.S. dominance in global economic policy. Although economic globalization as a tool of dominance would appear to have taken a backseat to military force under Bush II, these two (military and economic) have always gone and continue to go hand-in-hand in American imperial expansion. The Bush White House's September 2002 National Security Strategy document also included two chapters (6 and 7) on economic dominance: 'Ignite a New Era of Global Economic Growth through Free Markets and Free Trade' and 'Expand the Circle of Development by Opening Societies and Building the Infrastructures of Democracy'.

Chapter Six opens with the claim that 'a strong world economy enhances our national security by advancing prosperity and freedom in the rest of the world. Economic growth supported by free trade and free markets creates jobs and higher incomes. It allows people to lift their lives out of poverty...' The document continues, 'The lessons of history are clear: market economies, not command-and-control economies, are the best way to promote prosperity and reduce poverty.' Free trade is touted as a 'moral principle even before it became a pillar of economics.' The chapter outlines the following areas of action for U.S. security strategy: 1) Seizing the global initiative in the trade rules proposed by the World Trade Organization in areas of agriculture, manufacturing and services, 2) Press regional initiatives, such the Free Trade Area of the Americas, 3) Move ahead with bilateral free trade agreements with countries, such as Chile and Singapore, with Central America, Southern Africa, Morocco and Australia as principal focal points, and 4) enhance energy security. The chapter makes a small nod of recognition that intellectual property laws have prevented third world countries from getting affordable medicines for HIV/AIDs, tuberculosis and malaria, and should be made more 'flexible' in

28. See David Frum and Richard Perle, *An End to Evil: How to Win the War on Terror* (New York: Random House, 2003), pp. 18–19.

these cases. The connection between (First World) subsidies and dumping (cheap products in the Third World) and some concern for environment and stabilization of greenhouse gases are also acknowledged.

The seventh chapter opens by deploring world poverty in which half of the human race lives on less than $2 a day and calling for the United States to 'help unleash the productive potential of individuals in all nations.' The U.S. should seek to 'double the size of the world's poorest economies within a decade.' However, this assistance is restricted to those countries 'that have met the challenge of national reform;' i.e., countries that have abandoned socialist forms of economic development and accepted neoliberal market laws. This assistance includes efforts to 'improve the effectiveness of the World Bank and other development banks in raising living standards,' to 'open societies to commerce and investment,' and the promotion of agricultural development, including biotechnology. Ignored is the mounting evidence that these very policies have further impoverished the poor.

The World Bank and the International Monetary Fund were founded at the end of the Second World War to rebuild war-torn Europe and to create a global financial system that would avoid the economic rivalries that fueled the Depression in the 1930s. Since Europe, with the aid of the Marshall Plan, rebuilt itself without such assistance, the World Bank turned to development loans to the Third World. Many of these loans focused on large development projects, such as big dams, that did not facilitate integral economic development that helped the poorer classes. The mounting debts from such loans led to an international debt crisis in the early 1980s. The response to this debt crisis by the international banking system was the program of Structural Adjustment aimed at forcing countries (other than those of the developed world of the U.S. and European Union) to pay their debts at the expense of internal development.[29]

The formula for Structural Adjustment entailed the following: 1) devaluation of local currency, while adopting the dollar standard for international currency exchange, 2) a sharp rise in interest rates

29. Numerous studies have been done to describe these policies of the Bretton Woods institutions and their rise to global dominance in the 70s and 80s. See Bruce Rich, *Morgaging the Earth: The World Bank: Environmental Impoverishment and the Crisis of Development* (Boston: Beacon Press, 1994) and Susan George and Fabrizio Sabelli, *Faith and Credit: The World Bank's Secular Empire* (Boulder, Beacon Press, 1994).

on loans (the earlier loans having been negotiated with low interest rates), 3) removal of trade barriers that protected prices for local industries and agriculture, 4) privatization of public sector enterprises, such as transportation, energy, telephones and electricity, 5) deregulation of goods, services and labor; i.e., removal of minimum wage laws and state subsidies for basic foods, education, transportation and health services that aided the poor. Acceptance of this package of 'reforms' was mandatory in order to receive new loans to repay debts. Each country was directed to focus on a few traditional export commodities, such as coffee, tobacco or sugar, to earn money in international currency (dollars) to repay debts. This meant not seeking to diversify agricultural and industrial production for local consumption.

The World Bank and IMF claimed that these 'austerity' measures might cause temporary adversity, but through cutting back on what were pictured as 'bloated' national budgets for internal welfare, the whole economy would soon adjust and begin to grow, creating prosperity for all. The results were the opposite of these rosy predictions. By focusing on a few export products, the international market for these products was glutted. Prices fell, so that even though the country produced and exported more, they earned less on their exports. Local wages fell, prices rose. Devaluation of the currency made it worth much less. Government subsidies on basic foods, health, education and transportation were cut back or eliminated, meaning they became much more expensive, out of the reach of many of the poor. Gains in access to health and education were lost. There was a rise in poverty, malnutrition and unemployment. Crime increased as people turned to gangs and drugs for needed money.[30]

Pushing high interest loans to repay debts under the rules of Structural Adjustment created a spiraling debt trap. Both poverty and debts increased. Poor countries were able to pay only a portion of the interest on debts, with the rest added to the principal owed, so that even though countries continued to squeeze their resources to pay their debts, the debts mounted year by year. The result was a net extraction of wealth of billions of dollars from the poor countries to the wealthy developed world and international banks.

30. For the relation between structural adjustment rules, U.S. dominance and global poverty, see Walden Bello, *Dark Victory: The United States and Global Poverty* (Oakland, CA: Food First, 1994).

By dismantling trade protections, local production was devastated. Flooded by cheap products from multinational corporations, local industries went out of business and local farmers were forced off their land to become farm labor in agribusiness or cheap labor in multinational factories.

Intellectual property rules protected the patents of multinational corporations on new technology, not only in areas such as computers, but also agricultural biotechnology. Thus developing countries were barred from making clones of the technology of the developed world. Agricultural biotechnology was often based on traditional plants that had been grown for millennia, but once slightly modified and patented, local farmers were forbidden to grow them without paying fees to the agricultural multinationals. Instead of saving seeds from their own crops and recycling wastes as fertilizer, as had been traditionally the case, farmers now became dependent on agricultural multinationals to buy seeds year after year, as well as the fertilizers and pesticides to make them grow. [31]

Corporations were also buying up aquifers and forcing local people to pay for water they formerly used free from their own wells and streams.[32] These measures thus sought to destroy local economic independence and create a world system of dependency on multinational corporations. Trade investment rules sought to prevent governments from imposing local ownership or content rules, which would mandate that foreign firms that invest in a country have a certain percentage of local ownership and draw their materials locally. This allowed investment firms to invade a society and repatriate all profits without making any contribution to local development.

Advocates of this corporate system of 'free trade' and 'open markets' claimed to be creating an 'even playing field' where the same rules apply to all. But this claim was specious, since small

31. The devastating effects of Intellectual Property laws on third world agriculture has been a central theme of the writings of Vandana Shiva. See her *The Violence of the Green Revolution: Third World Agriculture, Ecology and Politics* (London: Zed Books, 1991), *Biopiracy: The Plunder of Nature and Knowledge* (Boston, MA: South End Press, 1997) and *Stolen Harvest: The Hijacking of the Global Food Supply* (Boston, MA: South End Press, 1997).

32. Multinational privatization of water is a major area of concern for various writers: see Maude Barlow and Tony Clarke, *Blue Gold: The Battle against the Corporate Theft of the World's Waters* (New York: New Press, 2002); also Vandana Shiva, *Water Wars: Privatization, Pollution and Profit* (Boston, MA: South End Press, 2002).

businesses and farmers were pitted against huge multinational corporations. Moreover, American and European agriculture remains highly subsidized, and trade barriers protect major first world industries, such as steel in the U.S. Thus, the multinationals are able to produce cheaply because they enjoy subsidies from their own governments which the 'developing' countries were not allowed to impose to protect their own development. Also questionable is the claim of neoconservatives that 'free trade' leads automatically to 'democracy,' a subject to which we will return later in this chapter.

The wealthy nations who now enjoy developed economies, not only the U.S. and Europe, but also the newly industrialized economies of Japan, Korea, Hong Kong and Singapore, all prospered through a cooperation of government and business in which local industry and agriculture was highly protected from outside rivalry. Technological innovations in areas such as computers advanced rapidly by cloning versions of the technology developed elsewhere, when no laws prevented such imitations.[33] The new trade, patent and investment laws being imposed by the World Trade Organization in the 1990s were kicking the ladder away from the developing world, preventing them from climbing toward modernization of their economies in the same way the developed world had done, maintaining these countries as places of cheap labor and resources for the developed world. In effect, neoliberal trade laws are a new form of first world colonization over the rest of the world.[34]

For most of the 1990s these world trade laws which buttress the take over of the world economy by western based corporations seemed to be accepted by third world countries without much protest. The fact that such trade rules favored local elites, even while impoverishing the majority, and were the established wisdom of the dominant economists who represented what came to be known as the 'Washington consensus' was intimidating enough. But also the World Bank could deny loans to any country that defied

33. The route to development of the Asian 'Tigers' through protective legislation and the crisis caused by the Western efforts to dismantle these protections has been a major theme in the writings of Walden Bello. See his *Dragons in Distress: Asia's Miracle Economies in Crisis* [with Stephanie Rosenfeld] (San Francisco, CA: Institute for Food and Development Policy, 1992).

34. A good summary of this criticism is found in Johnson, *Sorrows of Empire*, pp. 255–82.

its rules, making it a world economic pariah. Few countries wished to risk this 'punishment.'

In November, 1999 this seeming passivity changed. At the global meeting of the World Trade Organization in Seattle organized protest erupted that united labor representatives, peasant and farmer movements, environmentalists, alternative health, education and communication networks from around the world. The protests succeeded in shutting down the meeting without having negotiated any new agreements. These street protests would continue for the next two years, following the WTO meetings around the world.[35] Despite the efforts of the established media and political leaders to portray the protestors as violent anti-global nihilists, a worldwide justice movement had been born that would pursue alternatives to the dominant neoliberal economic model in annual meetings of the World Social Forum in Porto Alegre, Brazil and other forums.[36] New alliances of third world nations sprang up and began to organize within the meetings of the WTO itself. First world leaders no longer found it so easy to overwhelm delegates of the third world on issues of investment, services and agriculture.

One response of U.S. corporate and political leaders to this new resistance within the WTO was to bypass it with direct free trade agreements regionally. This had already been done in 1993 in the North American Free Trade Agreement that brought together the U.S. with Canada and Mexico. Despite rosy promises that Mexico would prosper and rapidly achieve 'first world' development, the results were a devastation for Mexican farmers many of whom lost their ability to survive on the land and became cheap labor in the *maquilas*.[37] But even employment in these 'free trade' factories built on the Mexican borders began to fail, as multinationals moved their factories to even cheaper labor in areas such as China.

The Central American Free Trade Agreement became the next effort of the U.S. to extend this pattern of economic colonization to the six Central American nations. Here the U.S. intentionally negotiated separate agreements with each Central American nation

35. See the account of these protests in Rosemary R. Ruether, *Integrating Ecofeminism, Globalization and World Religions* (Lanham, MD: Rowman and Littlefield, 2005), pp. 135–39.

36. Ruether, *Integrating Ecofeminism*, pp. 139–41.

37. See 'The Ten-year Track Record of the NAFTA-US, Mexican and Canadian Farmers and Agriculture,' Public Citizen-Global Trade Watch, NAFTA at Ten series: www.citizen.org/documents/NAFTA-10-ag.

to set them in conflict with each other and prevent the region working together to negotiate terms. Strong resistance developed at the grassroots in several Central American countries, but this was largely overwhelmed by the ability of elites, allied with the U.S., to deliver the vote on the agreement.[38] The U.S. also sought to extend this free trade zone to all of Latin American, through the Free Trade Area of the Americas, again using the divide and conquer method.[39] In Brazil, Venezuela, Bolivia and Chile grassroots organizing began to bear fruit in the election of regimes no longer willing to be subservient to American interests. Even as the U.S. sought to establish its control in the Middle East, Central and South Asia, its grip on its first region of imperial control, Latin America, appeared to be slipping.

Pentagon Capitalism and an Empire of Bases

The ideology of 'free trade' and 'free markets' assumed certain standards of economic efficiency in which those who could produce with the lowest costs got the jobs. But as American militarism spread its network of control around the world, it exhibited forms of 'crony capitalism,' and 'state capitalism' which were shocking expressions of rampant exploitation and waste. This had been the case for several decades. Already in the 1970s Seymour Melman's studies on 'Pentagon capitalism' showed how a system run on government funding tended toward maximizing costs (gold-plating), systemic inefficiency and waste.[40] But this pattern seemed to become rampant under the Bush II Administration.

Government contracts both for 'rebuilding Iraq' and for military support services are typically farmed out to a favorite list of companies without competitive bidding. In the Bush II Administration this was particularly Halliburton and its subsidiaries, such as Kellogg Brown and Root. Halliburton is the company for which Vice President Richard Cheney served as CEO and still retains large economic interests, including stock options worth millions. As Pratap Chatterjee, points out in his, *Iraq, Inc: A Profitable*

---

38. See CAFTA, Public Citizen-Global Trade Watch, www.citizen.org/trade/cafta.

39. On the Free Trade Area of the Americas, see FTAA-Public Citizen, Global Trade Watch, www.citizen.org/trade/FTAA.

40. Seymour Melman, *Pentagon Capitalism: The Political Economy of War* (New York: McGraw-Hill, 1970).

Occupation, this 'company practically designed the modern system of outsourcing the American military with the help of one man: Dick Cheney.'[41]

In 2003, Halliburton earned $3.9 billion from contracts with the military. Halliburton has established a pattern of high costs, spending far more for materials that could have been obtained much more cheaply from local sources, and sometimes charging for services that were not delivered. In February, 2004 the *Wall Street Journal* reported that in July, 2003 Halliburton billed the government for 42,042 meals a day but served only 14,053 meals daily. In the first seven months of 2003 Halliburton overcharged as much as $16 million for meals served to U.S. troops, according to military auditors.[42]

Halliburton and other companies, far from providing employment for the 70 per cent unemployed Iraqis after the American conquest, have established a pattern of avoiding giving jobs to Iraqis, preferring to bring in more expensive labor from areas such as India, and from the United States. Even for sweatshop labor, in which local Iraqis are paid $100 a month, Halliburton prefers to bring in Indians who are paid $300 a month and Texans who receive $8,000 a month.[43] As Chatterjee points out, 'Ultimately the company doesn't care how much it spends, because under its contracts, the military pays Halliburton for costs plus a small margin of profit of one per cent. In addition to its direct costs Halliburton can bill as cost a percentage of its overhead, all the way up to its Houston head office. …Thus the more money the company spends the more profit it can make, making a mockery of the private sector's highly touted efficiency.'[44]

The favored company for reconstruction projects in Iraq is Bechtel, also a company with close and long standing ties to the government. Former Secretary of State (under Reagan) George Shultz served as its President. Since its founding in 1898 Bechtel has worked on 20,000 projects in 140 nations on all seven continents. Its earnings were $16.3 billion in 2003. Even before President Bush declared the end to major conflict in April 2003, Bechtel received the contract from

---

41. Pratap Chatterjee, *Iraq, Inc: A Profitable Occupation* (New York: Seven Stories Press, 2004), p. 39.
42. Chatterjee, *Iraq, Inc*, p. 23.
43. Chatterjee, *Iraq, Inc*, p. 28.
44. Chatterjee, *Iraq, Inc*, p. 29.

USAID to repair sewage, water and school systems in Iraq. [45] Bechtel has an infamous record in many parts of the word of cost overruns, exploitative practices and lack of accountability.[46] Despite lucrative contracts, repair of sewage, electricity and water systems have moved with sickening slowness, leaving most Iraqis still without these services in 2006.

Bechtel insists on long studies and high standards while local Iraqis fume that they could have fixed these systems quickly if given the chance. 'Iraqis pointed out that the previous regime (of Saddam Hussein) got things up and running again after the First Gulf War in a matter of months, despite the fact that the damage was much more extensive because the United States and Britain strategically bombed the power infrastructure.'[47] Iraqis also see the American occupation as engaging in systematic privatization of former state enterprises, creating a take-over by foreign corporations and banks, saddling any future government of Iraq with huge debts for years to come. Two months after the establishment the Trade Bank of Iraq, under a consortium of foreign banks led by J.P. Morgan, the occupation authorities enacted Order 39 opening up all of Iraq's resources to foreign ownership except oil. New rules allowed foreign financial corporations to own 100 per cent of banks in Iraq. This means that locally owned banks are de facto excluded from forging the new economy. In the words of Rania Masri, Co-director of the Campaign to Stop War Profiteers, 'Are these the kind of laws that help Iraq rebuild for Iraqis or are these the kind of laws that open Iraq up for corporations to come and profit off Iraq's resources....It reeks of colonialism. It does not represent rebuilding.'[48]

In addition to such sweetheart contracts to American corporations (Russian, German and French corporations who actually built much of Iraq's infrastructure and had compatible parts were forbidden by the U.S. to bid for contracts since they had not supported the war), much of the security, police training and support services for the American military are contracted out to mercenaries, rather than supplied by soldiers themselves. Companies such as Dyncorp,

45. Chatterjee, *Iraq, Inc*, p. 63.

46. A infamous example is its take over of the water system in Bolivia, which was eventually taken back by a grassroots movement of Bolivians. Chatterjee, *Iraq, Inc*, p. 65.

47. Chatterjee, *Iraq, Inc*, p. 73.

48. Chatterjee, *Iraq, Inc*, p. 95.

founded in 1946 by returning U.S. pilots seeking to continue to use their skills, provides many such services for the U.S. government. 'Dyncorp employees make up the core of the police force in Bosnia; Dyncorp troops protect Afghan President Hamid Karzai and Dyncorp planes and pilots fly defoliations missions over co-ca crops in Colombia. Dyncorp is in charge of the border posts between the United States and Mexico. The company oversees many of the Pentagon's weapons-testing ranges, staffs the entire Air Force One fleet of presidential planes and helicopters and reviews security clearances applications of military and civilian personnel for the navy.'[49]

Such mercenaries can expect far higher salaries than the locals. While a Kurdish security guard protecting oil field receives $110 a month, their supervisors average $5,000 a month. Dyncorp and other such companies, such as Titan and CACI, have an evil reputation of sex trafficking, drunkenness and violence to locals. Both CACI and Titan were implicated in the shocking tortures that were revealed to have taken place at the Abu Ghraib prison. Twenty-nine contract interrogators at Abu Ghraib were CACI employees and were notorious for encouraging abusive treatment of prisoners.[50] Many had served in the police or prisons, including the military prison in Guantánamo Bay, before coming to Iraq.

The American military system that has been built over a hundred years of military-economic expansionism is described by Chalmers Johnson as an 'empire of bases.' Since the completion of the occupation of the continental U.S. 'from sea to sea' through purchases, Indian genocide and the Mexican American war, every subsequent expansion of American military-economic power has left a legacy of permanent military enclaves or bases, except in those cases where the American military was defeated and their presence ousted, as in Vietnam. From Guantánamo in Cuba, and bases in Puerto Rico and the Philippines, a legacy of the Spanish-American War in 1898, to Germany, Italy, England and Japan after the Second World War, to Korea with the Korean War, Saudi Arabia and the Persian Gulf, especially after the first Gulf War, to bases in Afghanistan, Kyrgyzstan and other Central Asian Republics into which the U.S. has moved with the war in Afghanistan (previously having been seen as USSR turf), and now Iraq, each expansion of

49. Chatterjee, *Iraq, Inc*, p. 110.
50. Chatterjee, *Iraq, Inc*, pp. 148–54.

American power adds to the empire of bases. Since the invasion of Iraq in 2003, where previously there were no American bases, 109 U.S. military bases have been established, four of them very large and apparently permanent.

This empire of bases gives the lie to the American claim that it is not an empire because it does not create 'colonies.' Rather it should be seen as building an empire, like the British Empire, 'on which the sun never sets' through military bases in as many strategic locations as possible throughout all parts of the world. From these bases it 'projects force' in the region, using military pressure to back up American neocolonial economic penetration of the surrounding countries. Johnson (before 2003) counted some 725 such bases in 38 countries of various sizes, 17 very large, 18 middle-sized and 690 small. These are only the bases officially acknowledged, since others are secret or disguised. Johnson sees five post-Cold War 'missions' now being served by these bases. These are: 1) maintaining absolute military preponderance over the rest of the world; 2) spying or eavesdropping on military and civilian communications of friends and enemies alike; 3) controlling as many sources of petroleum as possible; 4) providing work and income for the military-industrial complex (Halliburton, Bechtel, etc) and 5) providing members of the military and their families with a comfortable life.[51]

Using a legal fiction created in the nineteenth century as Europeans and Americans sought to establish enclaves of control in China, all these bases enjoy extraterritorial status, meaning that any crimes committed by their personnel are handled by American courts. The U.S. typically negotiates a 'status of forces agreement' with the presumably 'independent' host country that assures that its people will not be tried by local laws. Thus, the American empire of bases are something like 'micro colonies, in that they are completely beyond the jurisdiction of the occupied nation.'[52] Such bases are typically surrounded by bars and brothels to provide entertainment for the soldiers and thus are seen both as corrupting the local culture and its people and also being the spark for endless incidents; rapes, and drunken driving which cause injuries and deaths. Thus, in addition to their general role in neo-colonial control

51. Johnson, *Sorrows of Empire*, pp. 151–52, 154.
52. Johnson, *Sorrows*, p. 35.

of the region, they are the source of outrages which focus the anger of the country upon their presence. Nevertheless, once established, an American base proves very difficult for a local country to get rid of. For most Americans the existence of this empire is largely unknown.

The building of such bases and their servicing and security is outsourced to the corporations like Halliburton and Bechtel and security firms such as Dyncorp, so the same pattern of cost-overruns, exploitation and waste we have already discussed in relation to Iraq applies to this whole 'empire of bases.' Robert Higgs, senior fellow in political economy at the Independent Institute, characterizes this American military-industrial complex as 'a vast cesspool of mismanagement, waste and transgressions not only bordering on but often entering deeply into criminal conduct... The great arms firms have managed to slough off much of the normal risks of doing business in a genuine market, passing on many of their excessive costs to the taxpayer while realizing extraordinary rates of return.'[53]

Ideologies of Empire: Neoliberal, Neoconservative and Christian Fundamentalist

The rhetoric of American empire, starting with Ronald Reagan and renewed with George W. Bush, draws on three streams of ideological justification. These are: neo-liberal economic theory, neoconservative views of American role in the world and Christian fundamentalist visions of divine will in history. These three streams of ideological justification are both contradictory within themselves and with each other. This means that they are employed in public discourse in selective ways that mask these contradictions.

Neo-liberal Economic Theory

Neo-liberal economic theory is based on eighteenth-century English liberalism but is more narrowly materialistic and utilitarian. At least since the Cold War it has become the civil religion of the U.S. political and economic ruling class. Any critique of it or search for alternatives to it are seen as 'heresy' whose spokespersons lack 'scientific' seriousness. Economists who critique it, seeking social justice or

---

53. Quoted by Chalmers Johnson, *Sorrows*, p. 309.

ecological sustainability in their economic theories, may be denied employment, tenure or publishing opportunities in established journals.[54]

In neo-liberal anthropology humans are viewed as autonomous rational subjects who act solely to maximize their individual self-interest, qua economic possessions. This maximization of possessions is equated with well-being and happiness. The more one has the better off one is and the happier one will be. Earth's resources set no limits to endless growth and expansion of wealth. Humans are sovereign over the earth, so there is no need to factor in ecological destruction into the economic model. This drive to maximize individual self-interest is seen as self-regulating. Each person seeking to maximize their self-interest is met by others also seeking such maximization of self-interest, creating a system that automatically harmonizes these drives; i.e., the 'invisible hand.' Thus, there is no need for government to adjudicate the conflicts between such individuals. Indeed, government intervention is seen as distorting the mechanisms of such self-regulation and should be dismantled in order to create a 'free market.'[55]

Cynthia Moe-Lobeda analyzes this neo-liberal theory as based on several 'dogmas.'[56] First, economic growth benefits all humans. No account needs to be taken of the distribution of wealth. Thus, if the collective wealth is rising, everybody concerned is increasingly their well-being and happiness. One can ignore growing gaps between rich and poor, when growth takes place in a way that causes most of the increase in wealth to go to the top 10 per cent, mostly to the top 1 per cent, while the majority of people have grown poorer. Moreover, any economic activity is counted as growth, even oil spills or bombing, which demand expenditures to clean up or rebuild.

54. Information on the difficulties in publishing and tenure faced by economists who don't follow the dominant line was shared in a class in Spring, 2004 at the Graduate Theological Union by ecoeconomist, Robert Norgaard who teaches in the Energy and Resources Program at the University of California at Berkeley. See his article, 'Intergenerational Commons, Economics, Globalization and Unsustainable Development', *Advances in Human Ecology* 4 (1995), pp. 141–72.

55. This account of neoliberal ideology summarizes that found in my book, *Integrating Ecofeminism, Globalization and World Religions*, pp. 33–36.

56. Cynthia Moe-Lobeda, *Globalization and God: Healing a Broken World* (Minneapolis, MN: Fortress Press, 2002), pp. 63–65.

Second, free markets are equated with democracy and human freedom. Making choices in a free market cultivates a culture of freedom, what the 2002 National Security document calls, 'the habits of liberty.' Thus, one ignores the fact that the corporate economy in the world today does not consist of individual actors who are roughly equal in power to one another, but huge corporations pitted against small farmers, workers and businessmen. Since these corporations have come to control elections, what Americans call 'democracy,' both at home and the system they seek to install elsewhere, is basically a competition between plutocrats who represent the wealthy ruling class.

The third dogma is that this system is natural, normative and inevitable. It was what former British Prime Minister Margaret Thatcher defined as TINA, 'There is no alternative.' Market laws are seen as a kind of 'natural law,' the only way that economies can be organized to 'work' optimally. Any other ways of organizing economic relations, such as socialism or state regulated 'command economies,' must inevitably lead to inefficiency, waste and collapse. Socialism must inevitably die out because it defies this natural law of economic operation. In Francis Fukuyama's view, the collapse of socialism, leaving only American style free markets to rule the world, is the 'end of history,'[57] the final form of human society. Thus, neo-liberal economics, despite its secularity, contains an eschatology. It alone expresses the laws of human progress, leading to endless movement toward a better and happier world.

Neoconservative Imperatives

The neoconservative 'mind,' as described by one of its founding ideologues, Irving Kristol, is less a 'movement,' than certain habits of thought among those shaped during the Cold War in rejection of their former roots in Leftist movements of the 1930s. Gary Dorrien, a leading historian of neoconservativism, defines these habits of thought as militant anticommunism, capitalist economics, a minimal welfare state, rule by traditional elites, and a return to traditional values.[58] The end of the Cold War challenged many

57. Francis Fukuyama, *The End of History and the Last Man* (New York: Free Press, 1992).

58. Gary Dorrien, *The Neoconservative Mind: Politics, Culture and the War of Ideology* (Philadelphia: Temple University Press, 1993), p. 8.

neoconservatives whose worldview was shaped by the conflict with the USSR, with its good/evil polarization of the world. Many were reluctant to accept that the USSR was no longer an 'enemy' and indeed was about to unravel.

In the 1990s neoconservative ideologues, such as Paul Wolfowitz, began to pioneer a new vision of American world domination. We have already seen some keys to their worldview in the Project for the New American Century document (2000). Central to their thought is that America is now the sole superpower and should expand its defenses to be able to fight two wars at once, conduct 'constabulary' duties in all parts of the world and prevent any other country from even thinking of becoming a rival to the United States, particularly preventing any non-nuclear country from acquiring nuclear weapons. Neocons also believe that America is an exception in human history. Its empire is essentially benign, and thus its self-interests and the 'true' interests and well-being of all other nations and peoples coincide. All other people should be convinced that they had nothing to fear from accepting American hegemony.

For some neoconservatives, such as Wolfowitz, this thesis of the exceptional and benign nature of American global power is united with the belief that the United States should use its power to dismantle dictatorial regimes and 'impose democracy,' by force if necessary. The objection that democracy needs to grow from indigenous roots and cannot be 'imposed' by an occupying army did not deter neocons, since they believed that the U.S. had already shown that this could be done successfully; i.e., in Japan after World War II.[59] Not all neoconservatives were enthusiasts for an American mission to democratize the world. Some, such as Irving Kristol, believed in a more cynical approach, frankly seeking to serve American power interests without any moralistic veneer.[60] Others, such as Robert Kaplan, thought that many non-western people were not capable of, or 'ready' for democracy. The U.S. should impose an autocracy that would rule in its interests.[61]

As we have seen earlier in this book, American imperialism had not hesitated to overthrow democratically elected governments; i.e., in Chile in 1973, when the people elected leftist leaders the U.S. did not like. So why the enthusiasm for democracy as an agenda of

59. See Frum and Perle, *The End of Evil*, pp. 158–63.
60. Frum and Perle, *The End of Evil*, pp. 75–76.
61. Frum and Perle, *The End of Evil*, pp. 231–37.

American empire in the 1990s? Partly this arose with the unraveling of the USSR in which American-supported democratic nationalist movements in the former Soviet Union favored free markets and thus seemed to expand the circle of states accessible to American power.[62] This renewed the thesis that democracy naturally flows from capitalist free markets. Underlining the thesis is the assumption that free markets build a capitalist class who will control elections and determine who can be elected. For organizations such as the National Endowment for Democracy, elections should be understood as managed competition between elites that create a 'consensual domination' of the masses who are excluded from other choices.[63]

The Christian Right

The Christian Right represents traditional evangelical and fundamentalist Protestantism that had become marginalized by the liberal Protestant establishment in the 1930s to 60s and enclosed themselves in an apolitical opposition to the evolving secular American culture. In the 60s, evangelicals like Pat Robertson began to develop new media empires, such as the Christian Broadcasting Network. The politicization of Christian conservative evangelicals grew in the 70s with the anti-ERA (Equal Rights Amendment for women) campaign. It took a major new step in 1979 when televangelist Jerry Falwell joined with neoconservative organizers Richard Viguerie and Paul Weyrich to found the Moral Majority to elect Ronald Reagan. The union of the Christian Right with the Republican Party through the 1980s, renewed with the election of George W. Bush, has created a formidable block of voters for a combination of American imperial foreign policy together with conservative domestic values.

In earlier decades conservative American social values had included racism (white supremacy), hostility to labor and to welfare. In the 1970s overt racism became masked and hostility to labor and welfare subsumed under free market ideology. The Christian Right thus focused on three major areas of social conservatism, hostility to women's reproductive rights (with the focus on abortion), to

62. Mann, *Rise of the Vulcans*, pp. 129–37.

63. For the role of the NED, 'polyarchy' and elections as managed competition between elites, see Roger Burbach and Jim Tarbell, *Imperial Overstretch: George W. Bush and the Hubris of Empire* (New York: Zed Books, 2004), pp. 71–73.

gays and to secular public schools. Prayer in public schools (or Christian private schools or home schooling), criminalization of abortion (thus reversing the *Roe versus Wade* Supreme Court decision that legalized abortion) and prevention of legalized marriage for homosexuals, became the key social crusades for the Christian Right.[64] Neoconservatives shared much of the same conservative social agenda and so could make an easy marriage of convenience with the Christian Right.

The alliance of the Christian Right with the neocon project of American empire was more complex. Most of the Christian Right is premillennialist. That is, it believes that the world has entered the final period of tribulation in which things will get worse and worse, leading to the 'rapture' in which true believing Christian (evangelicals) will be caught up into the heavens, and Christ will return to conduct the war of Armageddon against the Satanic powers of the world.[65] In the Cold War these were seen as the Communist nations. In the 1990s these came to include the Islamic world and the European Economic Union. After the defeat of the Satanic forces, the dead will rise, there will be the last judgment, the evil will be sent to Hell and the true believers descend to reign on a renovated earth.

The Jews and the state of Israel play key roles in this apocalyptic scenario. The election of Israel by God remains permanent. All Jews must return to Israel to conquer all the land promised by God to the Jews and to rebuild the temple. When these tasks are completed, a predestined group of Jews will be converted to Christ and be protected during the battle of Armageddon, while the rest will die with unbelievers. Believing Jews will thus become part of the united elect people of God who will reign in the millennium to come.[66] This makes conservative evangelicals simultaneously militantly

---

64. See Ruether, *Christianity and the Making of the Modern Family*, (Boston: Beacon Press, 2000), pp. 163–80.

65. On the history of premillennialism, see Timothy P. Weber, *Living in the Shadow of the Second Coming: American Premillennialism, 1875–1925* (Oxford: Oxford University Press, 1979).

66. On Christian Zionism in American evangelicalism, see Rosemary and Herman Ruether, *The Wrath of Jonah: The Crisis of Religious Nationalism in the Israeli-Palestinian Conflict* (San Francisco: Harper and Row, 1989), pp. 86–91, 173–81. For Christian Zionist tracts, see Hal Lindsay, *The Late Great Planet Earth* (Grand Rapids, MI, Zondervan, 1970) and *The 1980s; Countdown to Armageddon* (New York: Bantam, 1981); Mike Evans, *Israel — America's Key to Survival* (Plainfield, NJ; Logos International, 1981).

Zionist and anti-Semitic, sharing the traditional Christian view that Jews (and other non-Christians) cannot be saved until converted to Christ. Since neoconservatives are generally strong Zionists as well, this was another area of alliance with the Christian Right (assuming one can ignore the final agenda of this vision — the conversion of an elect group of Jews and the annihilation of the rest).

But some neocons came to realize that some accommodation with the Palestinians in a mini-Palestinian 'state' would be necessary to prevent a worse evil; Palestinians becoming a majority in Israel. Christian fundamentalists, however, often take the most militant Zionist line of refusing to allow any land to be given to Palestinians. When hard line Likud leader Ariel Sharon acted to remove Jewish settlers from Gaza in 2005 and began to envision such a mini-Palestinian state cut off from Israel by a 'wall' that incorporated most of the Palestinian aquifers, Christian fundamentalists, such as Pat Robertson, deplored such accommodation. When Sharon suffered a massive stroke in January, 2006, Robertson did not hesitate to declare that God was 'punishing' him for giving Gaza to the Palestinians, an embarrassment to George W. Bush and most of the Christian Right who hastened to separate themselves from Robertson's views.[67]

A few groups in the Christian Right are postmillennialists; that is, they believe that Christians must build a millennial kingdom of God on earth that will culminate in the return of Christ. This was the position of the Social Gospel in the nineteenth century. Christian progressives generally adopt a liberal version of this view, linking social progress with the coming of a redemptive Kingdom of God on earth. Christian Right postmillennialists, such as 'dominion theology' and Reconstructionsts, however, marry social conservatism with a belief that Christians must build a better world to prepare for Christ's coming. They take a militant view that only Christians should rule in the U.S. and eventually in the whole world. Non-Christians (and liberal Christians) should be excluded from government. As Christians take over the reins of government, they should enact legislation that follows Old Testament Law (which they assume includes anti-feminist, anti-abortion and anti-gay laws).[68]

67. 'Evangelical Leaders Criticize Pat Robertson', *Los Angeles Times*, 7 January 2006. A8.

68. For Dominion Theology and Reconstructionism, see Bruce Barron. *Heaven on Earth: The Social and Political Agendas of Dominion Theology* (Grand Rapids, MI: Zondervan, 1992).

Although an extreme version of this view is repudiated by most of the Christian Right, a softer version persists in the view that Christians should rebuild a 'Christian America.' George W. Bush's efforts to portray himself as an evangelical Christian in the presidency was clearly a part of his electoral appeal for some of these conservative Christians (a view which he inadvertently undermined when he sent out a 'Happy Holidays' card, rather than a card celebrating the birth of Christ, as his official White House 25th December greeting for 2005). Such dominionist views would be totally unacceptable to neocons, many of whom are Jews, as well as to a multi-cultural America generally. Thus Bush II's hold on the Christian Right as key to his electoral success runs into several contradictions.

The rhetoric of George W. Bush blends elements of these three ideologies into a single package. The free market and individual choice are seen as the basis of the 'liberty' and 'prosperity' which the U.S. is spreading around the world. At the same time, the neocon agendas of American military preeminence and willingness to use preemptive force, including nuclear weapons, are adopted. These agendas of free trade and American imperial preeminence are clothed in religious language of the divinely elected role of America to redeem the world. The conflict between America and its enemies is defined as a struggle between good and evil, God and demonic powers, with Bush II himself being chosen by God for the presidency at this critical hour.[69] The final conquest of evil is the goal of this apocalyptic crusade, Thus, Bush's announcement of the 'war on terror' after 9/11 declared as his goal to 'rid the world of evil.' Echoing this language Richard Perle and David Frum titled their book on winning the war on terrorism as *The End of Evil.*

This apocalyptic messianic language was echoed in a speech by General William Boykin, the army leader charged with the hunt for Osama bin Ladin. In a speech to an American Christian audience, Boykin declared that America is the object of hatred by other nations because it is uniquely a 'Christian nation.' Boykin then claimed that 'our spiritual enemies can only be conquered when we confront them in the name of God' (i.e. they are Satan, God's enemies). He repudiated Islam as a true religion, saying Muslims worship an idol

---

69. For an insightful analysis of Bush's melding of the three ideologies, see Michael Northcott, *An Angel Directs the Storm: Apocalyptic Religion and American Empire* (London: Taurus, 2004), pp. 3–12, 140–41.

and not the true God. Boykin went on to say that God has put George W. Bush in the White House as uniquely chosen to carry out this divine mission to defeat the powers of evil. America's war against the Islamic world is thus a holy war against Satan. 'We are the army of God raised up for such a time as this.'[70]

After 9/11: Seizing the Moment

The terrorist attacks on the World Trade buildings and the Pentagon on September 11, 2001 were immediately seized upon by Donald Rumsfeld and Dick Cheney to convert George W. Bush into the front man for the neocon agenda who then happily became its iconic spokesman. As we have seen, leading neocons had sought a new military intervention to overthrow Saddam Hussein since 1997. The terrorist attack was immediately seen by them as the opportunity for this 'regime change' in Iraq, as well as an opening for 'regimes changes' in other 'axis of evil' states; i.e.. Iran, Syria, North Korea. This also facilitated massive expansion and technological renovation of the American military. There was a major obstacle to this rush to war with Iraq: there was no evidence of any connection between Saddam Hussein and the terrorists (most of whom were Saudis). Hussein's secular Ba'athist views were hostile to Islamic fundamentalists, whether of a Wahhabis or a Shiite persuasion, and he strictly kept them from gaining any foothold in Iraq. Rumsfeld repeatedly ordered the CIA to produce evidence of such a connection between Hussein and Al Queda, in vain.[71]

The Bush II government turned to an invasion of Afghanistan as the first military response to the attacks, since the Taliban allowance of Al Queda training camps in that country more credibly fulfilled Bush's criteria of a military response not only to the 'terrorists,' but also countries that 'harbored them.' The U.S. had, of course, funded and armed the Taliban and set the stage for the emergence of Al Queda in the 1980s when militant Islamists appeared a useful ally against the Soviet Union.[72] The U.S. hi-tech military assault

70. On Boykin's remarks see Brian Knowlton, *International Herald Tribune*, 22 October 2003.

71. See Dorrien, *Imperial Designs*, p. 183.

72. See Michael Northcott, *An Angel Directs the Storm*, pp. 31–35. Also Ahmed Rashid, *Taliban: Islam, Oil and Fundamentalism in Central Asia* (New Haven, CT: Yale, 2000).

quickly dislodged the Taliban from power, but at the expense of reinstalling the Afghan warlords, who the Taliban had defeated, back in power over most of the country. America's puppet government has so little control outside the capital city of Kabul, that USAID workers can only venture outside the city with a U.S. military escort.[73] Cocaine quickly returned to being Afghanistan's main export crop. Osma bin Laden continues to elude capture (as of February, 2007) and al Queda survives in the border area between Afghanistan and Pakistan, as well as continuing to recruit worldwide.

But regime change in Iraq remained the main agenda for the Bush II Administration. The only problem was building a credible case for the attack that would convince Americans, if not the international community. Lacking proof of a connection between Saddam Hussein and Al Queda, Dick Cheney simply took to asserting it repeatedly, which for most Americans was good enough.[74] But the main case for war was built by asserting that Hussein had amassed a huge arsenal of weapons of mass destruction (WMD), nuclear, biological and chemical. A major obstacle to this argument was the ten years of arms inspections carried out under the UN whose spokesmen insisted that such weapons had been effectively destroyed.[75] The Bush II Administration resorted to all sorts of covert, forged and dubious sources of information, such as the delusional Iraqi defector, 'Curveball,'[76] in order to make the case that Hussein posed an imminent danger, not only to his neighbors, but to the whole world; i.e., the United States, because of his WMD, which he not only had but was on the verge

73. USAID agent Keith Schultz spoke to the Pilgrim Place Community in November, 2005 on his recent visit to Afghanistan, revealing that he and other USAID workers could not go outside Kabul without an escort from the U.S. military.

74. Polls of the American public continually show that more than half believe that Hussein was linked with Al Queda and had weapons of mass destruction which he was about to use: On systematic deceit in the Bush II Administration, see John W. Dean, *Worse than Watergate: The Secret Presidency of George W. Bush* (New York: Little, Brown and Company, 2004), pp. 36–40.

75. See Scott Ritter, *Iraqi Confidential*, op. cit.

76. 'Curveball', is the code name of an Iraqi defector to Germany who claimed he had detailed information on Iraq's chemical weapons programs. The Bush Administration made copious use of this information, despite the German intelligence officials repeated warning that he was unreliable: See Bob Drogin and John Goetz, 'How the U.S. Fell under the Spell of "Curveball"', *The Los Angeles Times*, 20 November 2005, A1, A28–30.

of using.[77] Despite such hyped up rhetoric, the U.S. failed to make the case to the UN and thus had to accept going to war without its blessing, supported by faithful ally, Great Britain, plus handfuls of soldiers from several countries, dubiously dubbed the 'coalition of the willing.'

With the 'shock and awe' attack on Iraq begun on 19 March 2003, the U.S. Army quickly rushed to Baghdad with a minimum of American casualties, thus refuting the warnings of those who feared that Hussein would use his WMD to create an Armageddon in the Middle East. Confirming the reports of the weapons inspectors, no such weapons were found. The U.S. military clearly expected the invasion to be a relative 'push over.' This raises the suspicion that they actually knew Hussein had no such weapons or that they were sufficiently inaccessible and his army sufficiently weakened by ten years of sanctions, that they would have a relatively easy time.

Since the claim that Hussein had large and dangerous stores of WMD was the main argument of the Bush Administration for the war, giving up this argument because of the failure to find such weapons died hard. For some time Bush, Cheney and Rumsfeld kept insisting that they were there and would be found, or if he didn't have them, he was about to have them; i.e., he had 'programs' which were about to produce them. However, the Bush Administration soon turned to a new rationale that had not been in evidence during the build up for war, but post-invasion became its main justification to the American public; namely, that the United States intervened to remove a brutal tyrant and to install 'democracy.' This, as we have seen, had been a major argument of neocons, such as Wolfowitz, for American-imposed 'regime changes' around the world, but no international law condones invading a country because one regards its leader as a dictator, in order to impose 'democracy.' Such an argument cuts no ice with the international community, but its emotional appeal seems to have satisfied much of the American public, which needs to see America as an agent of 'good' in the world.

From April, 2003 into 2006, the United States expended enormous energy and treasure to create a new Iraqi constitution and to carry

---

77. The story of the hyped intelligence to make the case for war has been discussed in many recent accounts. For an excellent example, see Stephan Halper and Jonathan Clarke, *America Alone: The Neo-Conservatives and the Global Order* (Cambridge: Cambridge University Press, 2004), pp. 201–31.

out various public displays of 'free elections.' Many neocons thought this would be an easy matter, with Cheney and Rumsfeld, not to mention Wolfowitz and Perle, expecting to install their favorite Iraqi conman, Ahmed Chalabi, as puppet 'democratic' leader.[78] When it became apparent that he had no following, and was in fact despised by Iraqis, they turned to other acceptably secular and pro-American candidates, such as Iyad Alawi.

The American leaders failed to take seriously the obvious demographic fact that Iraq is 60 per cent Shi'ite, and is deeply divided between this Shi'ite majority, the 20 per cent Sunni groups that had ruled under Hussein and the Kurds in the North. The likely outcome of any election that even partly represents these three groups would be a Shi'ite dominated government, friendly to the Shi'ite Islamic regime in Iran. There was also the danger of a civil war between the three sections of the country, which had been pasted together in the 1920s to create Iraq, but never fully united.[79]

Four years after invading Iraq, the U.S. finds itself mired in a Sunni led insurgency that has taken the lives of 3080 American soldiers, wounded 23,114 (as of 28 January 2007) and killed at least 55,000 Iraqis (some would put the figure closer to 600,000). The destruction of property is vast. In 2005, the U.S. was spending $5.6 billion a month for operations.[80] Violence rules the streets daily with no end in sight. Basic services have not been restored for most Iraqis. A Shi'ite dominated government unacceptable to the Sunnis has been elected, although it is doubtful that it can create a united and stable government. Despite such a massive mess, the neocons are still talking of 'regime change' in other countries, particularly

78. In their 2003 book, *The End of Evil*, David Frum and Richard Perle, continue to deplore the U.S. failure to install Chalabi as the best candidate to rule Iraq; pp. 37–38. Chalabi has a long history of shady financial dealings. He was a major source of misinformation for the Pentagon's case for war against Iraq, claiming that Hussein had major weapons of mass destruction and that the US forces would be greeted as liberators. See 'How Ahmed Chalabi Conned the Neocons,' John Dizard, www.salon.com/news/feature/2004/05/04/Chalabi.

79. See Charles Tripp, *A History of Iraq* (Cambridge: Cambridge University Press, 2002), pp. 8–9, 45–52.

80. For costs and numbers of the killed and injured through August, 2005, see 'The Iraq Quagmire: The Mounting Costs of War and the Case for Bringing Home the Troops', Phyllis Bennis, Erik Leaver and the Institute of Policy Studies Iraq Task Force, Institute of Policy Studies, Washington, D.C., 31 August 2005: ips-dc.org/Iraq/quagmire.

Iran and the use of 'tactical' nuclear weapons against Iranian
weapons factories is being discussed.[81]

The Denouement of American Empire?

At the end of August, 2005 Hurricane Katrina swept over the levees
in New Orleans, flooding most of the city, destroying large areas
of its housing, particularly for its poor, black citizens. The
devastation wrought by Katrina made starkly obvious the delusion
under which the American government and its neocon leaders are
laboring in seeking to dominate the world. The aspiration to global
empire was revealed as a serious overstretch purchased at the
expense of impoverishing large sectors of the American people and
undermining the basic infrastructures of American life.

A lead editorial in the British journal, *The Economist*, summarized
the reaction of much of the world (although such criticism was less
likely to appear in the U.S. media): 'Even America's many enemies
around the world tend to accord it respect. It might be arrogant,
overbearing and insensitive, but, by God, it can get things done.
Since Hurricane Katrina, the world view of America has changed.
The disaster has exposed some of the shocking truths about the
place; the bitterness of its racial divide, the abandonment of the
dispossessed, the weakness of critical infrastructure. But the most
astonishing and most shaming revelation has been its government's
failure to bring succor to its people in their time of greatest need.'[82]

In reality, these shaming revelations have grown for decades,
indeed for centuries. This is the burden of this book. But the
contradictions between American global aspirations and ideology
of benignity and the actual harm it does to others and to its own
people have sharpened under the current administration, revealing
more starkly its violent underside. As we have already pointed out
in this chapter, the claims that extending the 'free market' to the
world would bring prosperity to all has been contradicted by the
growing divide of rich and poor worldwide.

This gap between rich and poor has steadily grown since the
mid-70s. In 1960, the richest 20 per cent of the world had thirty

81. See Seymour Hersh, 'Iran Plans,' *New Yorker*, 17 April 2006, pp. 30–37; also
Phyllis Bennis, 'Iran, the U.S. and Nukes in the Middle East', in *Z Magazine*, May, 2006,
pp. 6–8.

82. *The Economist*, 10 November 2005, p. 11.

times the wealth of the poorest 20 per cent. By 1995 this had grown to 82 times. Figures show 85 per cent of the wealth of the world is in the hands of 20 per cent of the world's population, much of this concentrated in the top 1 per cent. The remaining 80 per cent share the remaining 15 per cent, with the poorest 20 per cent living in misery and starvation. The richest 225 people in the world have a combined wealth of over $1 trillion, equal to the annual income of the poorest 50 per cent of humanity, over 2.5 billion people. The richest three people have assets that exceed that of 48 poorest nations. In terms of absolute levels of poverty, half of humanity live on less than $2 a day, and more than 20 per cent, 1.2 billion people, on less than $1 a day in 1999.[83]

The gap of rich and poor has also grown in the United States. Poverty rose sharply during the Reagan years, fell slightly during the Clinton years but under Bush II has steadily risen, reaching 37 million in 2004 or 12.7 per cent of American society. Since the poverty line itself is set at less than $19,157 for a family of four, the actual numbers of Americans in dire economic straits unable to meet basic needs for adequate housing, food, education and transportation is much higher.[84]

Ecological devastation is also growing worldwide, with some of its worst effects concentrated where poor people live. Dumping of toxic waste from rich countries and areas to poor countries and areas has itself become a 'growth industry.' Toxic wastes from industrial agriculture accumulates in soils and runs off into the rivers and oceans, threatening the fish population. Air pollution has become chronic in larger cities, especially in the Third World. The pouring of gases, such as carbon dioxide, from the burning of fossil fuels is also increasing the percentage of greenhouse gases in the atmosphere, creating rising global temperatures. In the twentieth century global temperature rose 1.4°F with a rise of as much as 9°F at the two poles. This rise will continue into the twenty-first century with perhaps as much as 5.4°F by mid-century.

The effects of such a rise of temperature is already having a dramatic impact on world climate. Global warming has increased ocean temperatures in the Gulf of Mexico by some 5°F, making these waters a 'veritable hurricane refueling station,' increasing the

83. On World Bank figures for poverty, see www.worldbank.org/poverty.
84. See Joe Feuerherd, 'War on Poverty', *National Catholic Reporter*, 12 August 2005, pp. 4–5.

force of hurricanes from category 1 or 2 to category 5; in other words, from hurricanes which blow shingles off roofs to hurricanes that blow entire buildings away.[85] Kerry Emanuel, professor of atmospheric science at MIT, estimates a 50–80 per cent increase in the strength of hurricanes over the last 50 years.[86] The Bush Administration has been notable for its stonewalling on the issue of global warming, withdrawing from the Kyoto agreement signed by most of the world's nations to reduce greenhouse gases, claiming that the scientific evidence is 'not in' to prove any connection between human activity and global warming. It is thus particularly poignant that the disasters caused by the hurricanes in August and September point to one of the most immediate effects of global warming on daily life in the U.S. itself. More disasters undoubtedly will follow, with melting ice caps causing sea levels to rise, flooding coastal areas and causing entire island nations to disappear. Many of the world's major cities, built along coastal areas will be grievously affected.

Bush II has not only stonewalled the issue of global warming. His administration in Washington, like his earlier rule as governor of Texas in the later 1990s, has been characterized by a continual undermining of environmental law. In his 2004 book, *Crimes against Nature*, environmental lawyer Robert Kennedy Jr, has detailed this history of George W. Bush's destruction of environmental law on behalf of his corporate economic cronies.[87] Two anti-environmental leaders stand out in Kennedy's account. One is Pat Robertson, Christian fundamentalist leader who characterizes environmentalists as 'evil priests of a new paganism.' Another is Tom Delay, Republican Congressman from Texas notorious for his violations of ethical standards, who claimed that DDT is as safe as aspirin and that the Endangered Species Act is the biggest threat to Texas after illegal 'aliens.' [88]

Delay's plans to subvert environmental legislation were laid in 1995 when he invited 350 lobbyists from the country's biggest polluting companies to collaborate in drafting legislation to

85. See cover story on global warming and increased hurricane strength by Jeffrey Kluger, *Time Magazine* (3 October 2005).

86. See Kerry Emanuel, *Divine Wind: The History and Science of Hurricanes* (New York: Oxford University Press, 2005).

87. Robert Kennedy Jr, *Crimes against Nature: How George W. Bush and his Corporate Pals are Plundering the Country and Hyjacking our Democracy* (New York: Harper-Collins, 2004).

88. Kennedy Jr, *Crimes against Nature*, 29–43.

dismantle federal health, safety and environmental laws. Although these efforts were blocked under the Clinton Administration, under Bush II most of these plans have been implemented. There has also been a systematic purge of scientists and responsible administrators from government agencies. Senior positions were then filled with industrial lobbyists, many drawn from the anti-environmental group, Wise Use, whose founder Ron Arnold, stated his intention as one to 'destroy, eradicate the environmental movement.' When Bush II was elected in 2000, he appointed Gale Norton of Wise Use to head the Department of the Interior and mining lobbyist, J. Steven Griles, as undersecretary. Timber lobbyists, Mark Rey, was appointed to head the forestry service. These officials have systematically allowed violations of pollution laws and have promoted legislation to annul them altogether.

At the same time corporate polluters are heavily subsidized. Big oil alone receives $65 billion each year in subsidies. Kennedy sums up his case against Bush and 'his corporate pals' thus: 'George W. Bush and his court are treating our country as a grab bag for robber barons, doling out the commons to giant polluters. Together they are cashing in our air, water, aquifers, wildlife, and public lands and divvying up the loot. They are turning our politicians into indentured servants who repay campaign contributions with taxpayer-funded subsidies and lucrative contracts and reign in law enforcement against a booming corporate crime wave.'

Equally worrying is the undermining of basic safeguards of human rights, within the United States and around the world. The passage of the Patriot Act shortly after 9/11 enshrined in law (which Bush II seeks to make permanent) permission to gather information from citizen's library records, book purchases, emails, phone calls and credit card records. The rights of Habeas Corpus are suspended not only for resident non-citizens, but even for American citizens who the administration deems to be 'enemy combatants,' allowing indefinite imprisonment without charges, trial or legal counsel. International laws against torture have been bypassed[89] and spying without warrants have become characteristics of the Bush II Administration which claims unlimited presidential powers as

89. See the articles by Anthony Lewis, Richard Kim, Jonathan H. Marks, Lisa Hajjar, Moustafa Bayoumi and Tara McKelvey on 'The Torture Complex', *The Nation*, 26 December 2005, pp. 11–42. On the roots of the practice of torture in the U.S., see Alfred McCoy, *A Question of Torture: CIA Interrogation from the Cold War to the War on Terror* (New York: Henry Holt, 2006). Karen Greenberg, *The Torture Papers: the Road to*

justified by the need to 'protect the people of the United States from terrorism.'

A January 2006 editorial in the *National Catholic Reporter* summarizes the case against the Bush II Administration:[90] — Led a country to war on false premises; — Continues to link the war against terrorism with the war in Iraq when the two had no relationship at the outset; — Dismisses the Geneva Conventions and holds prisoners incognito for years without charges or access to legal representation; — Places detainees on planes bound for foreign countries known for torture and abuse of prisoners; — Maintains secret CIA prisons on foreign soil; — Subverts laws guarding the civil liberties of U.S. citizens, including searches of personal records and infiltration of religious and peace groups by the FBI; — Defers to a Vice President who argues for legal exceptions so that U.S. personnel can engage in torture; — Plants false news reports domestically and overseas, most recently in the Iraqi press. Added to this list of human rights abuses and violations of civil liberties is the December 2005 revelation that shortly after 9/11 President Bush personally approved widespread electronic eavesdropping on Americans, without requesting warrants, as required by law.[91]

The American claim to run a 'benign empire' where U.S. interests and those of the rest of the world coincide has become rapidly unraveled in five short years. It has been unmasked as serving the interests only of a select group of the rich and powerful at the expense of the rest of the world, including most Americans. Americans are beginning to cry 'No!' They are beginning to suspect that the imperialists have turned America into a 'rogue nation' that is threatening the foundations of American democracy, and perhaps the basic standards of human civilization and the survival of humanity on the planet.[92]

Abu Ghraib (Cambridge: Cambridge University Press, 2005). For the responsibility of the torture policy in the top levels of the Bush Administration: see Seymour M. Hersh, *Chain of Command: The Road from 9/11 to Abu Ghraib* (New York: HarperCollins, 2004).

90. 'The Latest Bush Threat to Democracy', *National Catholic Reporter*, 6 January 2006, p. 24.

91. 'The Latest Bush Threat to Democracy', *National Catholic Reporter*, 6 January 2006, p. 24. See also an article on the recent report to Congress that Bush's defense of his spying program cannot be legally sustained: Siobhan Gorman, 'Legal Support for Bush's Spy Actions Thin, Report Says', *Los Angeles Times*, 7 January 2006, A15.

92. It is significant how many of these denunciations have come from formerly conservative thinkers. See, for example, Clyde Prestowitz, *Rogue State: American Unilateralism and the Failure of Good Intentions* (New York: Basic Books, 2003).

Chapter Seven

ALTERNATIVE VISIONS OF AMERICA:
THE PROTEST TRADITION

The claim that the United States is an elect nation chosen by God to dominate and redeem the world has deep roots in the Puritan traditions of the seventeenth century. These ideas of U.S. America's messianic role have been continually retooled to justify new imperial adventures. But the connections between visions of America as a people with a mission to the world and American imperial power have always existed in some contradiction with each other. Many Americans have rejected the idea of empire as 'un-American,' and imperialists have gone about their expansionist activities by constantly denying that they were engaged in building an empire.

Thus there had developed early on, from the time of the Indian wars to the Mexican American War to the Spanish American war to today a deep disconnect between what Americans think they have been about in their history and how other people, especially those on the underside of American imperial power, have actually experienced America. This also means that most Americans do not know their own history, particularly this 'underside' of American history. American ideologies justify military and economic expansion by speaking in an idealistic language of promoting 'freedom' that conceals what they are actually doing from the perspective of conquered and colonized peoples.

But this self-deception has always had its critics. In every generation there have risen up prophetic witnesses, sometimes loners, sometimes speaking for major movements, who seek to unmask this self-deception. They reveal that what is actually happening is deeply contradictory to these idealistic claims, and also restate visions of America that would more authentically promote freedom and justice for all American peoples equally, as well as more authentically affirm the right of other people to genuine self-determination.

These critics have not rejected the idea that America has a mission to pursue 'liberty and justice for all,' but have sought to use this vision critically to unmask its betrayal. They have also sought to bring real public policies more in line with these ideals. This chapter seeks to sketch some key figures in this critical prophetic tradition in successive eras of American history discussed in the first five chapters of this book: the Colonial period, the Revolutionary era, the 1840s to the Civil War, the 1890s to 1930s and the Cold War era. Each of the five chapters has alluded to such representatives of prophetic and protest traditions in their time. In this chapter we wish to gather them together, not only to discuss their views in greater detail, but also to see what visions of a more authentic American 'way of life' have animated them that might prove helpful for those seeking alternative visions today.

Roger Williams and Anne Hutchinson in the Colonial Period

Roger Williams (1603–83)[1] was a pariah in the Puritan world of his own time, but has been embraced in the last two centuries as the prophet of freedom of conscience and religious liberty. Since separation of church and state and freedom of religion were principles endorsed in the American Bill of Rights that became foundational to American constitutional law, Williams has been extolled as a forerunner of those American constitutional principles and a critic of Puritan 'intolerance.' Today, freedom of religion is seen as rooted in a liberal relativism that assumes that all religious beliefs are more or less equally good and equally irrelevant in the public arena. These views are far from Williams' operating assumptions.

On the contrary, Williams was and remained a deeply convinced Puritan, a strict follower of Calvinist theology. His teaching of freedom of conscience arose from pushing Calvinist theology to its radical conclusion. Moreover, Williams' views of freedom of conscience are rooted, not only in a vision of what the true church

---

1. Roger Williams' exact birth and death dates are uncertain. Reuben A. Guild puts his birth at 1599: 'Biographical Introduction', *The Complete Writings of Roger Williams* (New York: Russell and Russell, 1963), 1, p. 5. Edwin S. Gaustad gives 1603–1683 as his birth and death: *Roger Williams: Prophet of Liberty* (Oxford: Oxford University Press, 2001), p. 131.

is, but, equally importantly, what the state is not. For Williams the state is not and cannot be Christian and thus cannot be an enforcer of Christian faith. This also means that no state or nation can claim to be the political or national heir of the biblical Israel, as God's New Israel and chosen people. It is this witness against any notion that the American people are God's new Israel and elect nation that is the particular legacy of Roger Williams. This legacy has been mostly ignored by later American thought, but is most significant for us today in the light of how this idea has been used in American history.

Roger Williams grew up in the Puritan movement in England in the 1620s and quickly moved to the radical end of that movement as a puritan separatist.[2] This meant that he concluded that the Church of England was irreformably apostate. Those committed to belonging to the true church of Christ must leave this church and form new Christian communities based on personal conversion through the Holy Spirit. Most Puritans did not go this far. They saw themselves as reformers within the Church of England. The Puritans who settled the Massachusetts Bay Colony were of this non-separatist variety. When Williams and his wife immigrated to New England in 1631, he soon fell into conflict with the Puritan leaders, both ministers and magistrates, because of his insistence that only a church which separates from the Church of England can be the true church.

Williams tried to find a church home in some of the other more separatist churches of Plymouth and Salem but also found them insufficiently strict in their separatism. Williams insisted that true Christians must separate from the Church of England. Their personal conversion must include renouncing and repenting of their former membership in this Church. Williams also claimed that the King of England could not claim a right to Indian lands as a Christian King, and so he had no right to give Englishmen titles to Indian lands that overrode the Indians' own land claims. These and other teaching of Williams, such as his belief in liberty of conscience and his rejection of oaths using the name of God sworn in courts, so offended the Puritan leaders in the Massachusetts Bay Colony that they banished him from the colony in October, 1636.[3]

2. On Williams' early life, see Gaustad, *Roger Williams*, pp. 9–14.

3. Gaustad gives four main reasons for Williams' banishment: his views of Indian ownership of the American land, on oaths, on denouncing membership in the Church of England, and on freedom of conscience: see pp. 25–29.

Refusing to repent, Williams evaded the arresting officers by fleeing into the wilderness where he was sheltered by Indians with whom he had established friendly relations. Williams then negotiated for land with the Indians, establishing the colony of Rhode Island that would become a haven for dissenters, founded on the principle of freedom of religious conscience. Among the dissenters banished from the Massachusetts Bay Colony who made their way to Rhode Island was Anne Hutchinson, along with some eighty householders who followed her. Anne Hutchinson was banished for her teachings on the primacy of grace over works, and for leading religious assemblies in her house that included men as well as women. Such teaching in 'promiscuous assemblies' was seen as forbidden to women. Hutchinson's activities were condemned as neither 'tolerable nor comely in the sight of God nor fitting for your sex.'[4]

In Providence, Williams would work out a more radical version of his separatist view of the true church. In the process he also clarified his rejection of any Christian state which claims to act as an agent for protecting and promoting the true church. Williams followed the radical Protestant view that the true church founded by Christ had existed in apostolic times but had been totally destroyed when Constantine joined church and state to create Christendom. After the Constantinian establishment the anti-Christ reigned over the world, using the apostate state church is his vehicle. True Christians existed in scattered bands in the 'wilderness.' Protestants believed that they were reestablishing the true Church of Christ through correct teachings on faith and grace, personal conversion and departure from the false Church of Rome. Separatist Puritans like Williams extended this same critique to the Church of England.

But Williams came to the conclusion that these separatist churches also were not true churches. Christians in his time had no capacity to reestablish the true church simply by separating from apostate churches linked to the state and gathering an assembly of the converted to covenant together and establish a ministry. The apostolic church, wholly lost in the fourth century, could only be established by Christ in a new advent. This second coming was soon

4. See Rosemary S. Keller, 'New England Women: Ideology and Experience in First-Generation Puritanism, 1630–1650', in *Women and Religion in America: Volume 2: The Colonial and Revolutionary War Periods*, Rosemary S. Keller and Rosemary R. Ruether (eds.), (San Francisco, CA: Harper and Row, 1983), pp. 140, 165–75.

to come, but meanwhile Christians like himself remained as scattered witnesses in a wilderness of paganism and apostasy.[5] The wilderness he encountered in America was no worse than, and indeed in some ways better than, the wilderness and hypocrisy of an England that pretended to be 'Christian.' The task of Christian witnesses, such as himself, was to critique apostate churches and cultivate inner spiritual gifts, but not to evangelize, either English or Indians, since no true church can be gathered within the present fallen era.[6]

Williams drew several conclusions from this radical view of the church which had important implications for his understanding of the state and also for the relationship of the English settlers to the American Indians. To understand these conclusions one must understand his view of the 'natural man,' as distinct from humanity redeemed in Christ. Like many Puritans, Williams operated with a dichotomy between nature and grace, creation and redemption, reason and revelation or natural knowledge and morality as distinct from saving knowledge. God in creation had given humans natural reason, rooted in the inner voice of conscience, capable of understanding what God required of them as human beings.

Although human beings have fallen into sin and their reason has been dimmed and corrupted, nevertheless it has not disappeared. This gift of reason and moral conscience continues with sufficient adequacy that all humans can establish governments based on a social morality that forbids such basic violations as robbery, murder, lying, and adultery, and promotes honesty, fidelity, gratitude and other virtues conducive to the common good. This capacity to promote the common good lies on the plane of the natural man and the proper ends of earthly society. It has nothing to do with the supernatural ends of redemption and the life to come. People of all cultures and religions have this capacity to found true governments that share common understandings of social morality. Governments founded by people claiming to be Christians are in no way superior by those founded by pagans on this plane of natural morality.[7]

5. See Edmund S. Morgan, Roger *Williams: The Church and the State* (New York: Harcourt, Brace and World, 1967), pp. 28–56.

6. On Williams' millenialist view of the true church, see W. Clark Gilpin, *The Millenarian Piety of Roger Williams* (Chicago, Il: University of Chicago Press, 1979), pp. 56–62.

7. On William's anthropology, see James Calvin Davis, *The Moral Theology of Roger Williams: Christian Conviction and Public Ethics* (Louisville, KY: Westminster/John Knox Press, 2004), pp. 49–69.

This view was reinforced for Williams by his experiences with American Indians whose social life he found was equally valid on this plane of natural moral principles, and in many ways superior to that found among the English who claimed to be Christians. As he put it in his writing on Indian languages and customs: 'I could never discern that excess of scandalous sins amongst them which Europe abounds with. Drunkenness and gluttony generally they know not what sins they be, and although they have not so much to restrain them (both in respect to knowledge of God and Laws of men) as the English have, yet a man shall never hear of such crimes among them of robberies, murders, adulteries, etc as amongst the English.'[8] For Williams all peoples are basically equal and on a par with one another on this level of natural morality. States or governments were founded to safeguard and promote this natural morality of 'civility' or civic life. Pagans do as good a job of it as Christians.[9]

Williams' dichotomy between nature and grace also defined an irreconcilable divide between church and state. No Christian state is possible because Christianity can never be promoted by the state. It must exist in a wilderness of prophetic witnesses until Christ comes. Although religion and politics had been united in ancient Israel, this union was transcended in Christ, who established a spiritual people who must always stand as suffering witnesses against the state and its violent and coercive methods of rule. No 'New Israel,' no Christian state or nation, can exist as an expression of the reign of Christ that must witness against all worldly ways of life.[10] The state must accept liberty of conscience in religious matters, not because all religions are equally good, but because the state has no power to discern true Christianity from false. It must stick to its own sphere of natural morality and not pretend to promote a redeeming community that transcends its knowledge.[11] To ally church with state, and make the state an instrument to promote 'Christianity,' is simply to create an apostate church which has departed from true Christian life.

8. Roger Williams, 'Key into the Language of America', (1643), in *Complete Writings*, 1, p. 165: see also p. 81 where says 'Boast not proud English of thy birth and blood, Thy brother Indian is by birth as good, of one blood God made Him and Thee and All, as wise, as faire, as strong, as personall.'

9. On William's view of 'civility', see Davis, *Moral Theology*, pp. 91–115.

10. See Morgan, *Roger Williams: Church and State*, pp. 62–85.

11. On Williams' view of conscience, see Davis, *Moral Theology*, pp. 70–90.

From these principles Williams came to several startling conclusions. Since no Christian state can exist, and every state that claims to be Christian makes the church apostate, there can be no Christian king who can claim to override the rights of natural men in relation to land claims. Land claims are based on the rights of those who first settled the land. On this basis the land of the Americas belongs to the American Indians. The English can settle there only by negotiating with its owners, the Native Americans, receiving their acceptance and paying them a fair price.[12] This means that the English must become good neighbors with the Indians, living only on those lands which the Indians have conceded to them and for which they have paid fairly. They cannot claim to supersede Indian rights to the land on the basis of a grant given by a 'Christian' king.

Williams originally learned Indian languages to negotiate with the Indians in trade and land purchase, and also to converse with them about Christian faith with hopes of converting them.[13] But he came to the conclusion that since no true apostolic church exists, and because, on the level of 'civilization,' Indians are as good or better than the English, the English have no capacity to evangelize the Indians, either claiming to civilize them or to impart to them redemptive knowledge. Rather they should learn to live justly with the Indians as fellow humans, awaiting the re-founding of the millennial church by Christ in which pagans, both Indian and English, might be converted to the true church.[14]

Thus Williams, proceeding from very different principles than liberal humanism, came to conclusions that stand as a radical witness against any American creed of divine election. Not only did he champion freedom of religion, the non-interference of the state in matters of religious conscience, something Americans would later accept on a very different basis from Williams' principles. But he also rejected two foundational ideas which would shape America

12. See Gilpin, *Millenarian Piety*, pp. 40–42.

13. In Williams' preface to his 'A Key into the Language of America', he suggests that his purpose of learning Indian languages was to convert the Indians to Christ: *Complete Writings*, 1, pp. 19–28.

14. For Williams' repudiation of evangelization of the Indians through the present churches on the grounds that this would only bring them into apostate churches, see especially his 1645 treatise 'Christenings make not Christians', *Complete Writings*, VII, pp. 26–41. See also Gilpin, *Millenarian Piety*, pp. 128–32.

for the next four centuries and are still largely unquestioned today. First, he rejected the rights of Europeans to take Indian land because they were 'Christian' or more 'civilized.' He believed the Indians had the prior right to the land of the Americas and Europeans could obtain some land only through the consent of the Indians. Second, he rejected the idea of a Christian state or elect People of God as a nation is a contradiction in terms. To make such claims is idolatrous and blasphemous. To claim ruling power in the name of the God of Jesus Christ is to deny both Christ and God. From such apostasy flows all manner of bloody deeds of war, murder and oppression.

Tom Paine and Abigail Adams in the Revolutionary Era

The writings of the 'Founding Fathers' of the American Revolution and its Declaration of Independence, Bill of Rights and Constitution have continually inspired American critics of the movement toward empire. George Washington, Thomas Jefferson, James Madison are frequently cited in their statements against entanglements in European wars and enmities and the maintenance of standing armies.[15] There are indeed important traditions to be reclaimed from the thought of the founders for critical retrieval today. But the accomplishments of the founding generation were also ambivalent, as we have pointed out in Chapter Two of this book.

These leaders failed to abolish slavery and sanctioned wars of extermination against American Indians. Their perspective was shaped as men of property, slaveholding planters of the South and the elite merchant class of the North. Even while throwing off British control, these men were deeply committed to maintaining their own class privileges. Full citizenship and participation in voting and government excluded not only the Indian and the enslaved Negro, but also all property-less people, servants, apprentices, working men, skilled artisans without property. All women were excluded, even though some women who were independent property-holders had voted in colonial governments.

15. Objection to the maintenance of standing armies is one of the grievances cited against the British by the American Revolutionaries in the Declaration of Independence: see Lois G. Schwoerer, *No Standing Armies: The Antiarmy Ideology in 17th Century England* (Baltimore, MD: The Johns Hopkins University Press, 1974: also Jacob G. Hornburger, 'The Bill of Rights: Antipathy to Militarism', in *Freedom Daily*, September, 2004.

In this section I have chosen not to try to evaluate what is recoverable from the Founders (a very complex task) but to lift up two prophetic voices at the time of the American Revolution, Tom Paine and Abigail Adams, who sought to expand the citizen base of the American government to include all working men, including blacks, the abolition of slavery and the recognition of the rights of women.

Tom Paine (1737–1809) grew up in a Quaker working class family in Thetford, Norfolk, England. He was apprenticed to his father's business of stay-making, ran away to sea, returned to practice his craft, was employed as an excise officer and as a teacher and started a grocery business. Although an indifferent success in these occupations, he gained a political education in circles of dissenters, and began to write political poems. In November 1774 he immigrated to America, with a letter of recommendation from Benjamin Franklin whom he had met in London, settling in Philadelphia.

Paine hit the ground running in Philadelphia. All his accumulated resentments against the British government and hopes for a new human society found their right moment in an America on the brink of revolutionary war. He quickly made the acquaintance of leaders in the struggle against Britain, and became editor of Robert Aitken's *Pennsylvania Magazine*, where he was able to air his critical views. Within weeks of arrival he wrote a tract against African Slavery in America (written in late 1774 and published in the *Pennsylvania Journal* 8 March 1775).[16] He also edited for publication a tract attacking the oppression of women.[17] Paine's interest in the promotion of women is indicated by the fact that he originally came to America with the thought of opening a school for young women.

In January 1776 Paine published *Common Sense*, a tract which quickly became a publishing sensation throughout the American colonies. At a time when newspaper circulation averaged two thousand copies and pamphlets were printed in one or two editions of a few thousand copies, Paine's *Common Sense* went though 25 editions in a single year. At least 150,000 copies were sold, reaching many hundreds of thousands of readers. *Common Sense* transformed the American political discourse of 1776, making what had been

16. 'African Slavery in America', reprinted in Philip S. Foner (ed.), *The Complete Writings of Thomas Paine*. II. (New York: Citadel Press, 1945), pp. 15–19.

17. 'An Occasional Letter on the Female Sex', by an unknown author, but edited by Paine for publication in the *Pennsylvania Magazine*, August, 1775: *idem*, pp. 34–40.

seen as the dangerous and unacceptable ideas of a Republic and independence from Britain broadly acceptable. Above all Paine sought to break the deeply engrained American feeling of dependence on Britain as the 'Mother country' and respect for the English king as the sovereign authority, established by divine right, and to free the American mind to think in radically different ways about itself and its place in history.

In *Common Sense* Paine engages in a straightforward and furious attack on the legitimacy of monarchy and hereditary leadership. Paine would later attack the authority of the Bible in his *The Age of Reason* (1793–94). But in *Common Sense* he appeals to the authority of the Bible against kingship, citing the passages where the Jews, seeking to emulate the idolatrous customs of the heathen, are condemned for establishing a monarchy. 'Monarchy is ranked in Scripture as one of the sins of the Jews, for which a curse in reserve is denounced against them.' Before that time 'their form of government…was a kind of republic administered by a judge and the elders of the tribes.'[18] Paine thus established republican government as the original and true polity of the People of Israel, and defined monarchy as a sinful state of fallenness from divine intentions.

Paine went on to de-legitimize the British monarchy and aristocracy with savage ridicule. He describes William the Conqueror as 'a French bastard landing with an armed banditti and establishing himself King of England against the consent of the natives is in plain terms a very paltry rascally original — It certainly hath no divinity in it.' Those who venerate the descendents of such a lineage are described as 'promiscuously worshipping the ass and the lion.'[19] Monarchies, far from protecting the nation from foreign and domestic wars, are seen as continually fomenting wars. 'Monarchy and succession have laid (not this or that kingdom only) but the world in blood and ashes.'[20] Republics, by contrast, focus on commerce and cultivate peaceful relations between nations, according to Paine.

Paine seeks to discredit ideas that Americans should feel any attachment to Britain, that they should see it as their Mother

18. In Thomas Paine, *Rights of Man, Common Sense*, Everyman's Library (New York: Alfred A. Knopf, 1994), p. 258.
   19. Paine, *Common Sense*, p. 262.
   20. Paine, *Common Sense*, p. 264.

Country to which they owe a special allegiance and should seek reconciliation with it. He describes the diversity of places of origin of the immigrants in Philadelphia to argue that not just Britain but all of Europe is the source of the American people. Paine points out all the advantages of separation and independence and the absurdity of continued dependence on England who only exploits their wealth and involves them in unnecessary wars. Paine's argument is not only for independence. Above all, he hopes that America will use this independence to break with all forms of hereditary leadership and to establish a Republic based on the consent of the governed.

Paine sketches a process in which each county in each colony would elect delegates to a convention from which a Charter of Government could emerge that would truly represent the mind and will of the people for their own self-government.[21] By establishing such a democratically founded Republic the United States of America would found the only authentic and just form of human government, pointing the way for all other nations to follow. Paine was convinced that he lived in a kairotic moment in which tyrannical monarchies were about to be overthrown throughout the world and democratically founded Republics established. The United States was the harbinger of a new era of human history. Thus, he urges 'from the errors of other nations let us learn wisdom and lay hold of the present opportunity — *to begin government at the right end.*'[22]

Paine would remain all his life a rapturous admirer of the accomplishments of the American Revolution and Constitution, seeing them as having accomplished his fondest dreams. But his own vision of republican government was considerably more democratic than what most founding fathers had in mind. Leading revolutionary leader, John Adams of Massachusetts, read *Common Sense* with considerable irritation (his wife Abigail seems to have read it with much more pleasure[23]). In 1776, John Adams wrote a response to it, *Thoughts on Government*, in which he decried Paine's excessively 'democratical' biases. He claimed Paine's views of government flowed 'from simple ignorance and a mere desire to

21. Paine, *Common Sense*, p. 278.
22. Paine, *Common Sense*, p. 288.
23. See the reference to Abigail Adams' response to *Common Sense* in Rosemary Keller, *Patriotism and the Female Sex: Abigail Adams and the American Revolution* (New York: Carlson Publishing Co., 1994), p. 84.

please the democratic party in Philadelphia...I dreaded the effect so popular a pamphlet might have among the people, and determined to do all in my power to counteract the effect of it.'[24]

Paine had argued for a unicameral legislature that represented the whole people as one community. Adams and other founding fathers favored a bicameral legislature modeled after the British government's two houses of Lords and Commons. Adams believed that the desires of common people needed to be balanced by the wisdom of wealthy elites who he assumed would dominant the Senate. Adams saw the class interests of the wealthy and the popular classes as inherently in conflict; the structure of government needed to reflect checks and balances between the two.

Paine, by contrast, was associated with a democratic reform party in Philadelphia (as Adams noted in his comments) which sought to overthrow the power of the wealthy elite merchant class of the city. This elite constituted about 10 per cent of the city's population, but held about 50 per cent of the wealth. They controlled the trade between Britain, the port of Philadelphia and the Caribbean. While owning the great trading houses in the city, they also lived in elegant rural country estates where they aped the manners of the British aristocracy. They controlled both the economic and political life of the city.[25] Another 50 per cent of the city was the artisan class, ranging from elite craftsmen to more humble tradesmen. Together they controlled about 46 per cent of the wealth, but were largely shut out of political power. The remaining 40 per cent were day laborers, apprentices, indentured servants and slaves, although slavery was disappearing in Philadelphia at this time. This group were poor and powerless, sharing among them only 4 per cent of the wealth.[26]

In 1776, a radical group representing the interests of the artisan class seized power in Philadelphia and wrote a new democratic state constitution, which Paine had a hand in shaping. They established a unicameral legislature based on wide franchise. Property qualifications were abolished as a basis of voting, and all men over 21 who paid taxes were given the vote. This rule still excluded dependent persons; i.e., slaves, indentured servants,

24. See Eric Foner, *Tom Paine and Revolutionary America* (New York: Oxford University Press, 1976), p. 122.

25. Foner, *Tom Paine*, p. 21–23.

26. Foner, *Tom Paine*, p. 23–56.

apprentices, and women, but gave the vote to all working men with sufficient independence to be listed as a tax payer. The Pennsylvania Assembly based on this Constitution also voted to abolish slavery in March, 1780, with Paine writing the 'Preamble' to this act. While Paine had hoped for an immediate abolition of slavery, the Assembly voted for a more moderate policy of graduate emancipation.[27]

Paine's reasoning behind his advocacy of a broad franchise and the abolition of slavery was his deep belief that every (male?) human owned his own body and life as his personal property. If a man had no other property, he nevertheless owned his own self as inalienable personal property. No one had a right to take his rights to his own body and life from him and to subjugate him involuntarily. Although Paine accepted that people could voluntarily contract for periods of service as apprentices and indentured servants, this was a contract into which they entered willingly and which lasted for a fixed period of time. It did not become permanent servitude inherited by their descendents. Thus just as Paine rejected any hereditary lordship, he also rejected an inherited servitude.

It was this rejection of involuntary servitude that led Paine to write his tract against African Slavery in America within weeks of landing in Philadelphia on 30 November 1774. Paine was not the first to write against slavery in America, but few took up a pen against it with greater vehemence before his time. He begins with the cry:

> To Americans: That some desperate wretches should be willing to steal and enslave men by violence and murder for gain is rather lamentable than strange. But that many civilized, nay, Christianized people should approve, and be concerned in the savage practice, is surprising; and still persist, though it has been so often proved contrary to the light of nature, to every principle of justice and humanity and even good policy.[28]

Paine not only decried slavery as barbarous and contrary to all justice, but he suggested a plan of emancipation by which elderly slaves would be supported in their old age by their masters, while younger ones would receive land and/or salaried employment from their masters, with the assistance of state legislatures. Not only the

27. 'Preamble to the Act Passed by the Pennsylvania Assembly, March 1, 1780', in Philip Foner, *Complete Writings of Thomas Paine*. II, pp. 21–22.
28. Foner, *Complete Writings*. II, p. 16.

masters, but the whole society that had accepted slavery were seen by Paine as 'bound in duty to him and to them to repair these injuries.' Paine signed his tract in the name of 'Justice and Humanity.' On 14 April 1775, five weeks after the publication of this tract, the first anti-slavery society in America was founded in Philadelphia, with Paine among its members.[29]

Abigail Adams, wife of that John Adams who disapproved of Paine's too 'democratical' ideas, ironically has become a symbolic representative of those who spoke for widened rights of women at the time of the American Revolution. Her interventions were unknown at the time, taking place in the private realm of letters to her husband. Only with the late nineteenth and twentieth century feminist movement and women's revisionist history, has her voice become known publicly.

Abigail Smith Adams was the daughter of a respected minister of the First Church of Weymouth, Massachusetts. His wife, Elizabeth Quincy, came from an elite family of Massachusetts, as did John Adams. Although lacking any formal education, Abigail gained literacy through her family and was notable for her independence of mind and forthright self-expression. She and John Adams were wed in 1764. As the revolutionary struggle developed she took a keen interest in public affairs. Her husband was quickly drawn into leadership roles, as a delegate to the Constitutional Convention, then diplomatic representative to France, becoming the second President of the United States in 1797. During the long years when John Adams was away from home on public business, Abigail not only raised their family, but ran their farm and family business.[30] The letters which she and John exchanged during this period reveal her keen and critical mind.[31]

On 31 March 1776, while John was away in Philadelphia at the Constitutional Convention, Abigail wrote him a long letter inquiring about the process of the convention and the military struggle. Her opposition to slavery was expressed in a side comment in which she asked about 'what sort of defense Virginia can make against our common enemy,' given the class system of the state. 'Are not the gentry lords and the common people vassals?' She doubted

29. Foner, *Complete Writings*. II, pp. 15, 19.
30. Keller, *Patriotism and the Female Sex*, pp. 105–122.
31. Charles Francis Adams, *Familiar Letters of John Adams and his Wife Abigail Adams During the Revolution* (Cambridge, MA: The Riverside Press, 1876).

whether slaveholders would take up the cause of freedom with the same fervor of the people of her New England society. 'I have sometimes been ready to think that the passion for liberty cannot be equally strong in the breasts of those who have been accustomed to deprive their fellow creatures of theirs.'[32]

Later in the letter she takes up her concern that more liberal laws toward women will emerge from the Constitutional Convention. 'And, by the way, in the new code of laws which I suppose it will be necessary for you to make, I desire that you would remember the ladies and be more generous and favorable to them than your ancestors. Do not put such unlimited power into the hands of the husbands. Remember, all men would be tyrants if they could. If particular care and attention is not paid to the ladies, we are determined to foment a rebellion, and will not hold ourselves bound by any laws in which we have no voice or representation.' [33] Abigail here claims the same rights to independence as the revolutionary males of her society. Just as they reject any laws in which they have no voice or representation, so women will do the same to men.

Realizing the boldness of her voice, Abigail seeks to soften it by saucy humor, even as she deepens the seriousness of her demands, appealing to male chivalry, rather than women's 'natural' rights. 'That your sex are naturally tyrannical is a truth so thoroughly established as to admit of no dispute; but those of you as wish to be happy willingly give up the harsh title of master for the more tender and endearing one of friend. Why, then, not put out of the power of the vicious and the lawless to use us with cruelty and with impunity? Men of sense of all ages abhor those customs which treat us only a vassals of your sex; regard us then as being placed by Providence under your protection, and in imitation of the Supreme Being make use of that power only for our happiness.'[34]

On 14 April 1776, John Adams replied to requests for more liberal laws on women's status with a paternalistic rebuff, which reveals not only his views of women's innate dependency, but also his fears, and those of other men of his class, that the American Revolution might have awakened demands for a broader democracy from other disenfranchised groups: apprentices, youth, Indians and negroes:

32. Keller, *Patriotism and the Female Sex*, p. 148.
33. Keller, *Patriotism and the Female Sex*, pp. 149–50.
34. Keller, *Patriotism and the Female Sex*, p. 150.

'As for your extraordinary code of laws, I cannot but laugh. We have been told that our struggle has loosened the bonds of government everywhere; that children and apprentices were disobedient; that schools and colleges were grown turbulent; that Indians slighted their guardians and negroes grew insolent to their masters. But your letter was the first intimation that another tribe, more numerous and more powerful than the rest, were grown discontent.' Claiming that men know they are really powerless in the face of their women, John Adams insists that this is all the more reason to keep their male power intact. 'Depend on it we know better than to repeal our masculine systems.' Without this legal power, men would be helpless before the 'despotism of the petticoat.' [35]

On 7 May 1776, Abigail responded to this rebuff. Deeply disappointed that her husband failed to take her seriously, she took up his gambit that women do know how to wield their informal personal power. 'I cannot say that I think you very generous to the ladies; for, whilst you are proclaiming peace and goodwill to men, emancipating all nations, you insist upon retaining absolute power over wives. But you must remember that arbitrary power is like other things that are very hard, very liable to be broken; and notwithstanding all your wise laws and maxims, we have it in our power, not only to free ourselves, but to subdue our masters and, without violence, throw both your natural and legal authority at our feet. "Charm by accepting, by submitting sway, yet have our humor most when we obey. "'[36]

It would be almost 150 years before women would gain that legal status of citizens for which Abigail Adams appealed in 1776. Property-less white men, Indians and negroes would also wait many generations before their rights would even begin to be vindicated.

Abolitionists/Feminists in the 1830s–1860s

In the 1830s to 50s there developed in the U.S., especially in New England and the Northeast, a formidable community of radical reformers who brought together militant anti-slavery views, anti-racism, feminism and pacifism, with visions of alternative forms of

35. Keller, *Patriotism and the Female Sex*, p. 155.

36. Keller, *Patriotism and the Female Sex*, p. 169. On Abigail Adam's feminist convictions, see Keller, *Patriotism and the Female Sex*, pp. 89–103.

human society. Leading radical thinkers, white and black, men and women, allied, while also debating vigorously with each other around these themes. This period was remarkable for its intense criticism of American society and political order, as it had developed since the Revolution, with its preservation of slavery, oppression of Indians and lack of rights for women. Its foundational vision was the full humanity of every human being, regardless of sex or race.

The charismatic figure around which this collection of critics and visionaries assembled, organized and debated was founder and editor of the abolitionist newspaper, *The Liberator*, William Lloyd Garrison (1805–79). Given the space restraints of this brief section of one chapter, I will focus primarily on Garrison, with references to some of the other key figures interconnected with him, such as the feminists, Lucretia Mott and Elizabeth Cady Stanton, and black leader, Frederick Douglass.

Lloyd Garrison grew up as an impoverished son of a mother deserted by her husband. He was self-educated as an apprentice printer who read in his master's library in Newsburyport, Massachusetts. Garrison was converted to abolitionism by the Quaker anti-slavery organizer, Benjamin Lundy in 1828 and joined him in publishing the newspaper, the *Genius of Universal Emancipation*.[37] Gaining experience of the horrors of slavery primarily in Maryland and becoming friends with the free black community, Garrison's commitment grew, not only against slavery, but against the discrimination suffered by free blacks in the North. On 1 January 1831, Garrison founded *The Liberator* to advocate the immediate freedom of slaves and the elevation of the condition of free blacks. Of his first 450 subscribers, 400 were blacks.[38] Garrison would faithfully publish *The Liberator* every week until the passage of the thirteenth amendment abolishing slavery anywhere in the United States, putting out his last issue 29 December 1865.

Garrison quickly became highly controversial, suffering legal indictments and mob violence for his insistent advocacy of the immediate emancipation of all slaves. Those Americans who were against slavery in the 1830s and 40s thought in terms of a gradual

37. Henry Mayer, *All On Fire: William Lloyd Garrison and the Abolition of Slavery* (New York: St. Martin's Press, 1998), pp. 51–56.

38. *Documents of Upheaval: Selections from William Lloyd Garrison's The Liberator, 1831–1865*, ed. Truman Nelson (New York: Hill and Wang, 1966), p. 2.

process of emancipation in which blacks would be 'prepared' for freedom by education. They also generally believed that blacks could not coexist with whites as equal citizens in United States and so favored removing freed blacks to Haiti or to Africa. The American Colonization Society, founded in 1816 by Virginia Congressman, Charles Fenton Mercer, and supported by the 'respectable' establishment in the North, such as Princeton theologian Robert Finley, represented this view.

Garrison set himself to attack the colonization view, exposing its racism. In powerful speeches and articles in the U.S. and England, Garrison sought to discredit colonization. Garrison's campaign culminated in a 236 page book, *Thoughts on African Colonization: Or an Impartial Exhibition of the Doctrines, Principles and Purposes of the American Colonization Society, together with the Resolution, Addresses and Remonstrances of the Free People of Color* (1832). Garrison's technique was to expose the Society through quoting its own statements, revealing its racist and pro-slavery presuppositions. He also showed the utter opposition to colonization by free people of color who insisted that the U.S. was their country and demanded full citizenship in that country, not removal to Africa or some other country.[39] Although the supporters of colonization fought viciously against Garrison, tagging him as a crazy fanatic, colonization gradually lost its acceptability in anti-slavery circles in the U.S. and England, thanks largely to Garrison's efforts.

Garrison's demand for immediate emancipation without compensation to the slaveholders appeared totally untenable to most Americans at that time. It was taken for granted that slaves were unprepared and perhaps incapable of freedom and, if it was given all at once, there would be outbreaks of violence and chaos. Also slaves were property, and thus slaveholders had rights to protection of or compensation for their property. But Garrison's understanding of immediatism was not a political strategy, but a moral demand.

For Garrison slavery was a heinous crime, a sin against millions of human beings who were not only treated brutally, but denied their basic humanity as fellow humans made in the image of God. It was no more acceptable to respond to slavery by demands for gradualism than it would be to ask someone robbing and assaulting

39. Mayer, *All on Fire*, pp. 134–41.

another human being to desist 'gradually.' What Garrison demanded of the abolitionist movement and all Americans was that they unequivocally denounce slavery as a sin, as an intrinsic evil, and that they withdraw from it all moral legitimacy. Since slavery originated in 'man-stealing,' it no more deserved compensation than any other wealth acquired through robbery.[40] The politics of how it would be abolished was secondary and, he believed, would quickly follow, once all legitimacy was taken from it.

Garrison's greatest insight and enduring contribution to American social thought was his recognition that the roots of the legitimacy of slavery for most Americans was racism or what he called 'colorphobia.'[41] Most Americans thought (and some still think) that because African people have a dark skin, this means they are intrinsically inferior, incapable of the same intellectual and cultural prowess. For slave-owners slavery was appropriate for Africans as lesser beings incapable of equal citizenship with themselves. Many Northern whites shared the same view and wanted freed blacks either removed from the U.S. or else kept in an inferior status, educationally, socially and politically.

Nothing excited so much furious violence from anti-abolitionist whites as the practice of whites and blacks associating as equals in anti-slavery meetings. For such whites, the ultimate charge against Garrison and his group were that they were 'amalgamationists;' i.e., they sought an equal social association of blacks and whites that would lead to intermarriage (illegal at this time in the U.S.[42]) Cartoonists depicted for a horrified public images of blacks and whites courting each other.[43] Garrison refused to be deterred by these fears, insisting that the end of racial discrimination indeed meant that 'the time is to come when all the nations of the earth will intermarry and all distinctions of color will cease to divide mankind.'[44]

On 17 November 1837 *The Liberator* published what Garrison called 'A short Catechism, adapted for all parts of the United States' in

40. Mayer, *All on Fire*, pp. 72–73, 194.

41. Mayer, *All on Fire*, pp. 247, 525.

42. Jacqueline Battalora, *Toward a Critical White Race Ethics: the Construction of Whiteness in Anti-miscegenation Law* (PhD thesis, Northwestern University, Evanston, Illinois, 1999).

43. Mayer, *All on Fire*, see 11th page between 232–33.

44. Mayer, *All on Fire*, p. 82.

which he ironically exposed the 'colorphobia' that lay at the root of all race discrimination in the U.S. The 'catechism' contained 26 questions, each of which is answered by some version of the reply, 'because they are black.' Among these queries are: '1. Why is American slaveholding in all cases not sinful? Because its victims are *black*... 6. Why are our slaves not fit for freedom? Because they are *black*... 14. Why is Lynch law, as applied to abolitionists, better than common law? Because the slaves, whom they seek to emancipate, are *black*. 17. Why are they not created in the image of God? Because their skin is *black*... 19. Why are they not our brethren and countrymen? Because they are *black*. 20. Why is it unconstitutional to pity and defend them? Because they are *black*.... 26. Why is slavery the cornerstone of our republican edifice? Because its victims are *black*.'

In insisting on the centrality of color prejudice behind all the claims that upheld slavery, Garrison sought to make the obvious point, that if the 'slaves of the South should be today miraculously transformed into men of white complexion,' all these arguments would fall to the ground...' Then indeed immediate emancipation would be the right of slaves and the duty of the masters!'[45]

Garrison's most radical claim was that the Constitution itself was a proslavery document by virtue of its acceptance of the 'compromise' that allowed slaveholders to count slaves as 'three-fifths of a man' for purposes of political representation (of the slaveholders.) This compromise Garrison saw as the foundation of the political power which held the union ransom to slaveholders and committed the North to defend slavery as legitimate private property, believing this to be necessary to maintaining the union of free and slave states. For Garrison these compromises invalidated the Constitution, making it both a betrayal of its foundational values that 'all men are created equal,' and an abomination in the sight of God that created all humans in God's image.

Garrison never tired of quoting the verse from Isaiah 29:15 that equated the Constitution with a 'covenant with death and an agreement with hell.' Like the People of Israel, Americans counted on this false covenant to keep them safe, but the Lord God would sweep away their false foundations in violent judgment: 'Then your covenant with death will be annulled and your agreement with Hell will not stand' (Isa. 29:18).

45. Nelson, *Documents of Upheaval*, pp. 128–30.

Although Garrison became increasingly critical of the established churches because of their cooperation with slaveholders and gradualists, Garrison remained all his life deeply rooted in a biblical faith inherited from his evangelical mother.[46] His ultimate commitment to anti-slavery was his conviction that it was against God's law and Christ's commandment to create a redeemed people. To depart from all support for slavery, to disavow 'all union with slaveholders,' was to separate from sin and join the people of God from whom God is fashioning a redeemed creation. Like many 'come-outers' of his time, Garrison read the command to separate from a tainted society and church in the optic of the impending judgment on 'Babylon' found in the book of Revelations. Once again God calls: 'Come out of her, my people, so that you do not take part in her sins, and so you do not share in her plagues' (Rev. 18:4).

Since the Constitution was fundamentally invalid, the whole political system on which it was based was, for Garrison, false. He advocated that abolitionists not become partisan supporters of one political party over another, since both were tainted by the constitutional protection of slavery as the basis of the union. He also rejected running for political office or voting, although he was willing to accept different views on this point among the anti-slavery society members.[47] For most Americans these views were simply seditious, rejecting the most fundamental cornerstone of American national life. Even many abolitionists, such as Frederick Douglass, came to criticize Garrison as unrealistic. Douglass would defend the Constitution as fundamentally a liberation document, although it needed to be reformed on some points.[48]

But Garrison's radical and even millenarian 'come-outerism' was based on a deeper perception. The compromises with slavery that allowed the union to be created in 1787 committed both parties to protect slavery in slave states. No political party could abolish slavery while this compromise stood as the basis for the union. Only by dissolving the union, through repudiation both by

---

46. See Mayer, *All on Fire*, pp. 5–7, 10–22, 29–31 for the influence on him of his mother Fanny Lloyd.

47. Mayer, *All on Fire*, pp. 250, 254–57, 263–64.

48. Mayer, *All on Fire*, pp. 371–74, 431–33; also Frederick Douglass, chapter 25 in *My Bondage and My Freedom*, in *The Oxford Frederick Douglass Reader* (New York: Oxford University Press, 1996), p. 217.

abolitionists and by the slave-masters, could the basis of union be reconstituted without this compromise. Although Garrison hoped that this dissolution of the union and its reconstitution could take place peacefully, he always suspected that it could only happen through a violent upheaval in which the sin of slavery would have to be paid for. This view of slavery as a national sin that demanded a bloody atonement would be echoed in Abraham Lincoln's second Inaugural address:

> If we shall suppose that American slavery is one of those offenses which, in the providence of God must needs come, but which, having continued through His appointed time, He now wills to remove, and that He gives to both North and South this terrible war as the woe due to those by whom the offense came, shall we discern any departure from the divine attributes which the believers in a living God always attribute to Him? Fondly do we hope, fervently do we pray that this mighty scourge of war may speedily pass away. Yet, if God wills that it continue until all the wealth piled by the bondsman in two hundred and fifty years of unrequited toil shall be sunk, and until every drop of blood drawn by the lash shall be paid for by one drawn by the sword — as was said three thousand years ago so it still must be said, that the judgments of the Lord are true and righteous altogether.[49]

This deep sense of slavery as a sin 'which cries to heaven for vengeance' explains what is often seen as the 'contradictions' of Garrison's pacifism. Garrison was a firm believer in non-resistance. Christians, committed to the way of Christ, must not take up arms to fight their enemies, or in self-protection. The Christian must fight with the arms of truth-telling alone (which included the sharpest words Garrison could muster against his detractors). If their enemies attack them, they may not retaliate violently. But Garrison also rejected what he saw as the double standard of many pacifists, who celebrated the American revolutionary war to separate from Britain, but denied the right of blacks (or Indians)[50] to defend themselves against their attackers. For Garrison the tyranny blacks have experienced under slavery is far worse than anything white Americans experienced from their British rulers. So if white

49. Mayer, *All On Fire*, p. 587.
50. Unfortunately Garrison did not focus very much on the unjust treatment of American Indians by the American government, but he did take note of and condemn such episodes of violence as the removal of the Cherokees under President Jackson: See Mayer, Mayer, *All on Fire*, pp. 74, 138.

Americans had a right to take up arms against the British on the grounds of being treated unjustly, the negro slaves have a much better right to rise up against their masters.

This double view, that non-resistance is the norm for committed Christians, but if anyone had a right to take up arms, the slaves had that right far more than the white Americans against the British, and certainly more than the slave-masters against the slaves, explains what appears to be Garrison's inconsistency as a pacifist. While insisting on non-resistance for abolitionists, he nevertheless expressed sympathy for slave revolts, such as the Nat Turner Rebellion of 1831.[51]

This double-sided view came to a head with John Brown's conspiracy to foment a slave insurrection in 1859 in which several leading abolitionists, including Frederick Douglass, were complicit.[52] Garrison sought to express both sides of his complex view. While rejecting Brown's way of violence, he also insisted that if anyone has a right to pick up guns, slaves have that right preeminently. He also suggested that the time of fateful judgment for the sin of slavery was dawning with the Brown insurrection. Brown, in Garrison's view, 'In firing his gun, he has merely told us what time of day it is. It is high noon, thank God.'[53]

Garrison's principles of non-resistance and non-participation in politics under a pro-slavery system would find its final test with the political campaigns of Abraham Lincoln and in the Civil War. Sensing that the final test had come by which the American system would be judged, its fallacious union of free and slave dissolved, clearing the way for a new union, Garrison sided with the Republicans and Lincoln. His own son (not through his father's wish, but with his blessing) joined the army and went off to fight as an officer of a colored regiment from Massachusetts.[54] Lincoln himself was the first president to subscribe to *The Liberator*.[55]

---

51. Mayer, *All on Fire*, pp. 120–23; See also his speech to the Convention of the Free People of Color of Philadelphia and other writings on the Nat Turner Insurrection: Nelson, *Documents of Upheaval*, pp. 28–36.

52. Mayer, *All on Fire*, pp. 476–77, 494, 497–98.

53. On Garrison's speech on the evening of Brown's execution, see Nelson, *Documents of Upheaval*, pp. 263–69.

54. Mayer, *All on Fire*, pp. 551–56, 573–74.

55. Mayer, *All on Fire*, pp. 521, 540.

By the end of the war Garrison found himself in the unaccustomed position of being treated as an elder statesman to be invited to the White House. He also attended the flag-raising by which the U.S. took back Fort Sumner at the end of the war.[56] When the thirteenth amendment was passed by the U.S. Congress, Garrison ended the publication of *The Liberator*. Although he recognized that a new struggle for full equality of the freemen was still ahead, for him this would have to be the struggle of a new generation. The abolition of slavery for which he had fought for thirty-eight years was over.

But Garrison, at his best, fought not just for ending slavery, but for 'universal emancipation.' All oppressed people must go free. This led him to support the nascent women's rights movement that began in the mid-1830s with the Grimké Sisters and Lucretia Mott. Garrison would pay a heavy price for his support of women's rights, and for the equal participation of women in the anti-slavery movement. The anti-slavery society would split into two opposed groups in 1840 because of his appointment of Abbey Kelley to the committee of business of the Society. Those opposed to women's participation withdrew from the society, forming the American and Foreign Anti-Slavery Society.[57] Shortly after this schism, Garrison's society sent four delegates to the World Convention of anti-slavery movements in London, which included a black, Charles Remond, and Lucretia Mott. The London society refused to seat Mott. When Garrison arrived, he refused to take his seat in the convention, remaining in the gallery in solidarity with the women.

Denied official status as a delegate, Lucretia Mott spent much of her days in London getting to know the new bride of Henry B. Stanton (one of the leaders of the opposition to Garrison's radicalism[58]), Elizabeth Cady Stanton. The exclusion of women made Elizabeth Cady Stanton newly aware of women's oppression. She and Mott promised each other to do something to improve women's status. Although Elizabeth Cady Stanton was preoccupied with childbearing for the next few years, these promises bore fruit in July, 1848 when she and Mott organized the first women's rights convention in Seneca Falls, New York. Using the Declaration of

56. Mayer, *All on Fire*, pp. 518–85.
57. Mayer, *All on Fire*, pp. 282–85, also Nelson, *Documents of Upheaval*, pp. 163–68.
58. Mayer, *All on Fire*, pp. 254–58.

Independence as a model Mott, Stanton and others drew up the Declaration of Sentiments and Resolutions which was then passed at the convention on 19 July. The Declaration reflects the Garrisonian assumption that a constitutional system flawed by the exclusion of a major sector of humans, in this case women, can be dissolved, just as the American revolutionaries dissolved their covenant with Britain and instituted a new government that would rectify this failing.

The Declaration adopts this revision of the words of the Declaration of Independence:[59]

> We hold these truths to be self-evident: that all men and women are created equal; that they are endowed by their Creator with certain inalienable rights; that among these are life, liberty and the pursuit of happiness; that to secure these rights governments are instituted, deriving their just powers from the consent of the governed. Whenever any form of government becomes destructive of these ends, it is the right of those who suffer from it to refuse allegiance to it, laying its foundations on such principles and organizing its powers in such form, as to them shall seem most likely to effect their safety and happiness. Prudence indeed will dictate that governments long established should not be changed for light and transient causes; and accordingly all experience hath shown that mankind is more disposed to suffer, while evils are sufferable, than to right themselves by abolishing the forms to which they are accustomed. But when a long train of abuses and usurpations, pursuing invariably the same object, evinces a design to reduce them under absolute despotism, it is their duty to throw off such government and to provide new guards for their future security. Such has been the patient sufferance of the women under this government, and such is now the necessity which constrains them to demand the equal station to which they are entitled:

The Declaration then goes on to list a series of such abuses and usurpations, such as denial of the franchise, forcing women 'to submit to laws in the formation of which she has no voice,' 'taking from her all right in property, even to the wages she earns,' monopolizing all profitable employment and giving her scanty remuneration from those she is permitted to follow, denying women education, excluding her from the ministry and claiming even to speak for 'Jehovah himself' in assigning women her sphere of action. Having listed these grievances, the women demand (in the language

59. The Declaration of Sentiments and Resolutions, in Miriam Schneir, *Feminism: The Essential Historical Writings* (New York: Random House, 1972), pp. 77–82.

of Garrisonian immediatism) 'immediate admission to all the rights and privileges that belong to them as citizens of the United States.' The women then vow to pursue these ends with 'every instrumentality within our power,' employing agents, circulating tracts, petitioning State and National Legislatures and enlisting pulpit and press.

The Declaration goes on with a series of resolutions which declare null and void any laws that discriminate against women, dismissing the claims of women's incapacity for such rights, and finally calling for inclusion of women in the elective franchise. The resolution calling for the vote was opposed by some women, especially those like Mott who followed Garrison's rejection of voting, but it was passed when Frederick Douglass, present at the assembly, defended it from the floor.[60] A final resolution, proposed by Mott, calling for women's right to preach and the securing for women of 'equal participation with men in the various trades, professions and commerce' was also passed.

Most newspapers dismissed the convention or ignored it altogether. But Frederick Douglass gave it a warm endorsement in his paper, *The North Star* (28 July 1848). Reflecting that even those who have finally acceded that 'negroes' have some rights, 'have yet to be convinced that women are entitled to any,' Douglass goes on to insist on equal rights of women with men. 'We hold women to be justly entitled to all we claim for man. We go further, and express our conviction that all political rights which it is expedient for man to exercise, it is equally so for women. All that distinguishes man as an intelligent and accountable being, is equally true of woman; and if that government only is just which governs by the free consent of the governed, there can be no reason in the world to deny women the exercise of the elective franchise, or a hand in making and administering the laws of the land.'[61] It would be more than seventy years before this claim of the franchise was granted to women. Blacks would wait even longer for the franchise, stolen from them in Jim Crow Laws, to be restored.

60. Schneir, *Feminism*, p. 77.
61. Schneir, *Feminism*, pp. 86–89; see also Andrews, *Frederick Douglass Reader*, pp. 98–100. Douglass' consistent endorsement of women's rights has been traced by Philip S. Foner, *Frederick Douglass on Women's Rights* (Westport, CT: Greenwood Press, 1976).

Eugene Debs, Jane Addams and the Labor Question

Eugene V. Debs (1855–1926) was born and raised in Terre Haute, Indiana, the son of immigrants from Alsace.[62] Leaving school at 14, Debs went to work for the railroad, becoming a locomotive fireman at 16. He joined the local of the Brotherhood of Locomotive Firemen at twenty, soon becoming its local secretary and two years later the Grand Secretary and Treasurer of the whole union, as well as editor of the *Locomotive Firemen's Magazine*. In 1884, he entered electoral politics, being elected City Clerk and then to the Indiana House of Representatives as a Democrat, but was discouraged by his inability to get legislation passed that favored the working man.

Debs became convinced that the division of unions into different crafts made it impossible for them to win concessions from the owners. In 1893, he formed the American Railway Union to unify all railway workers and was successful in winning a major strike against the Great Northern Railway. The next year he took the side of Pullman workers in Chicago who were suffering from high rents and low wages imposed by George M. Pullman, owner of Pullman sleeping car factory and dictatorial ruler of the Pullman company town. Debs ordered the members of the Railway Union to uncouple Pullman cars from trains. Work stoppages spread along all the lines leading to Chicago. But this brought intervention from the Federal Government. Federal judges imposed an injunction forbidding the ARU from assisting the Pullman strike. President Cleveland sent troops to Chicago. Debs was arrested on charges of conspiracy to obstruct the mails and then for contempt of court for violating the injunction.[63]

Convicted on the second charge of contempt, Debs served six months in the county jail of Woodstock, Illinois. There Debs read extensively in American and European socialist literature, being particularly impressed by Lawrence Gronlund's, *The Co-operative Commonwealth* (1884). During this period Debs became convinced that the whole question of the working class in America must be rethought. It was not enough to wring concessions from the owners of corporations through strikes and negotiation, although that was still necessary. The workers needed their own party by which to win political power and change the system of ownership of the

---

62. The standard biography of Debs is by Ray Ginger, *The Bending Cross* (New Brunswick: Rutgers University Press, 1949). See pp. 1–19 for his boyhood and youth.
63. Ginger, *The Bending Cross*, pp. 109–67 on the Pullman Strike and Deb's conviction.

means of production. In 1897, Debs declared himself a socialist and helped found the Social Democratic party, running as their presidential nominee in 1900.

In 1901 he founded the Socialist Party of America, and was chosen as their presidential candidate in 1904, 1908, 1912 and 1920 (he declined to run in 1916). During the build up to and then American entrance into the First World War, Debs became an outspoken opponent of participation in the war, insisting that this was an imperialist war between capitalists which did not serve the interests of the working classes of any nation. Under the Espionage Act of 1917, strengthened in 1918, Debs was convicted of giving a speech in Canton, Ohio, 16 June 1918, opposing such wars in general (he did not actually mention World War I).[64] He was sentenced to ten years in prison. After the war President Wilson refused to commute his sentence, but he was released by President Harding on Christmas, 1921. After this imprisonment Debs became involved in issues of prison reform, but his health was broken and he died on 20 October 1926.

For Debs the issue of class struggle was not an abstract theory he learned from books, but a reality which he learned from the hard experience of the labor struggle itself, that was confirmed by socialist writings. The experience of the Pullman strike, in which Federal judges and the President collaborated to break the strike and destroy the railway union on behalf of wealthy industrialists like George M. Pullman, convinced him that the American system was deeply divided between a small wealthy class who owned the means of production and reaped huge profits and the impoverished masses who toiled for minimal pay under these owners and were crushed when they sought to protest and to gain more just wages and working conditions. As he put it in his article, 'How I became a socialist, "…in the gleam of every bayonet and the flash of every rifle *the class struggle was revealed*."'[65]

In Debs' experience, the political system, the newspapers, the courts, the universities and churches were all controlled by this ruling class and did their bidding. Workers, in order to win a more just society, must shape their own party, newspapers and educational

64. See Debs' Canton, Ohio speech, in *Writings and Speeches of Eugene V. Debs* (Introduction, Arthur M. Schlesinger, Jr; New York: Hermitage Press, 1948), pp. 417–33.

65. Debs, *Writings and Speeches*, p. 45.

system to serve the interests of the vast majority of the people by reshaping America from a system dominated by the capitalist class to one collectively owned by the workers, or what Debs would call, with Gronlund, the 'co-operative commonwealth.' Yet, Debs retained his faith in the democratic process. Despite having experienced the deliberate undercounting of the socialist vote by local elections authorities,[66] he continued to believe that if the working class became educated to an awareness of their class interests, they could win political power through the ballot box and shape a socialist society in America.

Debs saw socialism as thoroughly American, although also part of a worldwide revolutionary struggle. He continually presented it as the heir to the legacy of the American revolutionary struggle, manifest in the winning of American political freedom by the founding fathers in the late eighteenth century and the struggle against slavery in the abolitionist movement. Socialism was the next stage in this American struggle, seeking to overcome wage slavery and to establish economic democracy. He saw himself as part of a legacy that included Washington, Jefferson, Franklin and Paine in the revolutionary era, and John Brown, William Lloyd Garrison, Elizabeth Cady Stanton and Susan B. Anthony in the anti-slavery struggle. In his 12 September 1918 address to the jury in his trial under the Espionage Act, Debs defended himself on the grounds of the basic guarantees of freedom of speech, the press and assembly of the Constitution. He argued that the Espionage Act is unconstitutional, violating these basic guarantees: '...if Congress enacts any law that conflicts with this provision, that law is void. If the Espionage Law finally stands, then the Constitution of the United States is dead...'[67]

Debs has been criticized for his insistence on the primacy of class division in America, subsuming other differences, such as gender and race. But Debs did not ignore either the subjugation of women or that of American negroes. He repeatedly defended the equal membership of negroes in the Socialist party, against those that would exclude the negroes from the party, as they were typically excluded from most unions at the time. Racists who objected to the full equality of negroes were rejected in no uncertain terms. Unjust

66. On the undercounting of the socialist vote in the 1912 presidential campaign, see Ginger, *The Bending Cross*, pp. 283–84.

67. Debs, 'Address to the Jury', *Writings and Speeches*, pp. 433–37.

discrimination, not any innate inferiority, is responsible for the subjugation of negroes. For Debs, 'the history of the negro in the United States is a history of crime without parallel.' He spoke of white debasement of the negro as one 'that makes me blush for the unspeakable crimes of my own race.'[68]

Yet, he was also convinced that division of class between capitalist owning class and the oppressed 'wage slave' is the primary root of injustice, with race being a secondary discrimination within class division. He insisted that 'there is no negro question outside of the labor question — the working class struggle... The capitalists, white, black and other shades are on one side, and the workers, white, black and all other colors, on the other side.'[69] In a 1904 reply to an anonymous letter writer who objected to equality of blacks and whites, Debs cites the Negro Resolution passed at the last convention of the Socialist Party reaffirming such equality of black and white in the working class struggle as a basic principle of socialism.[70] Debs is equally insistent that women have no innate inferiority and will find their full citizenship and equality within the 'cooperative commonwealth.'[71]

Debs' views on religion, specifically Christianity, are significant. Although he is vehemently critical of clergymen who side with the capitalist establishment against the rights of labor, he is equally convinced that true Christianity is on the side of the workers. The church has betrayed the mission of Christ and the will of God in ever taking the side of the oppressor. 'When a rich and soulless corporation assaults its weary, worn, half-homed, half-fed workingman, the pulpit is dumb as death and no echo of the voice of Christ is heard in the temple that profanes his name. Can any doubt where the living Jesus would stand in such a struggle?'[72]

Debs frequently claims Jesus as a radical champion of the poor. As he wrote in a 1902 'Appeal to the Working Class,' 'The revolutionary Savior always and everywhere stood with and for the poor.' Debs compared the persecution of socialists with the

68. Debs, 'The Negro in the Class Struggle', *Writings and Speeches*, pp. 64, 55.

69. Debs, *Writings and Speeches*, p. 65.

70. Debs, *Writings and Speeches*, p. 68.

71. See his article in an undated pamphlet published by the Socialist Party, 'Woman — Comrade and Equal', Debs, *Writings and Speeches*, pp. 453–55.

72. 'Prostitution of Religion', *Christian Socialist*, 18 December 1915; quoted in Harold W. Currie, *Eugene V. Debs* (Boston: Twayne Publishers, 1976), p. 113.

persecution of Jesus: 'The Great Soul of Galilees was not only reviled but nailed to the cross by the pharisees two thousand years ago for his incomparably loving and loyal devotion to the lowly and oppressed.'[73]

Thus Debs, although not a churchgoer, is clear where true Christianity ought to be, even as he attacks what he sees as its hypocritical betrayal in the existing churches. He also echoes the language of millennialist redemptive hope in his conviction that the socialist 'cooperative commonwealth,' will bring about that reign of justice and love on earth for which all true believers long. Debs does not hesitate to speak of the 'emancipating gospel of the Socialist movement' and continually ends his speeches with a vision of a worldwide transformation of history that will bring 'freedom to all mankind.'[74]

Another important effort to address the labor question and the immigrant poor was the settlement house movement, led by socialist feminists, such as Jane Addams. Addams founded Hull House in Chicago in 1889 and lived there until her death in 1935.[75] She voted for Eugene Debs in 1920, her first opportunity to vote after women's enfranchisement through the 19th amendment. Although inspired by her Christian background, Addams eschewed evangelization of the mainly Catholic and Jewish immigrants of urban Chicago. Instead, she and her colleagues set up literacy centers, credit unions where the immigrants could save and manage their money, community housing for single working women, gymnasiums and youth clubs, kindergartens and day nurseries for working mothers and public kitchens to serve inexpensive hot meals for the working poor. Classes in sewing, nutrition and household management aided mothers in their domestic duties, while art classes, choral groups, debate clubs and libraries sought to lift immigrant's cultural horizons and also to honor their indigenous cultures. An employment agency and a meeting place for trade unions reached out to labor organizers.

The work of Hull House soon became transformed to address city reform issues. The women of Hull House led campaigns for safe playgrounds for children and to improve city services, such as

73. *Appeal to Reason*, 1 May 1909, p. 1. quoted in Currie, *Eugene V. Debs*, p. 118.

74. See Debs' acceptance speech for the 1904 presidential nomination of the Socialist Party, May, 1904, in *Writings and Speeches*, pp. 75, 95.

75. See Addams' two books, *Twenty Years at Hull-House* (New York: Macmillan, 1910) and *The Second Twenty Years at Hull-House* (New York: Macmillan, 1930).

trash and garbage pick up, and for the inclusion of music and art in the public schools. They set up teams that inspected factory conditions and food contamination, created a visiting nurse program and advocates for youthful law offenders, arguing for their separate treatment from adult criminals.

Hull House sought to institutionalize such programs as part of city and state government services. In some cases Hull House residents came to be employed by the city or state to head such programs. Florence Kelley, who led the inspection of working conditions in factories, won state regulations of factory conditions and was appointed chief factory inspector for the state of Illinois. Julia Lathrop's investigation of city funded asylums won her the appointment as head of the Illinois Board of Charities that supervised these institutions.[76]

Settlement house reform work became a new, primarily female, paid profession, social work. Hull House leaders, Sophronisba Beckinridge and Edith Abbott developed what became the School of Social Work of the University of Chicago, where they sought to professionalize social reform work and base it on careful sociological research and social analysis. Some settlement house women went on to head federal government agencies that sought to legislate such reforms nationally, such as the Children's Bureau, founded in 1912. Julia Lathrop was appointed to head this bureau and staffed it mainly with women from the settlement house movement, drawing on a state by state network of women's reform societies to implement its programs. Ironically, the work of these women to take social services out from under the churches with their evangelizing interests and to make them the responsibility of the government is being reversed today with the efforts of Ronald Reagan and George W. Bush to return the work of social services to the churches or 'faith based' organizations.

Jane Addams was also a pacifist. Throughout her life she argued for the abolition of war as a means of settling conflicts between nations, helping found the Women's Peace Party and Women's International League for Peace and Freedom after World War I.[77] Although not jailed like Debs, her patriotism was attacked during

76. See Robyn Muncy, *Creating a Female Domain in American Reform, 1890–1935* (New York: Oxford University Press, 1991).

77. See Marie Louise Degan, *The History of the Women's Peace Party* (Baltimore, MD: The Johns Hopkins University Press, 1939).

and after that war due to her anti-war views. When anti-women's suffrage forces argued that the vote was tied to the duty to bear arms for one's country, and therefore women were excluded (it was assumed that women could never be soldiers in the Armed Forces, even though women had actually fought in several previous wars), Addams attempted to turn the argument around. She argued that war represented a barbaric level of human development. Women's vote was needed in order to supersede war by negotiation as the more civilized way to deal with conflict between nations.[78]

Martin Luther King: Racism, Poverty, War and Sexism in the 1960s

Martin Luther King (1929–68) is perhaps the foremost spokesman for an American liberation theology, unifying in his powerful rhetoric the symbols of American civil religion, with its promises of 'liberty and justice for all,' with the prophetic language of the Bible. In his view Americans are sternly judged for their betrayal of their American and Christian ideals and called to repent and to create the just society that would begin to incarnate that 'beloved community' to which their civil and religious faith summoned them. It was a language long honed by the preaching of the black church in which King was nurtured.

King was the son and grandson of black preachers and social activists. His father, Martin Luther King Sr., was pastor of the influential Ebenezer Baptist Church in Atlanta, Georgia, and his grandfather, A.D. Williams, a founder of the Atlanta branch of the National Association for the Advancement of Colored People. Graduating from Morehouse College in Atlanta with a degree in sociology at nineteen, King went on to earn his Bachelor of Divinity degree from Crozer Theological Seminary in Pennsylvania in 1951 and his Ph.D. from Boston University School of Theology in 1955. Ordained to the Baptist ministry by his father in 1947, King was installed as pastor of the historic Dexter Avenue Baptist Church in Montgomery, Alabama, in the Fall of 1954. It was in this position that he would be precipitated into his career as civil rights leader of a rising movement of American blacks against the discriminatory Jim Crow Laws which had reigned in American, especially Southern, life for more than sixty years.

78. See Addams book, *Newer Ideals of Peace* (New York: Macmillan, 1907).

On 1 December 1955, Rosa Parks, a 42 year old civil rights activist, employed as a seamstress, refused to give up her seat on a bus to a white man in accordance with the Jim Crow Laws of Alabama. She was arrested and jailed. A group of black women declared a boycott, calling on the blacks of Montgomery to stay off the buses. A group of black ministers of Montgomery responded with their support and asked the 26 year old King to be spokesman for the boycott, dubbed the Montgomery Improvement Association. King was chosen because he was new in town and was not identified with any particular clique in the black community, but he quickly rose to the occasion. He positioned the boycott as a central expression of the struggle of the black community for full rights as American citizens. His words helped galvanize the 55,000 black population of the city into an historic struggle that would last more than a year and would end with a Supreme Court ruling making bus segregation unconstitutional.[79]

King recognized this as the historic moment to end all segregation in the South. He institutionalized the movement by founding the Southern Christian Leadership Conference in 1957, bringing together prominent church leaders across the South, with himself as President, a position he held for the rest of his life. The motto of the SCLC was 'to redeem the soul of America.' As its leader and spokesman King began to shape the vision of non-violent direct action as both a strategy and a philosophy of life. Against the skepticism of white and black leaders, King hammered out the key ideas of non-violent direct action.

First of all, he sought to make clear that non-violence was not passive submission to white violence. It is a method of active resistance to oppression. Secondly, nonviolence does not seek to defeat or humiliate the opponent but to win a change of heart. Thirdly, nonviolence seeks to attack systems of injustice as evil, not to attack the perpetrators as themselves evil. For example, in Montgomery it was laws of racial injustice that were evil, not white people. It seeks to avoid not only physical violence, but violence of spirit. Thus, nonviolence seeks to avoid reverse racial hate and to open the door for a reconciled community of whites and blacks.

79. See Martin Luther King, *Stride Toward Freedom: The Montgomery Story* (New York: Harper and Row, 1958). Also Adam Fairclough, *Martin Luther King, Jr.* (Athens, GA: University of Georgia Press, 1995), pp. 17–33.

Nonviolence also is willing to undergo suffering without retaliation, to accept blows without striking back, to go to jail if necessary. For King this willingness to accept violence without retaliation was also integral to the strategy of nonviolence. By committing violent acts against nonviolent protestors, the defenders of injustice reveal the evil of their system. When these acts are publicized through television and newspapers, the public is horrified and stirred to sympathy. More people join the protest, and government officials are impelled to act to change unjust laws.

Ultimately for King nonviolence was based on love. Love was not a sentimental feeling toward unjust people, but an agapic or self-giving love for the sake of the well-being of the neighbor and ultimately for a reconciled community, that 'beloved community' which was always King's ultimate vision. The exercise of such love for the sake of a new community was rooted in a faith that the laws of the universe were finally on the side of justice. God, the ultimate power of the universe, is on the side of justice and the creation of a beloved community. God is with the protestors in the struggle, no matter how much wrongly used power might be arrayed against them.[80]

It was difficult for many protestors to grasp the full dimensions of King's vision, much less to maintain non-violence in the face of vicious behavior by defenders of white dominance. The leaders of the civil rights movement developed training sessions to communicate the philosophy and discipline of non-violence. By the mid-sixties some of the younger organizers of the Student Non-Violent Coordinating Committee, such as Stokely Carmichael, began to challenge King with the slogan of Black Power. Although Black Power didn't necessarily mean armed violence, it signaled a more aggressive style than that seemingly promoted by King.

In his 1967 book, *Where Do We Go from Here: Chaos or Community?* King defended non-violent direct action not only as his personal faith, but the only practical strategy for a minority black community that would be totally outgunned by an armed white community and law enforcement system. To resort to violence could only lead to disaster, giving whites the excuse to wipe out blacks. But he also sought to affirm many aspects of Black Power which he saw as

80. King laid out this definition of non-violent direct action in several articles, such as an essay in *The Christian Century*, 6 February 1957. Its fullest development appeared in *Stride Toward Freedom*, pp. 66–71.

already implied by non-violent action. First, he clarified that non-violent direct action did not mean one could not defend oneself as an individual when one's person and home was attacked. Such right to self-defense of one's own home was recognized by American law.

Secondly, non-violence encourages self-esteem and self-confidence by blacks, overcoming fear and internalized passivity in the face of white aggression. Non-violence also encourages blacks to organize and to pursue their goals though many forms of political, economic and social development. But in public demonstrations, armed violence must not be used. Most of all, King objected to the implication that whites should be excluded from the civil rights movement. For King, the goal of the movement was integration of blacks and whites in a new society of justice and mutual well-being, not racial separatism. The dream of a separate black nation King saw as absurd in the American context. Ultimately he maintained his hope that non-violence was more than a tactic. He held out the vision of a new humanity beyond violence and counter-violence, a power rooted in justice and mutual love for one another as interdependent members of one human community.[81]

By 1965, the civil rights movement had won a number of campaigns in the south, despite several outbreaks of retaliatory violence by whites. King's famous speech at the climax of the August 28, 1963 March on Washington, 'I have a Dream,' had stirred the nation and won general approbation from liberal whites. The Kennedy brothers and Lyndon B. Johnson had intervened in support of King. Key legislation to abolish Jim Crow Laws, such as the Civil Rights Act (1964)[82] and the Voting Rights Act (1965) that defended full political rights for blacks, had been passed by Congress. But the outbreak of violence in several northern cities, such as Watts in Los Angeles in the summer of 1965, signaled a different problem among alienated urban blacks, not easily amenable to the techniques King had used in the South where smaller face-to-face communities and the power of the black church still existed.

In 1966, King sought to take the movement to the North by organizing in the black slums of Chicago. Here he was greeted with rocks and bottles hurled by white residents of areas adjacent to

81. See chapter 2 on Black Power, *Where do We Go From Here: Chaos or Community?* (New York: Harper and Row, 1967).

82. An expanded Civil Rights Act would be signed by President Johnson on 10 April 1968, after King's assassination and partly as a tribute to him.

black slums. He found it difficult to gain the same kind of response to his calls to loving community from alienated blacks, who suffered from more subtle and systemic forms of discrimination, rather than blatant Jim Crow Laws.[83] It also became evident to King that the escalating war in Vietnam was draining American resources in a way that left little hope of massive governmental funds for Johnson's proclaimed War on Poverty. King began to rethink his strategy and to envision a much wider movement that would aim at overcoming poverty across class. He would come to question American foreign policy as represented not only by the war in Vietnam, but imperialist wars in general.

King's two initiatives in the last year of his life signaled this new stage of the movement. One was his speech against the war in Vietnam, 'A Time to Break the Silence,' delivered on 4 April 1967 in Riverside Church in New York City at a meeting of the antiwar organization, Clergy and Laity Concerned[84]. The second was the announcement of the Poor Peoples Campaign unveiled in October, 1967. In his anti-Vietnam war speech on 4 April 1967, King detailed the history of U.S.-Vietnamese relations since the end of the Second World War as one of systematic betrayal of the legitimate Vietnamese aspirations for independence, contrary to American claims to be defending 'democracy.' He also indicated the links he saw between the U.S. failures to create a just society at home and its imperial adventures abroad. The war not only dragged poor young men, white and black, to murder Vietnamese people and destroy their society and land, but it also drained American resources needed to create a more just society at home.

But, most pointedly, King indicated that this war was not an exception to a generally benign U.S. history toward other nations, but rather part of a pattern in which the U.S. had continually intervened throughout the world, especially in Asia and Latin America, to undermine anti-colonial struggles for independence and to install brutal dictators subservient to the interests of the powerful

83. See Fairlough, *Martin Luther King, Jr.*, pp. 105–10, for the failure of King's Chicago Campaign.

84. This speech is found in James Melvin Washington (ed.), *A Testament of Hope: The Essential Writings and Speeches of Martin Luther King, Jr* (San Francisco, CA: HarperSanFrancisco, 1991), pp. 231–44. King's arguments against the war are elaborated in his book, *The Trumpet of Conscience* (New York: Harper and Row, 1967). See chapter 2 on conscience and the Vietnam War, reprinted in Washington (ed.), *A Testament of Hope*, pp. 634–40.

of U.S. society. In King's words, the U.S. had been for a long time on the 'wrong side of a world revolution.' To get on the right side of this world revolution America must 'undergo a radical revolution in values,' from a thing-oriented to a person-oriented society, placing the well-being of people over acquisition of wealth. King called on the U.S. to end bombing in North and South Vietnam, declare a unilateral ceasefire, prevent other battlefields from opening up in Laos and Cambodia, accept the National Liberation Front as the legitimate negotiating partner and set a date to remove all foreign troops, in accordance with the 1954 Geneva Agreement.

King's public attack on the Vietnam War and its links with general U.S. foreign policy dismayed many of his supporters and won the enmity of President Johnson. Many of his followers claimed that opposition to the war had nothing to do with King's main mission against racial discrimination in the U.S., but King stoutly insisted that these two realities were intimately interconnected.[85] The Poor People's Campaign also was greeted with veiled or open hostility by the federal government and ambivalence by many former admirers. This campaign clearly transcended the earlier basis of the civil rights movement as a crusade to dismantle racially discriminatory laws. It called for a broad class-based struggle that would unite poor communities, across all races and ethnicities in America.

The Poor People's Campaign implicitly appealed to an American tradition of Christian socialism found in the Social Gospel Movement of the era of Eugene Debs and Jane Addams. Although King avoided the word socialism, he spoke sardonically of the American tradition of 'socialism for the rich,' and called for 'poor people's power' and an 'economic Bill of Rights' that would give the poor a more equal share in American wealth that was theirs by right. The Campaign called for three thousand poor people to be recruited from each of ten different urban and rural areas across the U.S., to be trained in non-violent philosophy and discipline and to march on Washington, there to create an encampment and to remain indefinitely until Congress met their demands for legislation to address poverty in a root and branch manner.

This campaign was to be launched in the Spring of 1968. March 1968 saw King in Memphis in support of a strike by the city's sanitation workers seeking a wage rise and recognition of their

---

85. See *The Trumpet of Conscience*, in Washington (ed.), *A Testament of Hope*, pp. 634–36.

union. But a rally on March 28 went badly, with a group of young militants bent on disruption. King decided to continue his support for the workers. On April 3, he gave a poignant and powerful speech in which he speculated that he might die in the process, but that those committed to justice must continue the struggle, confident that a more just society was dawning:

> Longevity has its place. But I'm not concerned about that now. I just want to do God's will. And He's allowed me to go up to the mountain top. And I've looked over. And I've seen the Promised Land. I may not get there with you. But I want you to know tonight that we as a people will get to the Promised Land. So I am happy tonight. I'm not worried about anything. I'm not fearing any man. "Mine eyes have seen the glory of the coming of the Lord."

The next evening, as King stepped out on a balcony outside his motel room, chatting with staff members, a bullet tore into his face. Moments later King was dead.

The Civil Rights Movement of 1955–68 did more than end Jim Crow. It inspired a series of movements that sought redress of grievances of marginalized groups in the U.S., notably women, homosexuals, American Indians and Mexican-Americans. This critique went beyond the injustices within U.S. society. Americans opened up a deeply critical examination of American history and began to question, with King, whether we had not, for a long time, been on the wrong side of many world revolutions.

But these movements sparked vehement reaction from right wing forces, coalescing in a new union of religious and neoconservative reactionaries that swept into power with the election of Ronald Reagan in 1979. This coalition continues to expand its power into the twenty-first century with the administration of George W. Bush, committing the U.S. to new imperial adventures. The 'sixties' have been continually maligned by the Right, misrepresenting it as a time of break down of all values, rather than an affirmation of deeply held progressive values in American culture and religion. The Right has sought to silence critique of American society, both of poverty and injustice at home and of the pursuit of global domination abroad. But the excesses of the Bush II Administration have sparked a new outpouring of critical thought about American power within the U.S. itself, a critique that continues to grow in 2007, but has yet to unite into an effective movement for change. It is to this movement that I turn in the concluding chapter of this volume.

Chapter Eight

TOWARD A U.S. THEOLOGY OF LIBERATION AND LETTING GO

In 1977, Sister Marie Augusta Neal wrote a short book called *A Socio-Theology of Letting Go*.[1] This book made a strong impression on me since it seemed to articulate the other side of a liberation theology, the side of a liberation theology addressed to those who are holding oppressive power over others. For those who are oppressed to be liberated, those who hold oppressive power must 'let go' (or must be made to let go), must relax their grip on domination and so others can go free. Ultimately a transformation of both sides must take place so there is no more poor and rich, oppressed and oppressors, elect and non-elect, privileged and non-privileged, but a new society where all members enjoy dignity and access to the basic means of life. This is the 'civilización de pobreza' which martyred Jesuit theologian Ignacio Ellacuría spoke about in the last years of his life,[2] a phrase which might be translated a 'civilization of simple living.'

In this concluding chapter I will articulate something of what a theology of letting go might mean for North American power-holders, which would also be a theology of liberation, not only for dominated and impoverished peoples of countries victimized by the rich and powerful of the United States, but also for the vast majority of the people of the United States itself. Such a theology of liberation and letting go must involve, not only a transformed relationship between rich and poor in the United States and between the United States and the rest of the world, but also the relation of

1. The subtitle is *The Role of a First World Church facing Third World Peoples* (New York: Paulist Press, 1977).

2. 'Utopía y profetismo desde América Latina: Un ensayo concreto de soteriología histórica', *Revista Latinoamericana de Teología* 17 (1989), pp. 141–84; reprinted in I. Ellacuría and J. Sobrino, *Mysterium Liberationis* (Madrid: Editorial Trotta, 1990), 1, pp. 393–442.

rich and poor to the earth itself, to the eco-community of our common planetary home.

A theology of liberation and letting go today must be understood as a theology of ecojustice, just relations between humans to each other and between humans and the earth. Such a theology of ecojustice must include ecofeminism, not only in the sense of including women as equal humans in society, but transforming the way in which violent relations to nature and subjugated groups of humans have been shaped by the ideological patterns of sexism, of the masculine over the feminine, active over passive, virile over impotent.

This exploration of a theology of liberation and letting go for U.S. North America involves two parts. First, there must be explicit theological critique of those ideological themes that have been exploited by the theology of 'America' as elect nation, chosen by God to dominate and redeem the world. This involves questions such as the theological status of nation-states, the understanding of God, of good and evil and of messianic hope. Gender and hierarchical dualism will also be touched upon here. The second part involves our vision of an alternative society of just, peaceful and sustainable relations between humans and with the earth. This must involves such questions wealth and poverty, war and violence, ecological sustainability and global governance and some ideas of how we begin to get there from our present disastrous situation.

Dismantling the Theology of American Empire: The Chosen Nation

Already in the seventeenth century in the founding decades of Puritan settlement in New England, dissident thinker Roger Williams recognized the dangerous nature of belief in a 'Christian nation,' chosen by God to rule the earth that, by virtue of their representation of God's true faith and church, could push aside non-Christian people and take over their land. Williams raised his voice on behalf of the indigenous peoples of America as the owners of the land with whom the immigrants must deal fairly in order to themselves come and settle in this land. He was rejected by the Puritan leaders as a noxious heretic and banished to the wilderness. His voice was remembered and claimed by the American revolutionaries in regard to freedom of religion, but unfortunately what was not remembered or incorporated into the identity of the

American state was his protest against the idea of an elect Christian nation.

In 1966, Jewish dissident theologian Richard Rubenstein published his critique of traditional Jewish theology in the light of the destruction of the Jews by Nazism, *After Auschwitz: Radical Theology and Contemporary Judaism*.[3] In this book Rubenstein discards the concept of the Jewish people as an elect nation as a dangerous idea. Rubenstein deplored particularly the seductive effect of this idea on Christians who have incorporated themselves into the Jewish tradition while also claiming to supersede it. The idea of being an elect nation was appropriated by Christians to claim a unique status as God's favored people, superseding that of the people of Israel. In order to cut the root out from under this dangerous idea as it has been appropriated by Christians, Jews themselves must reject this primitive claim.[4]

Other Jewish theologians would not be as dismissive of the idea of election as Rubenstein. David Novak, professor of Judaic Studies of the University of Virginia, grapples with the idea of the election of Israel.[5] Novak sees the idea as essential to Jewish religious identity, but it should be understood as an interior idea of Israel's collective responsibility to God. It must not be appropriated as a way of giving Israel any kind of power or privilege over other peoples. Novak does not discuss Christian appropriations of this idea, but his critique would apply to any Christian use of this idea that would be construed as giving them power and privilege over other nations.

Thinkers among the peoples of the ancient Mediterranean world, both Jews, Greeks and Romans, were struck by the existence of different tribal groups (*gens*) with their distinct languages, cultures, social organizations and identities. As they came into contact with a plurality of such peoples different from themselves, they sought to place them in their theological universe. The Jewish tradition set themselves as elect people over against the other 'nations,' while also giving them their distinct place in relation to the God of creation that provides the basis for a universal morality for all humans.[6]

3. Richard Rubenstein, *After Auschwitz: Radical Theology and Contemporary Judaism* (Indiana: Bobbs-Merrill, 1966).

4. Rubenstein, *After Auschwitz*, see especially chapter 2, 'The Dean and the Chosen People,' pp. 47–58.

5. David Novak, *The Election of Israel: The Idea of a Chosen People* (New York: Cambridge University Press, 1995).

6. On the place of gentiles in a Jewish theology of election, see Novak, *The Election of Israel*, pp. 104–10, 182–90.

Jewish thought also speculated about distinct classes of angels in charge of different parts of the natural world and of each of the different nations: 'When the Most High gave to the nations their inheritance, when he separated the sons of men, he fixed the bounds of the peoples according to the number of the sons of God' (Deut. 32:8). Thus the number of nations are limited by the number of 'sons of God,' or angels (fixed in some traditions as seventy), each nation having a guardian angel. Christian thinkers, such as Origen in the late second century, picked up this Jewish theme and believed that each nation had its guardian angel.

This idea also figured in Greco-Roman political thought which sought to reconcile the cults and national gods of the conquered people with the universal Roman imperium representing the universal God. Thus, Julian the Apostate in the mid-third century BCE wrote 'Our writers say that the Demiurge is the father of all men and their common king. He has divided the peoples among various gods whose business is to watch over different nations and cities. Each of these gods rules over the portion that has fallen to him in accordance with his nature.'[7] The pagan apologist Celsus used this idea against Christianity by arguing that Christians had deserted their distinct national god.

Origen replied by claiming that humanity was once one, all under the one universal God. Separation into distinct nations, worshipping distinct national gods, was an effect of sin. Some of these angelic guardians departed from God and thus became the source of the idolatries. Only Israel remained faithful to the one God. But with redemption this separation is being overcome. Redemption through Christ is restoring original unity.[8] This Christian belief in restoration of the world to its original unity coincided nicely with the Roman imperial belief that the universal creator was the deity of the Roman imperium, thus paving the way to a fusion of these two ideas in the idea of a universal Christian empire.

While later Christianity discarded the idea of distinct guardian angels of each nation, it retained the idea of itself as the representative of universal empire in which human unity will be

7. See 'Angels of the Nations', http://www.home.zonnet.nl/chotki/angels_of_the_nations, 1–8. Also Julian, Emperor of Rome, 'Against the Galileans', *Works*, English translation, W.C. Wright (Cambridge, MA: Harvard University Press, 1961–68), III, p. 321.

8. Zonnet, 'Angels of the Nations', also Origen, *Contra Celsum*, Henry Chadwick (ed.), (Cambridge: Cambridge University Press, 1953), especially pp. 474–75.

restored. Other peoples and their distinct identities are thus dismissed as only representatives of idolatry or worship of false gods, while Christianity alone represents the universal God and religion. Judaism, while continuing to worship the one true God, only comes into its promised universality through converting to Christianity and accepting Christ as its promised Messiah. Judaism historically rejected this Christian construct of redemptive history, affirming its own distinct particularity, and the particularity of other peoples against Christian universalist imperialism.

How do we today sort out this heritage of opposition between nationalist particularity and the claim of a universal destiny of one messianic people destined to unify all people by destroying their differences from the ruling nation? There are several aspects to the rethinking of these opposing paradigms. One must start with the affirmation of the *equal* value each one of the diverse peoples, their heritages and cultures. Each people is a distinct expression of human creativity. We need to value each culture and language and seek to preserve it. To lose any language, and those who speak it, is like a species of animal going extinct; it is to rip a page from the Book of Life.[9]

At the same time we recognize that, unlike distinct species which deviate from each other over a long period of time through biological mutation, cultural entities are much more quickly mutable. Cultural identities are human cultural constructs, which means both that they are powerful centers of group identities and yet members of this group can assimilate into other cultures in a generation or two, becoming hybrid groups, partly retaining their earlier identity and partly taking on that of the group into which they have assimilated. This becomes increasingly complex as peoples of different cultures migrate and assimilate into political entities with other languages and cultures.

Today the concept of distinct 'nation-states,' i.e. each language and cultural group should become a distinct political entity, cannot be realized and has always been fallacious. What actually exists under the misleading term 'nation-state' is larger or smaller political entities produced by complex processes of expansion and colonialism, all of which have within them a variety of minority cultures and

9. See Art Davidson, *Endangered Peoples* (San Francisco, CA: Sierra Club Books, 1993).

peoples, even though one culture and language may assert itself as the dominant culture of that nation (or occasionally, as in Canada, claiming a bicultural identity). Thus, the problem of nationalism today is how to affirm the equal citizenship of peoples of a plurality of cultures within each political entity, without privileging one national culture in ways that discriminates against those of other cultures.

No state, including the United States, has solved this in a fully satisfactory way. Ethnic genocides continue to break out as one group seeks to eliminate the equal claims of other groups. The United States refused the invitation to become a bilingual nation after the Mexican American War in 1848 when it first promised and then rejected the terms of the Treaty of Guadalupe-Hidago to give Spanish equal status with English in the half of Mexico it was appropriating into the United States. But the continued migration of Hispanics to the U.S., while claiming the right to continue speaking their own language, continues to erupt in battles over 'immigration' of 'illegal aliens,' concepts which falsify what is really at stake. The animus toward recognizing Spanish as a national language is shown in the movements for English as the sole national language and the anger that erupted in April 2006, when some Mexican-Americans translated the U.S. national anthem into Spanish.

What is needed is to affirm the equal value of each culture, without universalizing the messianic identity of any one culture, mandated to dominate and assimilate all others. Each state then must be recognized as a provisional reality in which the plurality of cultures of the peoples within it are accorded equal citizenship within that state. Each state thus must meet other states as equals in a United Nations. At the same time each state must negotiate the equal status of the diverse cultures within itself. A universal humanity exists only through the dialogue and mutual respect of the many, not the suppression of the many by one dominant identity. No one people is God's favored people. God stands in relation to each people, inviting them to affirm their distinctiveness and their mutuality with the other peoples with whom they share community.

God and the Nations

If no nation is especially elected by God, it follows that the only universal God that can be affirmed without making God into a racist nationalist is a God of all nations, a God who affirms the unity of all peoples of earth in and through their diversity, a God who relates intimately to each of these distinct cultures, without setting any one culture above the others. Is it possible to conceive of God in such terms?

The concept of God that Christians inherit from Judaism and Greek philosophy is a complex and contradictory construct. As we now realize, monotheism did not leap full-grown from Hebrew religion, but evolved from earlier roots which were polytheistic (many gods) and henotheistic (one god for us). The concept of angels as 'sons of God' reflects earlier traditions which assumed a plurality of gods, under a 'head god.' The presence of a goddess as wife of the head god, was inherited from the Canaanite El, whom the Hebrews identified with Yahweh. El had a wife, Asherah, who lingered in Hebrew popular religion into the sixth century BCE.[10] A new female deity, Wisdom, was born in Jewish scholarly tradition in the post-exilic period and flourished into the first century BCE in writings such as the Wisdom of Solomon.[11] Jewish mysticism pursued a concept of deity that was multidimensional, both male and female.[12]

Monotheism evolved from henotheism. Yahweh was first seen, not so much as the only deity that exists, but the only one for Israel, a tribal god of a particular people. While Hebrew thought came to insist that 'He' is the only God, the creator of the universe, there still remains the assumption that 'He' is preeminently the God of Israel, the god of a particular people, choosing them and relating to them in a particular way different from all other nations. Christianity appropriated this quasi-tribal god into Greek philosophical ideas, the universal creator of Plato and the 'unmoved mover' of Aristotle. But there also remains a sense that this God, the father of Jesus Christ, is the Christian God in a way that excludes the religious

---

10. On the evolution of the Hebrew view of God, see Mark S. Smith, *The Early History of God: Yahweh and Other Deities* (San Francisco: Harper and Row, 1989); also Marjo C. Korpel, *Monotheism in Ancient Israel and the Veneration of the Goddess Asherah* (Sheffield: Sheffield Academic Press, 2001); Judith M. Hadley, *The Cult of Asherah in Ancient Israel and Judah: Evidence for a Hebrew Goddess* (New York: Cambridge University Press, 2000).

11. See Judith M. Hadley, 'Wisdom and the Goddess,' in John Day *et al.*, *Wisdom in Ancient Israel* (Cambridge: Cambridge University Press, 1991), pp. 234–43.

12. See Raphael Patai, *The Hebrew Goddesses* (New York: Ktav Publishing House, 1967), pp. 137–206.

experiences of other people. The Christian God is still a tribal god writ large.

The Greek philosophical God is constructed around metaphysical dualisms of spirit and matter, symbolically expressed as male versus female. When Hebrew and Greek views are fused in Christianity the resulting idea of God reflects anthropocentric, androcentric and ethnocentric biases. God is seen as anthropomorphic, uniquely related to the human spirit and intelligence as the image of God. The rest of creation lacks this direct relation to God and is related to God through the human which exercises dominion over nature. God is also seen as male, typically imaged as an elderly white male king. 'He' is fully disclosed only through Jesus, who uniquely incarnates God's Logos or Mind. Thus, the full presence of God is found only in Christianity. These anthropocentric, androcentric and ethnocentric biases distance God from non-human nature, from all women, from non-elite males and non-Christians.

How then to speak the name of God without these biases? Monotheism is plagued by the dualism of the One and the Many, seeking oneness by excluding manyness. The emphasis on oneness lines up with the oneness of the elite group who claim God as their God, who are us and not them; male, not female; human, not plant or animal; spirit, not body. The Trinitarian understanding of God could help this problem since it brings together manyness and oneness. But if this is seen as a super-celestial three-personed transcendent being outside the cosmos, the problem persists. Trinitarian thought must recover what was traditionally called 'the economic trinity,' an understanding of deity as dynamic process that underlies the creative gestation of differentiation, interrelation and communion. God as trinity encompasses all the manyness of cosmic, planetary and human plurality and their interconnection.[13]

Liberation theology's affirmation of God's preferential option for the poor calls the believing community to respond through solidarity with the poor. This is a useful correction to the distorted assumption that God is on the side of the elites and is represented

13. The best example of an effort to rethink Trinitarian thought in these terms is Ivone Gebara, 'The Trinity and Human Experience', in Rosemary Ruether (ed.), *Women Healing Earth: Third World Women on Ecology, Feminism and Religion* (Maryknoll, NY: Orbis Press, 1996), pp. 13–23. This is a condensed version of a longer essay in Portuguese, *Trinidade, palavra sobre coisas velhas e novas; uma perspectiva ecofeminista* (Sao Paulo: Paulinas, 1994).

by the rulers. But the concept of preferential option for the poor had typically been misunderstood among first world elites as a kind of 'election' of the poor against the rich, or a theological class war.

There is, of course, truth to the Marxist idea of class struggle. The bifurcation of society into rich and poor is not due to some people being hard working and others lazy (as U.S. ideology has it), but rather an organized system of exploitation which makes the rich rich through making most people poor. As Ellacuría put it, the relation of rich and poor is a dialectical relation, not a 'natural' differentiation.[14]

Preferential option for the poor recognizes that the extreme maldistribution of resources between humans is due to unjust and exploitative human social structures. God is seen as standing in judgment on this unjust structure, in solidarity with the excluded and impoverished and calling the privileged to repent of this injustice, side with the poor in their own struggles for liberation and seek to fashion a new society where resources as more justly shared. An ecofeminist liberation theology would make a parallel analysis of the marginalization of women and the impoverishment and pollution of nature in patriarchal extractive societies.

We need to interpret God's 'option for the poor' less anthropomorphically. I suggest that it means that cosmic interactive creativity tends to a mutuality of relations where the means of life are shared equitably by all. Human evil creates unjust distortion in these relations, making some very rich at the expense of others who are impoverished, privileging men at the expense of women, and using nature in a way that undermines its own processes of sustainability. God, as the underlying process of mutual generativity, thus 'stands' against these unjust distortions and constantly 'calls us' to correct them, to reestablish relationship of mutual sharing. God as the source of all life, from the distant galaxies to the multiplicity of species of microbes, plants and animals to the many human cultures, does not 'choose' one group against others, but calls all life into mutually life sustaining relations. To 'obey' God is to convert ourselves from every form of unjust discrimination, to struggle against systems that bias human society for some against

14. Ignacio Ellacuría, 'Los Pobres: Lugar teológico en América Latina,' in *Escritos Teológicos* (San Salvador: UCA editorial, 2001), I, pp. 141–42.

others and to seek to recreate systemic and personal relations of mutual flourishing.

Good and Evil

The legacy of the Christian fusion of Greek and Hebrew traditions has created two problematic biases of the view of good and evil: ethnocentrism and metaphysical dualism. The ethnocentric bias locates evil in the 'other' as cultures that worship other gods (idolaters) or have inferior cultures (barbarians versus Hellenes). The bias of metaphysical dualism locates evil in finitude and materiality which resists and subverts eternal Being. Women, pagans, barbarians, the body all are seen as expressions of inferiority that must be controlled and are expressions of evil when uncontrolled.

From the Hebrew prophetic tradition, however, there is an alternative view that denounces injustice by God's own people, criticizes self-serving religion and calls for repentance and return to obedience to God's commands for just and harmonious relations between peoples and between humans and the rest of creation. It is this tradition that has inspired liberation and ecofeminist theologies today. Prophetic faith does not project evil on the other, as body or social group, but turns the critique on its own community as the source of distortion, as those who oppress the poor and use religion for self-aggrandizement.

Evil as distorted relationship needs to be distinguished from natural finitude and mortality. Humans share with all other earth creatures limits and finitude. There was no perfect deathless utopia of the beginning, nor is it possible to create some perfect time of the future when all death, disease and tragedy will disappear. But humans ever strive against these limits and seek to create 'better' conditions of physical comfort and security. Unfortunately, one major tendency of human striving for betterment is for some to appropriate the lion's share of resources by exploiting others, taking over the fruits of their labor and impoverishing them, so that a powerful elite can enjoy wealth, leisure, power and prestige. One group protects itself from insecurity and maximizes its well-being by transferring heightened poverty and vulnerability to others. Thus are generated hierarchical societies of nobles over slaves or serfs, men over women and one race over another.

Such unjust hierarchies justify themselves by ideologies that claim that the exploited others are 'naturally' inferior, fitted only for brute labor and incapable of higher culture. Religion is a major tool in such justifying ideologies, making God or the gods in the image of the ruling class and constructing laws mandating such exploitative relations as having been handed down by God or the gods. Movements of prophetic faith critique these unjust social practices and their justifying ideologies. They call for a dismantling of such hierarchies in order to recreate societies of just sharing for all members of the society.

The American idea of itself as God's elect nation has functioned mostly as such a false ideology that justified appropriation of Indian and Mexican land and the expulsion or destruction of these people or their reduction to exploited labor. Identifying the elect nation as Anglo-Saxon Protestants privileged this group against Indians, African-Americans, Mexicans, Filipinos, Chinese and other people defined as 'non-white.' A cult of militarist virility sought to locate women as dependents and domestic labor and decried any efforts of women to seek equal rights. Feminists were blamed for making women 'viragos,' emasculating males, and thus threatening national security.

During the Cold War era, anti-communism became the national religion. Capitalism was conflated with liberty, freedom and democracy, while any way of communalizing social resources to create greater economic equality for all was decried as totalitarian, producing slavery and dictatorship. The American way was seen as the epitome of 'good,' communism the epitome of evil. This same dualism of America the good versus the forces of evil has now been transferred to the 'war against terrorism.' This dualistic thinking makes it very difficult for Americans to sort out the ambiguities on both sides. Communist systems have curtailed civil liberties in ways that we should decry, but also provided subsidized housing, education and medical care lacking in the U.S. 'free enterprise' system. Unfortunately, for American ideology and foreign policy, victory over communism has been understood to mean destroying not only its evils, but its positive accomplishments, reducing former communist areas to colonized and impoverished dependents on American colonialism.

The rhetoric of innocent and good America against irrationally evil terrorists was unleashed full throttle after the 9/11 terrorist attacks on the World Trade Center in New York and the Pentagon in Washington D.C. George W. Bush particularly favors a religious rhetoric that weaves together the language of apocalyptic warfare with that of messianic mission. The war against terrorism, against Al-Queda in Afghanistan and then against Saddam Hussein in Iraq (who had nothing to do with the 9/11 terrorist attacks) is depicted as episodes in an apocalyptic drama of good against evil, the angels of light against the forces of darkness. America, God's chosen people, is once more pitted against God's enemies. This language of apocalyptic warfare assumes an American redemptive mission to the world. America in general, and Bush in particular, are seen as God's messianic agents in combating evil and establishing good on earth.

Some American military leaders do not hesitate to pose this apocalyptic war as a struggle of the true religion, Christianity, against false religion, Islam. As we saw in Chapter six, General William Boykin, in speeches to conservative Christians, declared that America is an object of hatred because it is uniquely 'a Christian nation' that must confront and conquer their enemies 'in the name of God.' Muslims, Boykin said, worship an idol and not the true God. Moreover George W. Bush had been chosen by God to carry out this messianic mission at this time in history. 'We are an army of God raised up for such a time as this.'[15]

George W. Bush's rhetoric of apocalyptic warfare mirrors that of his iconic adversary, Saudi Arabian mastermind of anti-American attacks, Osama bin Ladin. Both imagine themselves as avenging angels of righteousness against an embodiment of evil. However, Bush, commanding the vast weaponry of the largest military power on earth, has wreaked far more death and destruction in the last four years than Osama bin Laden in his mountain hideout. Measured by sheer levels of killing, maiming and destruction of the means of daily life, Bush has done far more evil than Osama bin Laden. Bush claims that such destruction is an unfortunate necessity for a good end, but bin Laden claims also that he kills for a good purpose, to force Americans out of Saudi Arabia and Palestine. The worst evils are done by those who justify destruction for redemptive purposes.

15. On Boykin's remarks see Brian Knowlton, *International Herald Tribune*, 22 October 2003. Also Odai Sirri, *Aljazeer Net*, 19 October 2003.

In his 2005 book, *Rogue State*, William Blum chronicles such destructive violence by the United States over the fifty years since World War II (although the story could have been extended back to the colonial era of the seventeenth century, as is evident in this volume). With careful citation of sources Blum lists such evils as the training of terrorists, targeted assassinations of disliked leaders of other countries, the use of torture, bombings, chemical and biological weapons, undermining elections, spying, looting and kidnapping, the pursuit of the drug trade by the CIA and finally undermining civil and human rights for those resident in the United States itself.[16] In Blum's view it is the United States government that is the primary force for 'evil' in the world today. Ironically, in a recent video released by Osama bin Ladin from his mountain hideout, he held up this book, encouraging Americans to read it so they would understand why he is anti-American. Americans rushed to read it, making it a temporary best-seller. While not wishing to fall into a reverse demonization of America, when the evils of the world in the last fifty years are weighed out, the U.S. has surely done more than its share.

Messianic Hope

Given the dangers of messianic rhetoric for justifying imperialist violence, is part of the critique of theology that is needed a rejection of messianic hope itself? American culture, perhaps more than any other national culture in the world today, had been deeply shaped by messianic thinking. Everything from selling new cars and electronic trinkets to justifying military crusades employs the language of messianic hope for a future time of redemption assumed to be dawning today. Most important, for the purposes of this book, American prophetic critics, as much as American imperialists, have employed the language of messianic hope. To refer only to those critics lifted up as examples of the 'Protest tradition: Alternative Visions of America,' in chapter seven of this book, we see the ready resort to messianic hope by American critics of their country.

Roger Williams in the seventeenth century rejected the idea of a true church and Christian society in the present, but held out a fervent hope of Christ's imminent return to reestablish such a true

16. *Rogue State: A Guide to the World's Only Superpower* (Monroe, ME: Common Courage Press, 2005).

church in the near future. Thomas Paine in the revolutionary era decried the lack of full democracy, rights for women, and the existence of slavery in the plans for the new American revolutionary government. But he also fervently believed that the American Revolution and constitution was both reestablishing the original republic of Israel before it fall into monarchy, and lighting the way for a new era of just government which all nations should follow.

William Lloyd Garrison in the 1830s–60s weighed in with the deepest criticism of American racism and legalization of slavery, judging the Constitution a 'covenant with death and agreement with hell.' Yet his radical separatism from the American system, as it had been founded to allow slave states to be part of the union, was based on a belief that America must align itself with the true way of righteous living demanded by God for a redeemed people. By abolishing slavery, America was refounding itself as a redeemed people and creation.

For socialist Eugene Debs in the 1890s–1920s, America had deeply betrayed its democratic promise through a class warfare waged by the super rich owning class against the workers. Yet he also held out a fervent hope for a 'co-operative commonwealth' that would come about when a democratically elected American socialist government would reorganize the ownership of the means of production on behalf of the vast majority.

Martin Luther King's 'dream' for a new non-racist America was based on hope for a dawning 'beloved community' to be created through non-violence, direct action and the rescinding of Jim Crow Laws. Then black and white could finally walk hand in hand together and share equally in the promise of American abundance. In the last years of his life King broadened this hope to include equal rights for poor people across races and the ending of imperialist wars led by the United States. Neo-conservatives, who have distorted the image of the 'sixties' into an outbreak of hedonistic and valueless youth, fail to reckon with the actual spirit of the civil rights and anti-war movements of those years. In fact the sixties' radical hopes were classically American, shaped by utopian hopes in the possibility of a better world dawning just beyond the next Spring 'offensive.'

Messianic rhetoric sets up a dualism between some great evil to be defeated and the promise of a redemptive era to come. This pattern of thought has been typical in American culture. Yet no people can do without hope. Hope is the life giving edge of every human life, individually and collectively. No person or people can live without some renewed hope for future betterment. The issue is not to reject hope for a better future, but to recognize the way in which messianic hope can be abused, but also how it might be rightly used. How has messianic hope been used to justify the aggrandizement of one's own group, often entailing vast destruction of others? How do we sort out the difference between true and false messianism, good and bad use of future hope?

I suggest, as an initial rule of thumb, that any claim to be founding a redeemed society in a 'promised land,' will always be deeply flawed and productive of vast new evils, if it is built on one people claiming its future hope through the elimination of another people. Any vision of redemption in which our 'good news' creates 'bad news' for another is false redemption. Thus, an American promised land and redeemed people built on eliminating Indians, maintaining the enslavement of Africans, pushing aside Mexicans and banning Chinese was fraught with contradiction from the beginning. One can say the same of an Afrikaner South Africa whose claims for a promised land was built on marginalizing Zulus and taking their land, or an Israel that claimed to redeem Jews through eliminating Palestinians and confiscating their land.

Such redemptive dreams tend to produce more and more violence and destruction until the false starting point is deeply criticized and revised to include the previously excluded 'others.' Thus South Africa made a new beginning by rejecting apartheid. The U.S. rejected Jim Crow for a more racially inclusive society. Although the evils produced by the previous patterns are hardly fully overcome, these changes were essential for each society to go forward on a new basis. Israel, unfortunately, has not yet given up its hope of a greater Israel built through marginalizing and literally walling in the Palestinians.

A key flaw of messianic thought is the way it is built on 'end time' absolutes of ultimate evil and final good. This dualism absolutizes both the evil to be combated and the good that one hopes to achieve. End time messianism was built on an ancient apocalyptic belief in six thousand years of conflictual history followed by a crisis and show down between good and evil, and then a millennium of redeemed blessedness. Whether one thinks in terms of pre-millennialism or post-millennialism (i.e., Christ coming at the beginning of the millennium or at the end of it), the model of history here is untenable. It assumes that we are always at the point of final crisis, at the show down between absolute good and absolute evil and the beginning of a redemptive era when all evil will be overcome. But we are never at this point within history. We are rather always at a moments when some evils need to be redressed, some urgently so, but in ways that are partial rather than ultimate, which may allow society to be reconstituted on a somewhat more viable basis.

A better model for future hope, in my view, comes from the Jubilee tradition of Hebrew Scripture (Leviticus 25:8–17). The idea of Jubilee, which comes from the Jewish sabbatical tradition, assumes that there needs to be periodic renewal, every seven days, every seven years and every seven times seven years (50th year). Each of these stages represents a more radical renewal. We need to renew ourselves weekly with rest and worship, a period of being rather than doing. Every seven years there are more radical reforms, allowing for renewal of soil, rest for the workers and provision for wild animals. The great renewal every fiftieth year provides for return of land unjustly appropriated, release of captives, forgiveness of debts. This is a kind of periodic revolution to undo the unjust accumulations of wealth for some and oppression for others that have accumulated over the last several generations, reestablishing the basis for a viable society of equitable sharing of the means of life.

This is not a 'once-for-all' redemption, but a partial and periodic righting of balances that is more in keeping with historical possibilities. While not taking the fifty year period literally, it is interesting that in U.S. American history, roughly every fifty to sixty years or every second generation, there has been an acute sense of a need for a new start. We can trace this periodic eruption of demands for change from the American Revolution and Constitution (1776–1785) to the abolitionist era (1830s–1865), to the progressive era (1890–1910) to the civil rights era (1958–1970) to the first decade of the twenty-first century. Each of these moments of crisis and renewal have focused on different issues: independence and new Republican government; the abolition of slavery; the rights of labor; racism and sexism. Each period of intense revolutionary/ reform activity has made some significant changes that allowed society to go forward on a new basis. But other social evils not addressed in an earlier era grow into a crisis and become the concern of a later period.

Today I suggest the urgent issues have to do with extreme economic disparities worldwide, environmental destruction and inflated American military power. What is needed is a new era of revolutionary reform struggle to redress these extreme imbalances and to allow global society to function more justly, peacefully and sustainably. These are not once-for-all transformations that will usher in the Kingdom of God, or the final redemptive era of world history, however apocalyptically both Right and Left (including environmentalists) tend to see the crises of the present situation. Rather we are searching for how to effect some very deep reforms in relationships between humans with each other across economic classes and ethnic groups and between humans and the planetary ecosystem that will allow a new era of human history to proceed in a more peaceful, just and sustainable way.

Re-imagining America's Place in the World Community: Curbing American and Global Militarism

Since the American creation of the atomic bomb at the end of World War II, dropping it on two Japanese cities, the world has been held hostage to the fear of the possible use of 'weapons of mass destruction.' The United States has continually taken the lead in producing these weapons of greater and greater destructive power, as well as expanding its willingness to use them. Today, under the present Bush Administration, the willingness to use 'tactical' nuclear weapons in warfare against a non-nuclear power is again being contemplated by American political policy makers.[17]

Any hope of lessening this escalation of weapons of greater and greater capacity for mass destruction has been thwarted by a basic fallacy, primarily on the part of the United States. Curbing the expansion of such weaponry, much less disarmament, has always been blocked due to the insistence of the United States and its allies on maintaining a monopoly of such weapons, while denying such weapons to those considered our political and ideological enemies. This means a division of the world into elite nations who possess

17. See the article by Seymour M. Hersh, 'The Iran Plans: Would President Bush go to War to Prevent Teheran from Getting the Bomb?' *The New Yorker*, 17 April 2006, pp. 30–37.

those weapons and second class nations who do not. The obvious and inevitable result is a rising demand for such weapons as a status symbol. Every nation that wishes to establish itself as a first rank power, and to protect itself against other nuclear powers, specifically the United States, believes it must have such weapons. To demand that a nation desist from acquiring such weapons by holding such weapons to its head as a threat only fuels a feeling of urgent need to have them.

The curbing of nuclear proliferation, not to mention of other weapons of mass destruction, biological and chemical, is a losing game under these rules. There is only one way that the expansion of such weapons can be curbed, and that is to recognize that such curbing and reduction must apply equally to all nations. In the Middle East, Iran can only agree to disarm if Israel agrees to disarm. On the world stage, Iran and North Korea can only disarm if the United States and its allies disarm. Those who have not yet produced such weapons can be persuaded not to acquire them only if those who have them begin a process of giving them up.

This point is so obvious that it is hard to understand how it is continually avoided. The first step is to insist that this be the terms of discussion. Universal disarmament is the only way to curb such weapons. What will never curb them is a system in which some nations demand a monopoly of possession of such weapons, threatening to use them against those who do not yet have them, but might begin to acquire them.

If genuine disarmament of the nuclear nations could begin, it would be possible to initiate a discussion of real efforts to move away from war as a way of solving international problems. This was a topic on the agenda of progressives, such as Jane Addams, in 1910–30. For Addams and other feminist-pacifists of the Progressive era, war was a barbaric method of dealing with international conflict. It needed to be superseded by negotiation within a world forum of nations. Yet today this hope is not even on the table for discussion.

The United States has built the most enormous military system in world history, and has also helped to arm many other nations it regards as allies. Vast stockpiles of arms and chronic wars characterize the world. The United States is ringing the world with military bases. Since the invasion of Iraq there are now 109 military bases in that country, including four very large and apparently permanent ones.[18] A new military base was set up in the Dominican Republic in 2006, apparently as the base for possible invasion of Cuba and/or Venezuela.[19] World disarmament must demand the reduction and eventual elimination of these bases.

This, for the U.S. also means cutting back huge military spending that consumes more than half of the federal budget and is the major cause of national debt and the starving of every social program. Reducing the military budget would free American resources to address poverty, health, education, repair of critical infrastructure and environmental devastation. How do we begin to roll away the stone that is crushing us and allow new life to come forth?

Poverty

The human species has never before in its history experienced such vast disparities of wealth and poverty. As we saw in Chapter Six, some 20 per cent of humanity control 85 per cent of world resources, much of it concentrated in the top 1 per cent. This means that 80 per cent of the world shares about 15 per cent of the wealth and the poorest 20 per cent a mere 1.3 per cent, living in dire misery. Discussion of disparities in income only begin to touch on the extremes of the disparity between the very rich 20 per cent and the very poor 20 per cent.[20] One is talking about abundance of means of transportation, fleets of cars, access to frequent air travel, huge houses, advanced technology, medical care, high walls and guards protecting this elite, versus extreme lack of access to decent housing, medical care, education, housing, food and potable water, a daily vulnerability to violence, and disease.

Although not with quite the same extremes of poverty, this disparity also exists in the United States. In 1996, the top 1 per cent of Americans held 38 per cent of the wealth. The top 20 per cent held 76 per cent of productive wealth in the form of ownership of businesses, stocks, bonds and money market accounts, two-thirds of this concentrated in the top 1 per cent. The Forbes 400, the wealthiest Americans, possess 40 per cent of the fixed capital. The

18. See 'Extended Presence of U.S. in Iraq Looms Large', 21 March 2006, Associated Press: www.commondreams.org/headlines06/0321-10.htm.

19. See article in *Los Angeles Times*, 21 April 2006, p. 23.

20. See Rosemary Ruether, *Integrating Ecofeminism, Globalization and World Religions* (New York: Rowman and Littlefield, 2005), pp. 7–8.

other 80 per cent of Americans together own 24 per cent of the wealth, mostly in the form of houses and cars, and the poorest 30 per cent have debts that exceed their assets.

How do societies begin to address these disparities of wealth and poverty? In the United States in the last thirty years the wealthiest have paid less and less of a percentage of their income in taxes, and the minimum wage has been allowed to languish at less than two-thirds of what would be necessary for basic needs. A redress of these two scandalous trends is necessary, raising of the minimum wage to $10 an hour and the restoration of a progressive income tax in which the wealthy and large corporations would pay a much higher percentage in taxes to fund basic social needs. Reducing the military budget and freeing these funds for social needs would contribute much to this.

Taxing the rich and raising the income of the poor, as well as rebuilding the welfare roles of the state to subsidize health, education, sanitation and public transportation (which were dismantled by the World Bank and International Monetary Fund's programs of Structural Adjustment in the 1980s[21]) are also needed worldwide. This would alleviate the pressure of immigration from poor to wealthy countries, as well as the ability of corporations to profit by exploiting low wages of workers around the world.

Worldwide there needs to be a lessening of the economic reach of large corporations and the redevelopment of local economies for local distribution. Land reform is needed to redistribute land to the landless. Cooperative farming and factory projects should be encouraged where all workers share in the management and profits. Poverty alleviation cannot simply come from the top down, but demands a redevelopment of the basic means of life at the grassroots level.

Environmental Devastation

Environmental devastation is the context for economic destitution and war worldwide. It needs to be seen as the interaction of many factors. These include exponential growth of population which has grown from 1 billion in 1930 to over 6 billion in 2006, and could well double in another thirty years, causing increasing death from

21. Ruether, *Integrating*, pp. 4–6.

malnutrition, disease, including pandemics such as AIDS, unclean water, war and social violence. Another key factor is the use of fossil fuels, especially petroleum, as the chief energy source. The world industrial system is facing the depletion of petroleum in another 10–20 years. This growing scarcity is key to the oil wars in the Middle East and elsewhere.

Burning fossil fuels is also the chief source of air pollution and acid rain that destroys soil fertility and forests. It is also the main cause of global warming that is creating increasingly violent weather patterns (such as stronger hurricanes), and melting ice caps that threaten to inundate low lying islands and coastal areas where many cities are located. The ocean current that brings temperate weather to Europe could also be affected, as well as increased tropical heat devastating for farming in these regions.[22] Thus humanity stands on the edge of huge global disasters in the next few decades.

Soil erosion, and the pollution of soil and water from industrial and domestic wastes, are also major causes of decreasing fertility of the soil, toxic water supply and diseases conveyed to humans and animals through such pollution. This also affects the ability of humans to increase the food supply for growing populations, although the major source of famine is maldistribution of food due to poverty, rather than lack of adequate food to feed the world population. An elite few feast on a global food procurement system that markets products worldwide, while the rural poor lack adequate food for daily life. The urban poor are malnourished by innutritious 'fast food,' such as sodas/fizzy drinks and potato chips.

World deforestation is also unsettling world weather, causing drought and soil erosion. Destroying forests is the major cause of the rapid extinction of many species of animals and plants, greatly reducing the diversity of the planetary ecosystem. World food supply is threatened by a corporate agricultural system which is destroying the variety of species of foods, while specializing in a few species of food crops that are engineered to demand high levels of irrigation, pesticides and petroleum fertilizers.

All of these interlocking ecological crises need to be addressed both locally and as a world system of human life on the planet. I will mention a few obvious steps that need to be taken in each country and worldwide.

22. See issue on global warming, *Time*, 3 April 2006.

Population

The main issue here is to promote a culture of reproductive choice (often at variance with traditional patriarchal religions) that entails the education and empowerment of women, valuing of children, and community health and improved employment for the local community. In the context of such improved health, education and economic wellbeing, a variety of contraceptives need to be made available inexpensively and everyone encouraged to use them as a normal way of life. The creation of children needs to be seen as a planned decision when there is adequate means and social support structures to raise each child optimally.

Energy

A first step to redressing the problem of disappearing fossil fuels is to develop ways of using it much more efficiently through energy conserving machines and environmental design of buildings. But this must be seen as a transitional step toward rapid conversion from fossil fuels to renewable and less polluting fuels; solar, wind, thermal and biomass. Organic decentralized communities where living, work, production, trade and cultural amenities are within reach of walking, biking and public transportation need to be developed, to eliminate the private car and greatly lessen long distance travel and shipping. Electronic communication should replace much of the air travel that forces business people and communicators to fly long distance on a regular basis.

Food

Local food production must be greatly diversified, replacing monocrops with a variety of foods grown locally for local trade. There should be a great reduction of national and global food transportation chains which ship and fly food around the world. This would mean a return to canning and drying of foods for winter and eating in season. The human diet needs to be converted to eating lower on the food chain, primarily vegetables, grains and fruits, rather than meat, This would greatly expand the grain foods available for humans which are presently being fed to animals for meat. Food needs to be grown organically, using organic fertilizer and pest control and recycling all wastes to rebuild soils, feed animals and make fuel and other products.

Pollution

Eliminating the burning of fossil fuels for housing, transportation and factories, eliminating petroleum fertilizers and pesticides for organic methods, recycling all industrial and domestic wastes, eliminating wastes that cannot be reintegrated into production or composted (fluorocarbons and nuclear wastes) would greatly reduce the threat to human and planetary life from air, water and soil pollution and stabilize climate warming. Human societies should function like healthy forests or meadows in which the death or waste side of the life system is fully integrated into the production of new products, renewal of fertility of soils or feeding of animals.

Protecting Forests and Biodiversity

Existing forests where wild life exists need to be protected, using indigenous people who have traditionally lived and used such forests in moderation, rather than only parks and forest management agencies that are sometimes tied to lumber companies. But wetlands and green areas need to be redeveloped in a way that is interspersed with human habitation, renewing habitat for a variety of plants and animals, as well as protecting human habitat from storms and floods that are aggravated from the loss of forests and wetlands.

How Do We Get There from Here?

These key steps to ecologically sustainable living will demand enormous effort and cooperation worldwide on local, regional and global levels. How to generate the will for such a change? This will demand the mobilization of human cultural resources, neighborhood associations, unions, schools and religious communities (churches, synagogues, mosques, temples). Religious institutions could play a key role here. Religious institutions, especially in Christianity and Islam, are presently being hijacked by 'fundamentalists' who have made anti-feminism and backlash against women's reproductive rights their key issues. Progressive religion needs to redefine these issues so they are understood as key elements in healthy cooperative families, based on egalitarian cooperation of men and women and planning for and good care of children.

All the religions have traditions that promote social justice and see the natural world as sacred and/or the creation of God for whose care humans are accountable. Just, peaceful and ecologically sustainable societies need to become the ethical duty of religious persons. Religious faiths need to band together on an interfaith basis locally and globally to promote such just, peaceful and sustainable ways of life. Religions might also consider utilizing their traditional methods of condemning transgression of norms to question those promoting poverty, ecological devastation and military havoc.

Thus the World Alliance of Reform Churches (the world body of Presbyterian and Reform churches) has defined the crisis of world poverty created by corporate globalization as a *statis confessionis*; i.e., a situation in which every church body must take a principled stance against such evils.[23] This parallels the position of the World Alliance of Reform Churches in 1982 in which *apartheid* in South Africa was declared a *statis confessionis* calling all churches to renounce *apartheid* or be regarded as out of communion with the world body. Buddhists have also used their traditional ways of protecting religious beings from harm by wrapping trees in the orange sash of a monk, thus making it a sacrilege to cut down such trees.[24]

These dramatic gestures must be accompanied by campaigns of education in each local religious community to educate themselves on ecological, military and social justice issues and to take steps in their local communities to lessen such violence. Planting community gardens and using the produce for community meals for the poor (drawing in the participation of the poor themselves to do this), opposing local military bases, developing new forms of cooperative employment for the needy are some of the ways in which religious communities could address these issues. Liturgy and worship can also incorporate ecological and social justice consciousness. In urban areas where there are a variety of religious groups, churches, synagogues, temples and mosques, might band together neighborhood by neighborhood to work on local ecological and

23. See the document GC 23-e of the World Alliance of Reformed Churches, 24th General Council, Accra, Ghana, 30 July–13 August 2004.

24. See Mary Evelyn Tucker and Duncan Ryuken Williams, *Buddhism and Ecology: The Interconnection of Dharma and Deeds* (Cambridge, MA: Harvard University Press), p. xxxv.

justice issues, as has been the case in the Interreligious Sustainability Project for Metropolitan Chicago.[25]

Some believe there will be no massive shifts in these patterns without some vast breakdown in the present system. This may be the case, but large collapses and outbreaks of chaos do not necessarily fuel healthy responses. This can be seen in the 9/11 attacks which sparked new excuses for American military adventures and national security state repression at home, or the Hurricane Katrina floods in New Orleans which are been met with opportunistic efforts to eliminate much of the poor black population of that city. There needs to be widespread education and alternative community practice developed now through schools, churches, cooperative organizations and neighborhood associations in order to prepare for alternatives before and as the present system breaks down.

A new global political balance of power needs to emerge as well. There are signs that this is beginning to happen. Instead of one superpower, the United States, running the world as the dominant economic power, backed up by its huge military, regional alliances are beginning to emerge. African nations, Latin American nations, Asian-Pacific nations, Middle Eastern and European nations are banding together in alliances of regional cooperation. As Filipino economist, Walden Bello, puts it, 'regional economic collaborations among Third World countries — or, in the parlance of developing economics, "South-South cooperation" — are the wave of the future.'[26] Such alliances also need to promote more ecological and social justice policies and to curb unilateral American military interventions. Regional and global NGOs on environmental health, peace and local development need to communicate and work with each other to encourage such regional alliances to promote healthy policies for regional and global cooperation.

Are we too late? There is no way of knowing whether humans can act together to avert the impending tragedies. Many world trends are going in exactly the opposite direction. America as a world power is a major source of these wrong-headed policies, which makes it a special responsibility for Americans to work for reform of their own government and society. We can only work

25. See Ruether, *Integrating*, pp. 174–75; See also the website for the Center for Neighborhood Technology: www.cnt.org.

26. See Walden Bello, *Dilemmas of Domination: The Unmaking of American Empire* (New York: Henry Holt and Company, 2005), p. 212.

from where we are. While we cannot be optimistic, we can and must be hopeful that human creativity will rise to the task of saving one another and our beautiful planetary home. This, as Thomas Berry has said, is the 'great work' of our generation.[27]

27. Thomas Berry, *The Great Work: Our Way into the Future* (New York: Bell Tower, 1999).

BIBLIOGRAPHY

Adam, David Wallace, *Education for Extinction: American Indians and the Boarding School Experience, 1875–1928* (Lawrence, KS: University of Kansas, 1995).

Addams, Jane, *Newer Ideals of Peace* (New York: Macmillan, 1907).

_____ *Twenty Years at Hull House*. New York: Macmillan, 1910).

_____*The Second Twenty Years at Hull House* (New York: Macmillan, 1930).

Bacevich, Andrew J., *American Empire: The Reality and Consequences of U.S. Diplomacy* (Cambridge, MA: Harvard University Press, 2002).

_____ *The New American Militarism: How Americans are Seduced by War* (New York: Oxford University Press, 2005).

Bailyn, Bernard, *Ideological Origins of the American Revolution* (Cambridge, MA: Harvard University Press, 1967).

Barlow, Maude and Tony Clarke, *Blue Gold: The Battle against Corporate Theft of the World's Water* (New York: New Press, 2002).

Barron, Bruce, *Heaven on Earth: The Social and Political Agendas of Dominion Theology* (Grand Rapids, MI: Zondervan, 1992).

Barsh, Russel Lawrence and James Youngblood Henderson, *The Road: Indian Tribes and Political Liberty* (Berkeley, CA: University of California Press, 1980).

Barth, Gunther Paul, *Bitter Strength: A History of the Chinese in the United States, 1850–1870* (Cambridge, MA: Harvard University Press, 1964).

Battis, Emery, *Saints and Sectaries: Anne Hutchinson and the Antinomian Controversy in the Massachusetts Bay Colony* (Chapel Hill, NC: University of North Carolina Press, 1962).

Bauer, K. Jack, *The Mexican War, 1846–48* (New York: Macmillan, 1974).

Beaume, Colette, *The Birth of an Ideology: Myths and Symbols of Nation in Late Medieval France* (Susan Ross Huston, trans. Berkeley, CA: University of California Press, 1991).

Beisner, Robert L., *Twelve Against Empire: The Anti-Imperialists, 1898–1900* (New York: McGraw-Hill, 1968).

Bello, Walden, *Dark Victory: The United States and Global Poverty* (Oakland, CA: Food First, 1994).

_____ *Dilemmas of Domination: The Unmaking of American Empire* (New York: Henry Holt and Co., 2005).

Blum, William, *Killing Hope: U.S. Military and C.I.A. Interventions since World War II* (Monroe, ME: Common Courage Press, 1995).

Bogle, Lori Lyn, *The Pentagon's Battle for the American Mind: The Early Cold War* (College Station, TX: Texas A&M University Press, 2004).

Bonner, Raymond, *Weakness and Deceit: U.S. Policy and El Salvador* (New York: Times Books, 1984).

Booth, John A., *The End and the Beginning: The Nicaraguan Revolution* (Boulder, CO: Westview Press, 1992).

Borne, Russell, *The Red King's Rebellion: Racial Politics in New England, 1675–1678* (New York: Athenaeum, 1990).

Brock, Gene M., *Mexico Views Manifest Destiny, 1821–1846: An Essay on The Origins of the Mexican War* (Albuquerque, NM: University of New Mexico Press, 1975).

Brands, H.W., *The Reckless Decade: America in the 1890s* (New York: St. Martin's Press, 1995).

Branfman, Fred, *Voices from the Plain of Jars: Life Under an Air War* (New York: Harper and Row, 1972).

Bremer, Francis J., *The Puritan Experiment: New England Society from Bradford to Edwards* (Hanover: University Press of New England, 1995).

Bullard, Robert D., *Confronting Environmental Racism: Voices from the Grassroots* (Boston: South End Press, 1993).

Burbeck, Roger and Jim Tarbell, *Imperial Overstretch: George W. Bush and the Hubris of Empire* (New York: Zed Books, 2004).

Chadbourn, James H., *Lynching and Law* (Chapel Hill, NC: The University of North Carolina Press, 1933).

Chalmers, David M., *Hooded Americanism: The First Century of the KKK, 1865–1965* (New York: Doubleday, 1965).

Cherry, Conrad, (ed.), *God's New Israel: Religious Interpretations of American Destiny* (Chapel Hill, NC: The University of North Carolina Press, 1998).

Churchill, Ward, *A Little Matter of Genocide: Holocaust and Denial in the Americas, 1492 to the present* (San Francisco, CA: City Lights Books, 1997).

Collinson, Patrick, *The Elizabethan Puritan Movement* (London: Jonathan Cape, 1967).

Davies, Daniel S., *Struggle for Freedom: The History of Black Americans* (New York: Harcourt, Brace Jovanovich, 1972).

Davies, F. James, *Who is Black: One Nation's Definition* (University Park, PA: Pennsylvania State University Press, 2001).

Davis, James Calvin, *The Moral Theology of Roger Williams: Christian Conviction and Public Ethics* (Louisville, KY: Westminster John Knox Press, 2004).

Deloria, Vine and Clifford M. Lytle, *American Indians, American Justice* (Austin, TX: University of Texas Press, 1983).

Deverell, William, *Whitewashed Adobe: The Rise of Los Angeles and the Remaking of its Mexican Past* (Berkeley, CA: University of California Press, 2004).

Dickason, Patricia, *The Myth of the Savage and the Beginning of French Colonialism in the Americas* (Edmonton, Canada: University of Alberta Press, 1984).

Dobyns, Henry E., *Their Numbers Became Thinned: Native American Population Dynamics in Eastern North America* (Knoxville, TN: University of Tennessee Press, 1983).

Dorrien, Gary, *Imperial Designs: Neoconservatives and the New Pax Americana* (New York: Routledge, 2004).

_____ *The Neoconservative Mind: Politics, Culture and the War of Ideology* (Philadelphia, PA: Temple University Press, 1993).

Douglas, William, *Mr. Lincoln and the Negroes: The Long Road to Equality* (New York: Athenaeum, 1963).

Douglass, Frederick, *The Oxford Frederick Douglass Reader* (New York: Oxford University Press, 1996).

Drinnon, Richard, *Keeper of Concentration Camps: Dillon S. Meyer and American Racism* (Berkeley, CA: University of California Press, 1987).

Du Bois, W.E.B., *John Brown* (New York: International, 1962).

Eccles, William John, *France in America* (East Lansing, MI: Michigan State University Press, 1990).

Fall, Bernard, *Hell in a Very Small Place: The Siege of Dien Bien Phu* (Philadelphia, PA: Lippencott, 1967).

Flexner, Eleanor, *Century of Struggle: The Women's Rights Movement in the United States* (New York: Athenaeum, 1972).

Foos, Paul, *A Short, Offhand, Killing Affair: Soldiers and Social Conflict During the Mexican War* (Chapel Hill, NC: University of North Carolina Press, 2002).

Foner, Eric, *Tom Paine and Revolutionary America* (New York: Oxford University Press, 1976).

Foner, Philip S., *The Complete Writings of Thomas Paine* (New York: Citadel Press, 1945).

Gaddis, Lewis (ed.), *Containment: Documents on American Policy and Strategy, 1945–1950* (New York: Columbia University Press, 1978).

George, Susan and Fabrizio Sabelli, *Faith and Credit: The World Bank's Secular Empire* (Boulder, CO: Westview Press, 1994).

Gilpin, W. Clark, *The Millenarian Piety of Roger Williams* (Chicago, IL: University of Chicago Press, 1979).

Ginger, Ray, *The Bending Cross: A Biography of Eugene Victor Debs* (New Brunswick, NJ: Rutgers University Press, 1949).

Goulden, Joseph C., *Truth is the First Casualty: The Gulf of Tonkin Affair: Illusion and Reality* (New York: Rand McNally, 1969).

Griswold del Castillo, Richard, *The Treaty of Guadalupe Hidalgo: A Legacy of Conflict* Hernandez, José M., *Cuba and the United States: Intervention and Militarism, 1868–1993* (Austin, TX: University of Texas Press, 1993).

Halladay, Fred, *The Making of the Second Cold War* (London: Verso, 1986).

Haller, William, *The Elect Nation: The Meaning and Relevance of Foxe's Book of Martyrs* (New York: Harper and Row, 1963).

Halper, Stephen and Jonathan Clarke, *America Alone: The Neoconservatives and the Global Order* (Cambridge: Cambridge University Press, 2004).

Haynes, Sam W., and Christopher Morris (eds.), *Manifest Destiny and Empire: American Antebellum Expansionism* (College Station, TX: Texas A&M Press, 1997).

Heizer, Robert F. and Alan F. Almquist, *The Other Californians: Prejudice and Discrimination under Spain, Mexico and the United States* (Berkeley, CA: University of California Press, 1977).

Hendershot, Cyndy, *Anti-Communism and Popular Culture in Mid-Century America* (Jefferson, NC: McFarland and Co., 2003).

Hernandez, José M., *Cuba and the United States: Intervention and Militarism, 1868–1933* (Austin, TX: University of Texas Press, 1993).

Hill, Christopher, *Puritanism and Revolution: Studies in the Interpretation of the English Revolution in the Seventeenth Century* (London: Secker and Warburg, 1958).

_____ *A Century of Revolution, 1603–1714* (Edinburgh: Thomas Nelson and Sons, 1961).

_____ *Anti-Christ in Seventeenth Century England* (London: Oxford University Press, 1971).

Hoganson, Kristan L., *Fighting for American Manhood: How Gender Politics Provoked the Spanish-American and Philippine-American Wars* (New Haven, CT: Yale University Press, 1998).

Hoover, J. Edgar, *Masters of Deceit: The Story of Communism in America and How to FIght It* (New York: Holt, Rinehart and Winston).

Horsman, Reginald, *Expansion and American Indian Policy, 1783–1812* (Lansing, MI: Michigan State University, 1967).

_____ *Race and Manifest Destiny: The Origins of American Racial Anglo-Saxonism* (Cambridge, MA: Harvard University Press, 1981).

Hoxie, Frederick, *The Final Promise: The Campaign to Assimilate the Indians, 1880–1920* (Lincoln, NE: The University of Nebraska Press, 1985).

Ignatiev, Noel, *How the Irish Became White* (New York: Routledge, 1995).

Jacob, Matthew F., *Whiteness of a Different Color: European Immigrants and the Alchemy of Race* (Cambridge, MA: Harvard University Press, 1999).

Jaynes, Gerald D., *Branches without Roots: Genesis of the Black Working Class in the American South, 1862–1882* (New York: Oxford University Press, 1986).

Jennings, Francis, *The Invasion of America: Indians, Colonialism and the Cant of Conquest* (Chapel Hill, NC: North Carolina University Press, 1975).

Johnson, Chalmers, *The Sorrows of Empire: Militarism, Secrecy and the End of the Republic* (New York: Henry Holt Co., 2004).

Jonas, Susanne, *The Battle for Guatemala* (Boulder, CO: Westview Press, 1991).

Karlsen, Carol, *The Devil in the Shape of a Woman* (New York: Norton, 1987).

Karnow, Stanley, *In our Image: America's Empire in the Philippines* (New York: Random House, 1986).

Keller, Rosemary, *Patriotism in the Female Sex: Abigail Adams and the American Revolution* (New York: Carlson Publishing Co., 1994).

Kennedy, John Hopkins, *Jesuit and Savage in New France* (New Haven, CT: Yale University Press, 1950).

Kennedy, Robert Jr., *Crimes Against Nature: How George W. Bush and his Corporate Pals are Plundering the Country and Hijacking our Democracy* (New York: Harper Collins, 2004).

Kraus, Clifford, *Inside Central America: Its People, Politics and History* (New York: Summit Books, 1991).

LaFeber, Walter, *America, Russia and the Cold War* (New York: McGraw- Hill, 1993).

Landau, Saul, *The Dangerous Doctrine: National Security and U.S. Foreign Policy* (Boulder, CO: Westview Press, 1988).

Langley, Lester D., *The Banana Wars: United States Intervention in the Caribbean, 1898–1934* (Lexington, KY: University of Kentucky Press, 1985).

Lens, Sidney, *The Futile Crusade: Anti-communism as American Credo* (Chicago: Triangle Books, 1964).

Lopez, Ian F. Haney, *White by Law: The Legal Construction of Race* (New York: New York University Press, 1996).

MacEoin, Gary, *No Peaceful Way: Chile's Struggle for Dignity* (New York: Sheed and Ward, 1974).

McCoy, Alfred, *A Question of Torture: CIA Interrogations from the Cold War to the War on Terror* (New York: Henry Holt, 2006).

McDonnell, Janet A., *The Dispossession of the American Indian, 1883– 1934* (Bloomington, IN: Indiana University Press, 1991).

Mann, James, *Rise of the Vulcans: The History of Bush's War Cabinet* (New York: Viking, 2004).

Marshall, Jonathan, Peter Dale Scott, and Jane Hunter, *The Iran Contra Connection: Secret Teams and Covert Operations in the Reagan Era* (Boston: South End Press, 1987).

Mayer, Henry, *All on Fire: William Lloyd Garrison and the Abolition of Slavery* (New York: St. Martin's Press, 1998).

Merk, Frederick, *Manifest Destiny and Mission in American History: A Reinterpretation* (New York: Alfred A. Knopf, 1963).

Miller, Perry, *Errand into the Wilderness* (Cambridge: Harvard University Press, 1956).

Miller, Stuart C., *'Benevolent Assimilation': The American Conquest of The Philippines, 1899–1903* (New Haven, CT: Yale University Press, 1982).

Moe-Lobeda, Cynthia, *Globalization and God: Healing a Broken World* (Minneapolis, MN: Fortress Press, 2002).

Monge, José Trias, *Puerto Rico: The Trials of the Oldest Colony* (New Haven, CT: Yale University Press, 1997).

Morgan, Edmund, *Roger Williams: Church and State* (New York: Harcourt, Brace and World, 1967).

Muncy, Robyn, *Creating a Female Dominion in American Reform, 1890–1935* (New York: Oxford University Press, 1991).

Musicant, Ivan, *The Banana Wars: A History of United States Military Intervention from the Spanish-American War to the Invasion of Panama* (New York: Macmillan, 1990).

Nelson, Bruce, C., *Beyond the Martyrs: A Social History of Chicago's Anarchists 1870–1900* (New Brunswick, NJ: Rutgers University Press, 1988).

Nelson, Truman (ed.), *Documents of Upheaval: Selections from William Lloyd Garrison's The Liberator, 1831–1865* (New York: Hill and Wang, 1966).

Niebuhr, Reinhold, *The Irony of American History* (New York: Charles Scribner's Sons, 1954).

Northcott, Michael, *An Angel Directs the Storm: Apocalyptic Religion and American Empire* (London: Taurus, 2004).

O'Gorman, Edmundo, *The Invention of America: An Inquiry into the Historical Nature of the New World and the Meaning of its History* (Westport, CT: Greenwood Press, 1961).

Pearce, Jenny, *Under the Eagle: U.S. Intervention in Central America and the Caribbean* (Boston: South End Press, 1982).

Pestana, Carla, *Quakers and Baptists in Colonial Massachusetts* (New York: Cambridge University Press, 1991).

Pettipas, Katherine, *Severing the Ties that Bind: Government Repression of Indigenous Religious Ceremonies in the Prairies* (Winnipeg: University of Manitoba press, 1994).

Phelan, John Leddy, *The Millennial Kingdom of the Franciscans in the New World* (Berkeley, CA: University of California Press, 1970).

Pitt, Leonard, *The Decline of the Californios: A Social History of the Spanish-Speaking Californians, 1846–1890* (Berkeley, CA: University of California Press, 1998).

Porter, Gareth, *Perils of Dominance: Imbalance of Power and the Road to Vietnam* (Berkeley, CA: University of California Press, 2005).

Prestowitz, Clyde, *Rogue Nation: American Unilateralism and the Failure of Good Intentions* (New York: Basic Books, 2003).

Rashid, Ahmed, *Taliban: Islam, Oil and Fundamentalism in Central Asia* (New Haven, CT: Yale University Press, 2000).

Rich, Bruce, *Mortgaging the Earth: the World Bank, Environmental Impoverishment and the Crisis of Development* (Boston: Beacon Press, 1994).

Ritter, Scott, *Iraq Confidential: the Untold Story of the Intelligence Conspiracy to Undermine the UN and Overthrow Saddam Hussein* (New York: Nation Books, 2005).

Robinson, Cecil, *The View from Chapultepec: Mexican Writers on the Mexican-American War* (Tucson, AZ: University of Arizona Press, 1989).

Ruether, Rosemary R., *Integrating Ecofeminism, Globalization and World Religions* (Landam, MD: Rowman and Littlefield, 2005).

Ruether, Rosemary R., and Herman J. Ruether, *The Wrath of Jonah: The Crisis of Religious Nationalism in the Israeli-Palestinian Conflict* (Minneapolis, MN: Fortress Press, 2002).

Saxton, Alexander, *The Indispensable Enemy: Labor and the Anti-Chinese Movement in California* (Berkeley, CA: University of California Press, 1971).

Schlesinger, Arthur M. (ed.), *Writings and Speeches of Eugene V. Debs* (New York: Hermitage Press, 1948).

Schlesinger, Stephen and Stephen Kinzer, *Bitter Fruit: The Untold Story of The American Coup in Guatemala* (New York: Doubleday, 1982).

Segal, Charles M., and David C. Stineback, *Puritans, Indians and Manifest Destiny* (New York: G.P. Putnam and Sons, 1977).

Shiva, Vandana, *The Violence of the Green Revolution: Third World Agriculture, Ecology and Politics* (London: Zed Books, 1991).

Shoemaker, Nancy, *American Indian Population Recovery in the Twentieth Century* (Albuquerque, NM: New Mexico University Press, 1999).

Schoonover, Thomas, *The War of 1809 and the Origins of Globalization* (Lexington, KY: University of Kentucky Press, 2003).

Slotkin, Richard, *Gunfighter Nation: The Myth of the Frontier in the Twentieth Century* (New York: Athenaeum, 1992).

_____ *Regeneration through Violence: The Mythology of the American Frontier, 1600–1860* (New York: Harpers, 1996).

_____ *The Fatal Environment: The Myth of the Frontier in an Era of Industrialization, 1800–1890* (Norman, OK: Oklahoma University Press, 1998).

Starkey, Marion, *The Devil in Massachusetts* (New York: Alfred A. Knopf, 1949).

Stern, Kenneth, *Loud Hawk: The United States Versus the American Indian Movement* (Norman, OK: Oklahoma University Press, 2002).

Stebner, Eleanor, *The Women of Hull House: A Study of Spirituality, Vocation and Friendship* (Albany, NY: SUNY Press, 1997).

Stockwell, John, *In Search of Enemies: A CIA Story* (New York: W.W. Norton, 1978).

Straudenraus, Philip J., *The African Colonization Movement, 1816–1865* (New York: Columbia University Press, 1961).

Thornston, Russell, *American Indian Holocaust and Survival: A Population History Since 1492* (Norman, OK: University of Oklahoma Press, 1987).

Tinker, George E., *Missionary Conquest: The Gospel and the Native American Cultural Genocide* (Minneapolis, MN: Fortress Press, 1993).

Tuveson, Ernest Lee, *Redeemer Nation: The Idea of America's Millennial Role* (Chicago, IL: University of Chicago Press, 1968).

Wade, Mason, *The French Canadians, 1790–1945* (London: Macmillan and Co., 1955).

Wagenheim, Olga Jiménez de, *Puerto Rico: An Interpretive History from Pre-Colombian Times to 1900* (Princeton, NJ: Markus Wiener Publishers, 1998).

Walsh, Lawrence, *Firewall: The Iran Contra Conspiracy and Cover-up* (New York: Norton, 1997).

Washington, James Melvin (ed.), *A Testament of Hope: The Essential Writings and Speeches of Martin Luther King, Jr* (San Francisco, CA: HarperSanFrancisco, 1991).

Weber, Timothy P., *Living in the Shadow of the Second Coming: American Premillennialism, 1875–1925* (Oxford: Oxford University Press, 1979).

Weinberg, Albert K., *Manifest Destiny: A Study of Expansionism in American History* (Chicago: Quadrangle Books, 1935).

Wiarda, Howard J., and Michael J. Kryzanek, *The Dominican Republic: A Caribbean Crucible* (Boulder, CO: Westview Press, 1992).

Welter, Barbara, *Dimity Convictions: The American Woman in the Nineteenth Century* (Athens, OH: Ohio University Press, 1976).

Winthrop, Jordan D., *White Over Black: American Attitudes Toward the Negro, 1550–1812* (Chapel Hill, NC: University of North Carolina Press, 1968).

Woodward, C. Vann, *The Strange Career of Jim Crow* (New York: Oxford University Press, 1966).

Zakai, Avihu, *Exile and Kingdom: History and Apocalypse in the Puritan Migration to America* (Cambridge: Cambridge University Press, 1992).

Zinn, Howard, *SNCC: The New Abolitionists* (Boston: Beacon Press, 1964).

Index of Biblical References

General Index